A-Z BRIG[HTON]

CW00343694

Key to Map Pages	2-3
Map Pages	4-43
Large Scale City Centre	44

Index to
Villages,
and sele[...]

REFERENCE

A Road	A27	Car Park (selected)		P
B Road	B2123	Church or Chapel		†
Dual Carriageway		Cycleway (selected)		🚲
One-way Street		Fire Station		■
Traffic flow on A Roads is also indicated by a heavy line on the driver's left.	➤	Hospital		H
Road Under Construction		House Numbers (A & B Roads only)	10	124
Opening dates are correct at the time of publication.				
Proposed Road		Information Centre		i
Restricted Access		National Grid Reference		⁵30
Pedestrianized Road		Park and Ride	Withdean	P+R
Track / Footpath		Police Station		▲
Residential Walkway		Post Office		★
Railway	Station / Level Crossing / Tunnel	Toilet		▽
Built-up Area	MILL RD.	Educational Establishment		
		Hospital or Healthcare Building		
Local Authority Boundary	— · — · — · ·	Industrial Building		
National Park Boundary		Leisure or Recreational Facility		
Postcode Boundary	— — — — -	Place of Interest		
		Public Building		
Map Continuation	12 / Large Scale City Centre 44	Shopping Centre or Market		
		Other Selected Buildings		

SCALE

Map Pages 4-43   1:15,840

0   ¼   ½ Mile

0   250   500   750 Metres

4 inches (10.16cm) to 1 mile   6.31cm to 1km

Map Page 44   1:7,920

0   ⅛   ¼ Mile

0   100   200   350 Metres

8 inches (20.32cm) to 1 mile   12.63cm to 1km

Copyright © Collins Bartholomew Ltd 2020 © Crown Copyright and database rights 2020 Ordnance Survey 100018598.

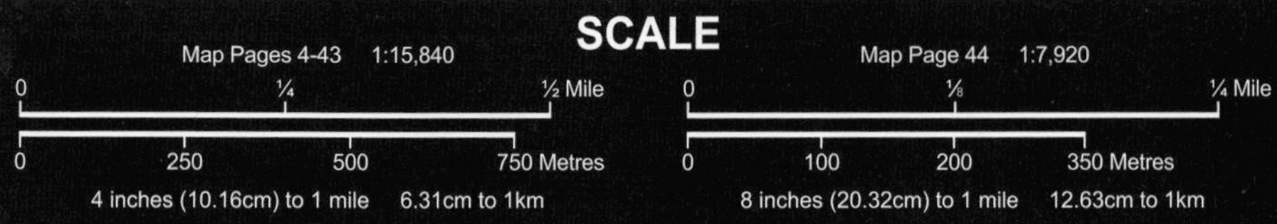

EDITION 7   2021

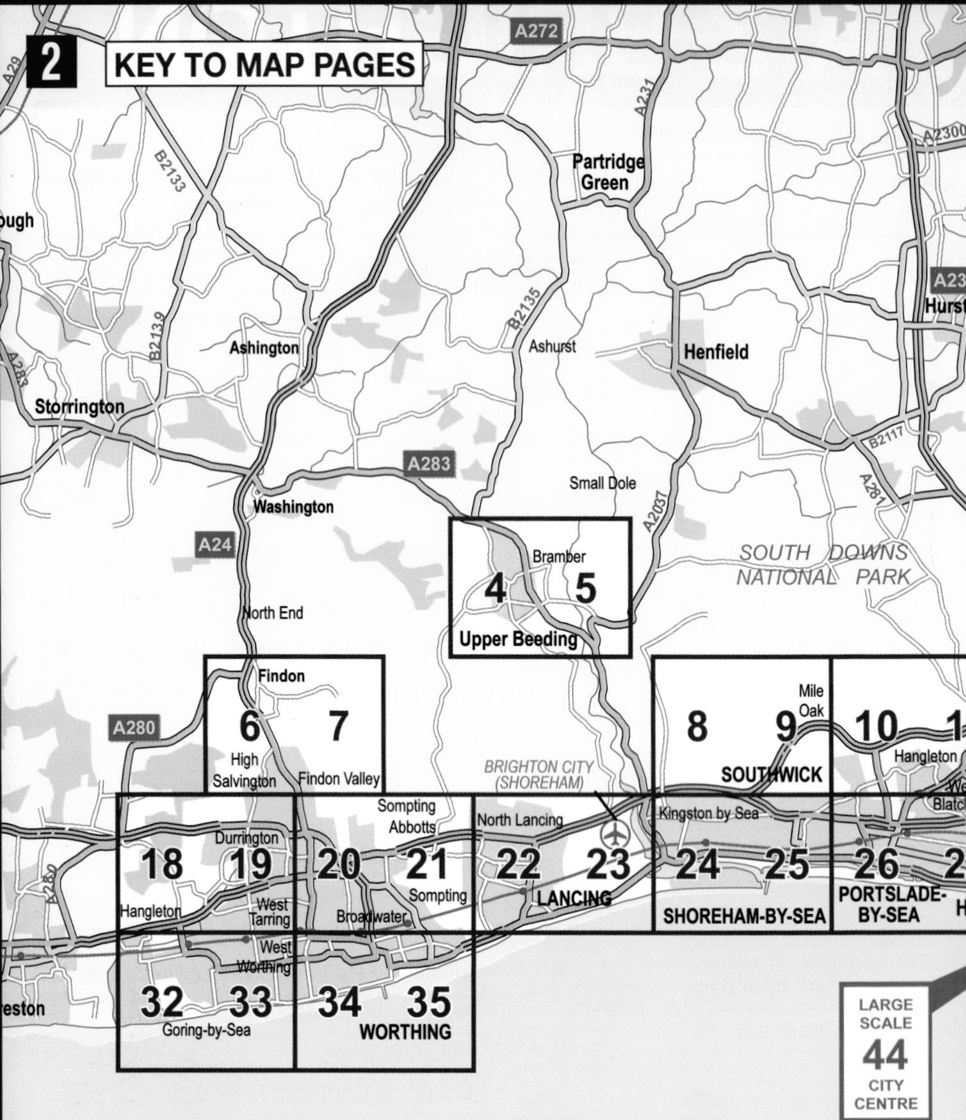

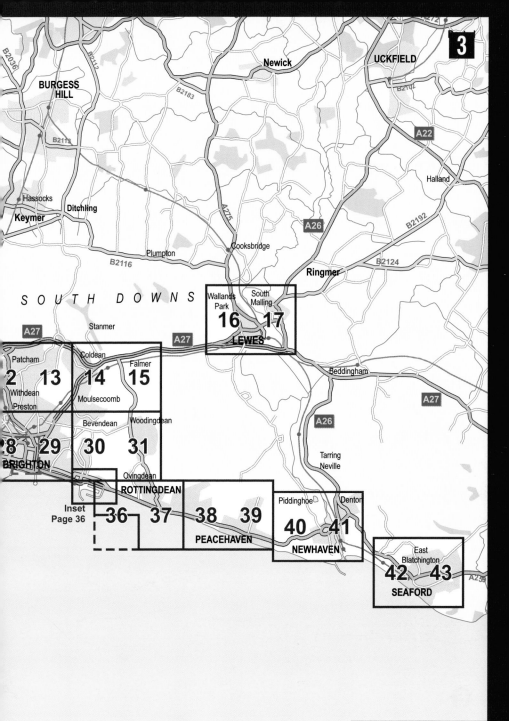

3

Newick

UCKFIELD

BURGESS HILL

B2036

B2112

B2183

A22

B2102

Halland

Hassocks

Ditchling

Keymer

B2119

A275

A26

Cooksbridge

Plumpton

B2116

B2124

B2192

Ringmer

S O U T H   D O W N S

Wallands Park

South Malling

16 **17**

LEWES

A27

Stanmer

Coldean

A27

Beddingham

A27

Patcham

2 **13** **14** **15**

Falmer

Withdean

Moulsecoomb

Preston

A26

Bevendean

Woodingdean

Tarring Neville

8 **29** **30** **31**

BRIGHTON

Ovingdean

ROTTINGDEAN

Piddinghoe

Denton

Inset Page 36

36 **37** **38** **39**

40 **41**

PEACEHAVEN

NEWHAVEN

East Blatchington

42 **43**

A259

SEAFORD

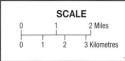

SCALE

0		1		2 Miles

0	1	2	3 Kilometres

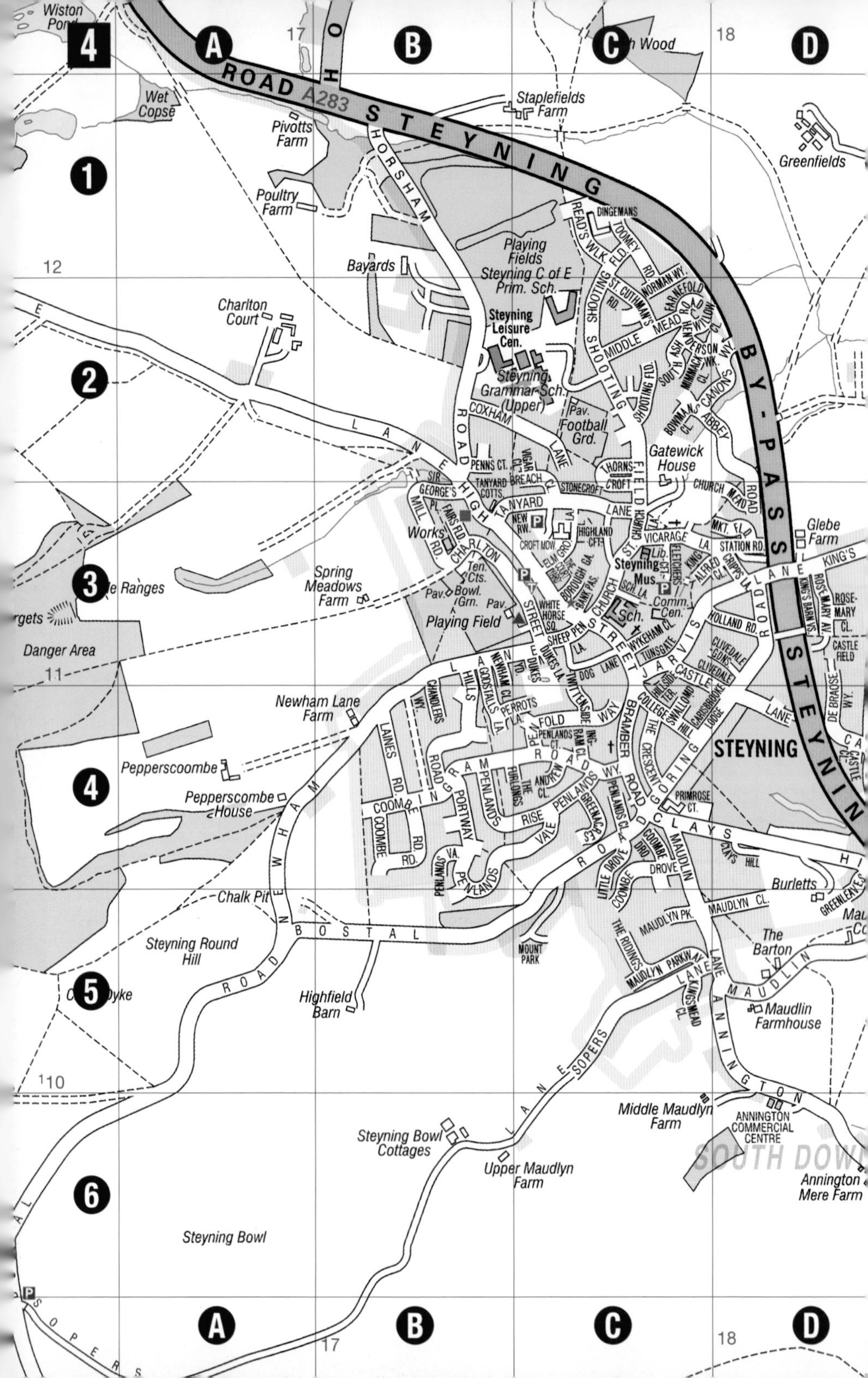
STEYNING ROAD A283
STEYNING BY-PASS
Wiston Pond
Wet Copse
Pivotts Farm
Staplefields Farm
Greenfields
Poultry Farm
Bayards
Playing Fields
Steyning C of E Prim. Sch.
Charlton Court
Steyning Leisure Cen.
Steyning Grammar Sch. (Upper)
Football Grd.
Gatewick House
Glebe Farm
Spring Meadows Farm
Works
Playing Field
Steyning Mus.
Comm. Cen.
Danger Area
Newham Lane Farm
Pepperscoombe
Pepperscoombe House
STEYNING
Burletts
Chalk Pit
Steyning Round Hill
Highfield Barn
The Barton
Maudlin Farmhouse
Middle Maudlyn Farm
ANNINGTON COMMERCIAL CENTRE
Steyning Bowl Cottages
Upper Maudlyn Farm
Annington & Mere Farm
Steyning Bowl
SOUTH DOWN
HORSHAM ROAD
HIGH STREET
CHURCH STREET
NEWHAM LANE
BOSTAL ROAD
SOPERS LANE
ANNINGTON LANE
MAUDLIN LANE
CLAYS HILL
KING'S BARN LANE
BRAMBER ROAD
GORING ROAD
JARVIS LANE
CASTLE LANE
MAUDLYN PARKWAY
MAUDLYN CL.
MOUNT PARK
A B C D
1 2 3 4 5 6
12 11 110 17 18

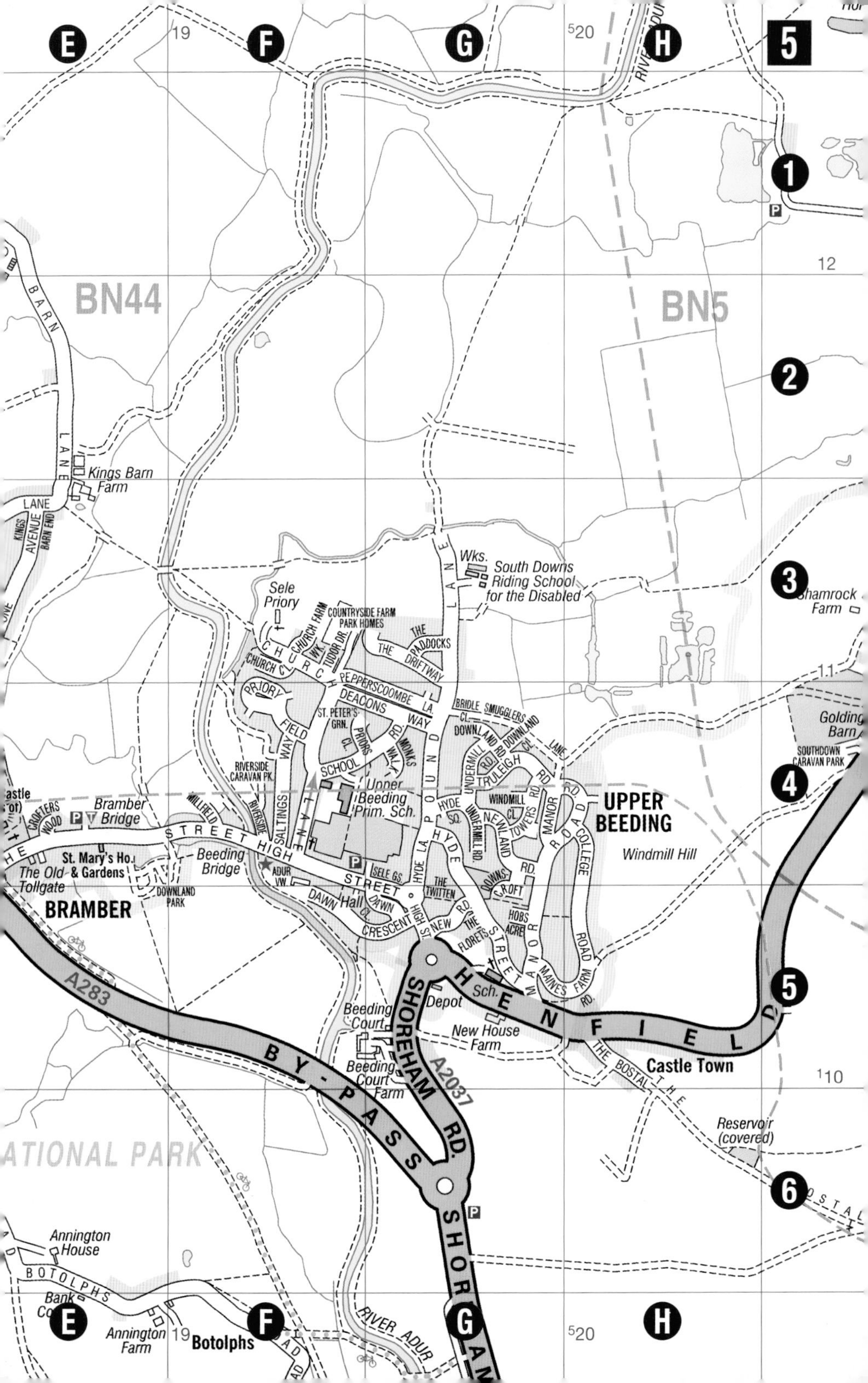
E
F
G
H
19
520
BN44
BN5
12
11
110
Kings Barn Farm
Sele Priory
Wks.
South Downs Riding School for the Disabled
Shamrock Farm
Golding Barn
SOUTHDOWN CARAVAN PARK
Upper Beeding Prim. Sch.
UPPER BEEDING
Windmill Hill
Bramber Bridge
Beeding Bridge
St. Mary's Ho. & Gardens
The Old Tollgate
BRAMBER
Hall
Sch.
Depot
New House Farm
Castle Town
Beeding Court
Beeding Court Farm
Reservoir (covered)
A283
BY-PASS
SHOREHAM RD.
A2037
HENFIELD
THE BOSTAL
ATIONAL PARK
Annington House
Annington Farm
Botolphs
RIVER ADUR
HIGH STREET
CHURCH LA.
DEACONS WAY
POUND LANE
SCHOOL LANE
MANOR ROAD
COLLEGE ROAD
Bank Co

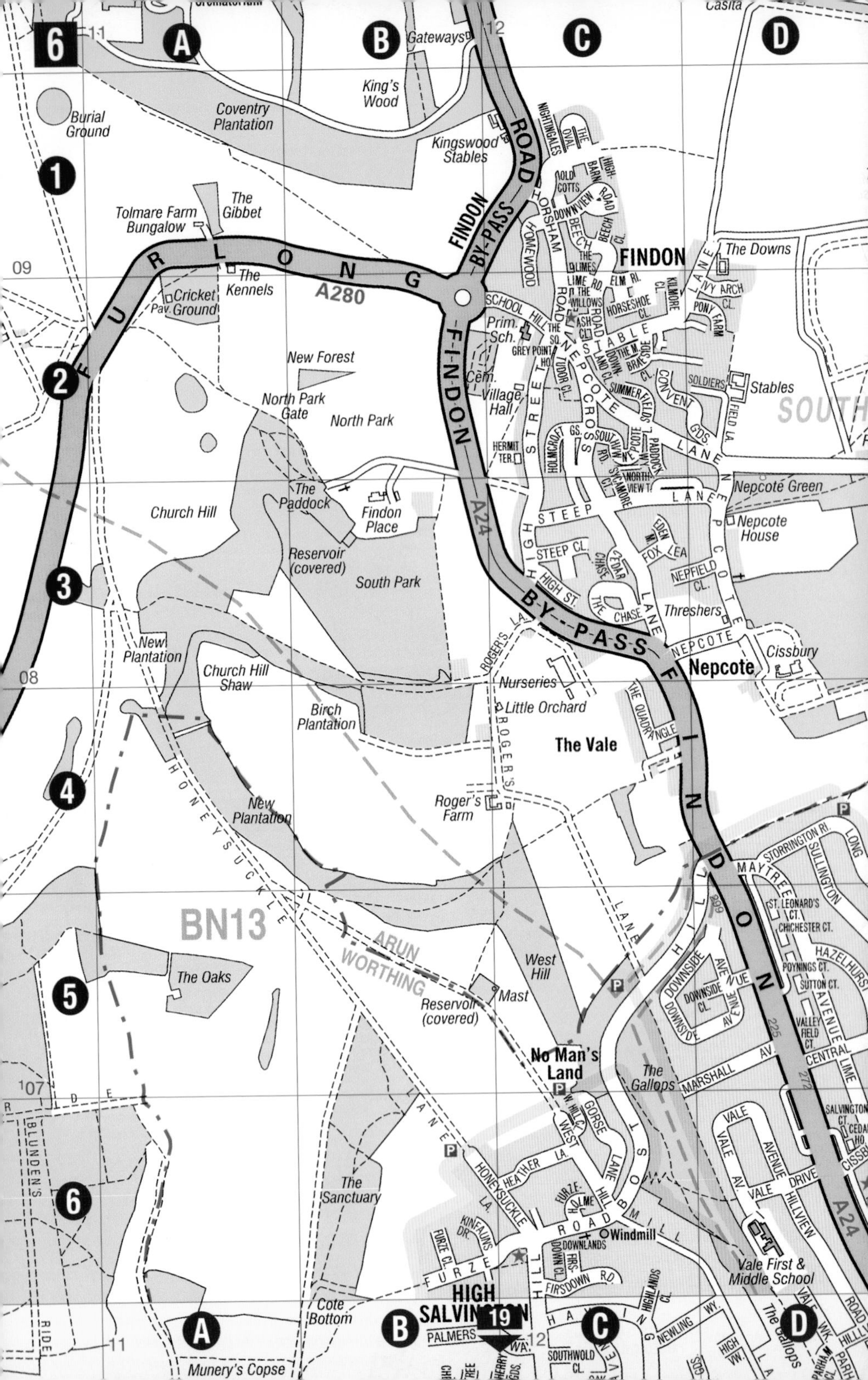
6
A
B
C
D
1
2
3
4
5
6
Burial Ground
Coventry Plantation
King's Wood
Gateways
Kingswood Stables
Tolmare Farm Bungalow
The Gibbet
FURLONG
A280
The Kennels
Cricket Ground
Pav.
FINDON ROAD BY-PASS
FINDON BY-PASS
A24
FINDON
New Forest
North Park Gate
North Park
Church Hill
The Paddock
Findon Place
Reservoir (covered)
South Park
New Plantation
Church Hill Shaw
Birch Plantation
Nurseries
Little Orchard
The Vale
Roger's Farm
ROGER'S LA.
HONEYSUCKLE
BN13
ARUN
WORTHING
The Oaks
West Hill
Mast
No Man's Land
The Gallops
The Sanctuary
Cote Bottom
Munery's Copse
HIGH SALVINGTON
19
Windmill
Vale First & Middle School
Prim. Sch.
Cem.
Village Hall
The Downs
Stables
Nepcote Green
Nepcote House
Threshers
Nepcote
Cissbury
SCHOOL HILL
HIGH STREET
NEPCOTE LANE
STEEP LANE
HORSHAM ROAD
HOMEWOOD
STABLE LANE
CROSS LANE
CONVENT GDS.
SOLDIERS FIELD LA.
FOX LEA
NEPFIELD CL.
THE QUADRANGLE
THE CHASE
STORRINGTON RI.
SULLINGTON
MAYTREE
ST. LEONARD'S CT.
CHICHESTER CT.
HAZELHURST
POYNINGS CT.
SUTTON CT.
DOWNSIDE AVENUE
DOWNSIDE CL.
VALLEY FIELD CT.
CENTRAL AV.
MARSHALL AV.
VALE AVENUE
VALE DRIVE
HILLVIEW
GORSE LANE
HEATHER LA.
WEST HILL
FURZE RD.
FIRSDOWN RD.
HIGHLANDS CL.
NEWLING WY.
SOUTHWOLD CL.
PALMERS WA.
BOSTAL
MILL ROAD
HILL ROAD
KINFAUNS DR.
FURZE CL.
DOWNLANDS
BLUNDEN'S RIDE
SOUTHWOLD
The Gallops
09
08
107
11
12

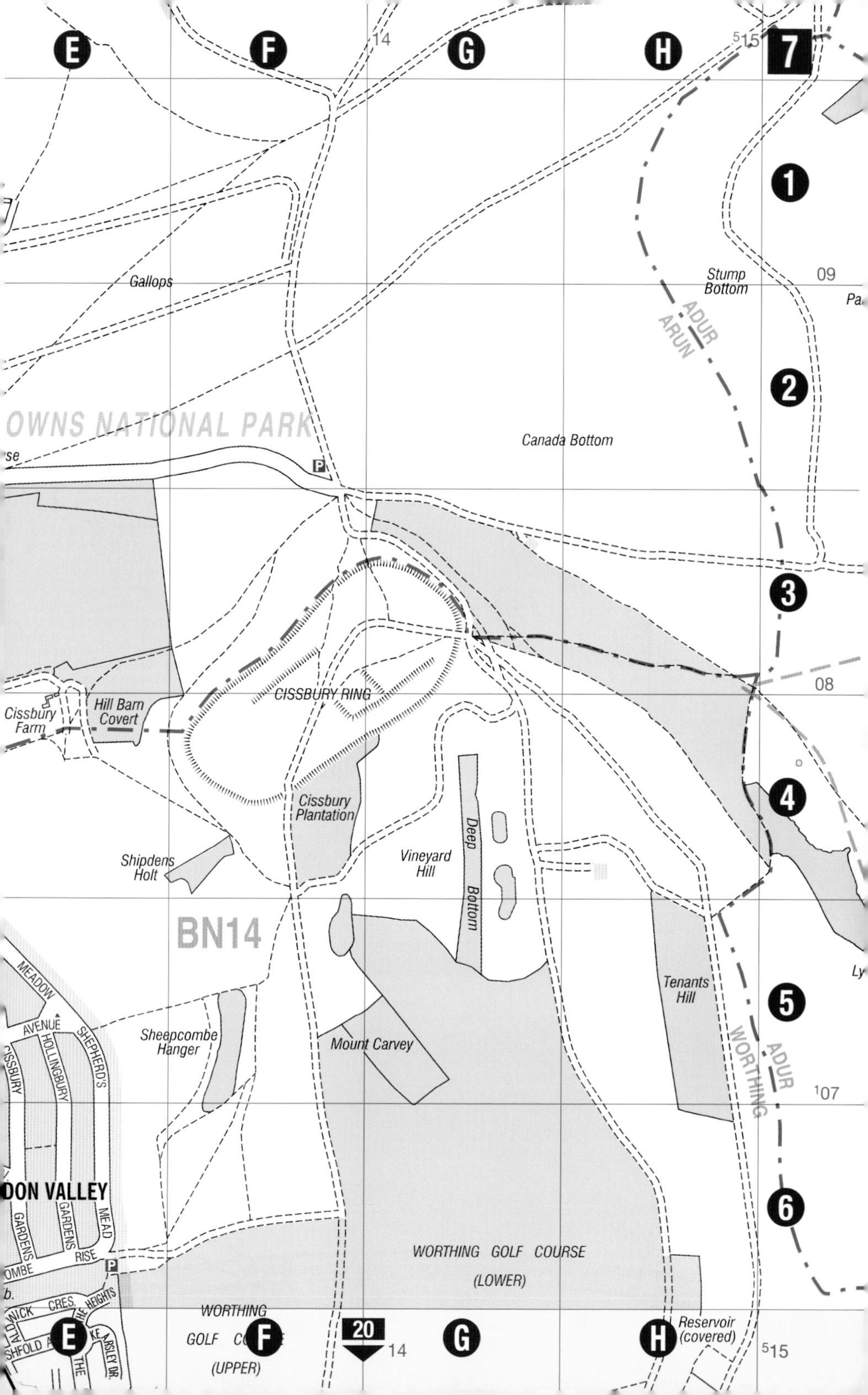

1

Gallops

Stump
Bottom

ADUR
ARUN

09

Pa

2

OWNS NATIONAL PARK

se

Canada Bottom

P

3

08

Cissbury
Farm

Hill Barn
Covert

CISSBURY RING

4

Cissbury
Plantation

Shipdens
Holt

Vineyard
Hill

Deep
Bottom

BN14

Tenants
Hill

5

ADUR
WORTHING

107

Sheepcombe
Hanger

Mount Carvey

MEADOW
AVENUE
HOLLINGBURY
SHEPHERD'S
ISSBURY

DON VALLEY

GARDENS
GARDENS
MEAD
RISE

6

P

OMBE

b.

WORTHING
GOLF COURSE
(LOWER)

WORTHING
GOLF COURSE
(UPPER)

Reservoir
(covered)

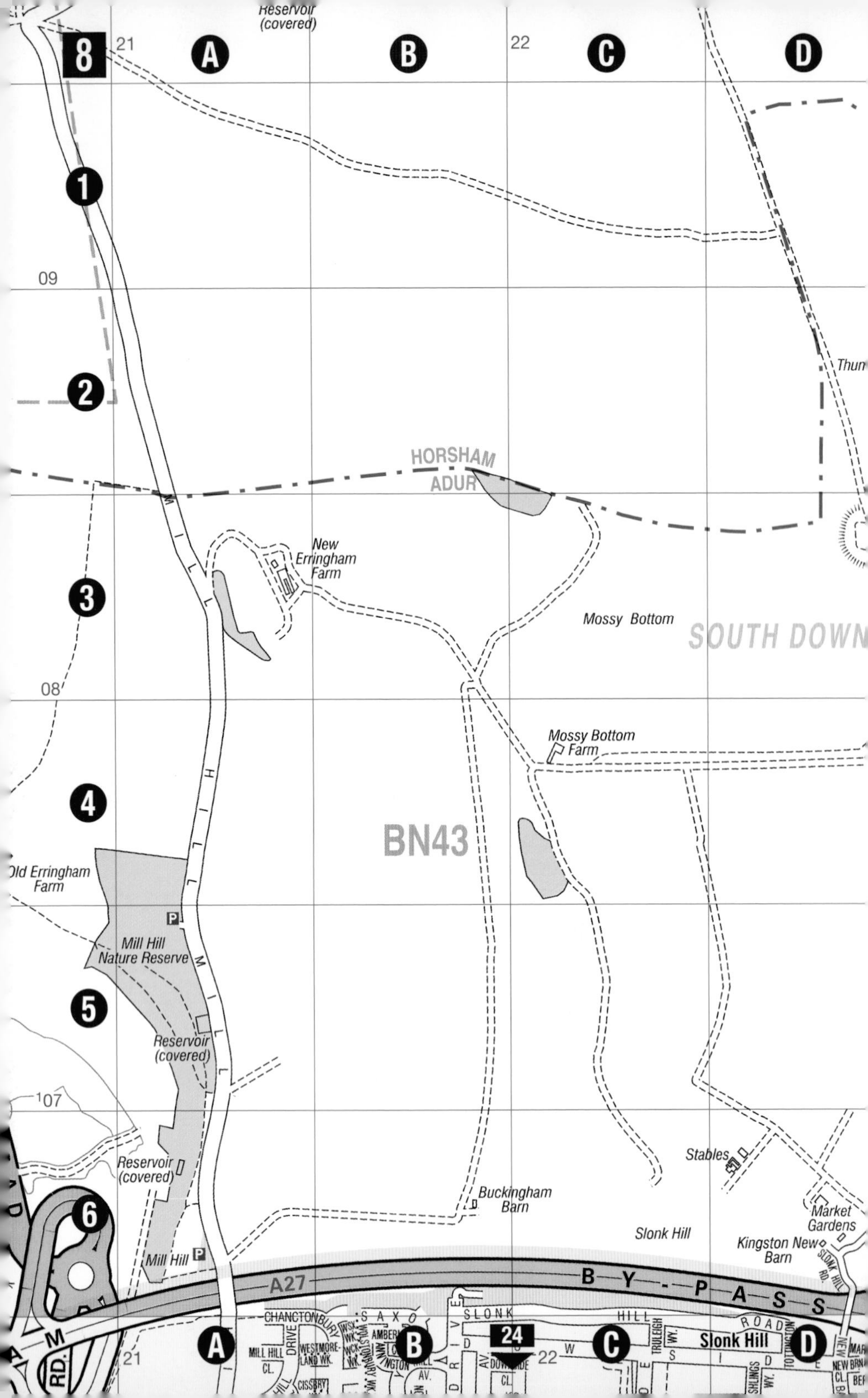
Reservoir (covered)
A
B
C
D
21
22
09
08
107
1
2
3
4
5
6
HORSHAM
ADUR
New Erringham Farm
Mossy Bottom
SOUTH DOWN
Mossy Bottom Farm
BN43
Old Erringham Farm
Mill Hill Nature Reserve
Reservoir (covered)
Reservoir (covered)
Mill Hill
Stables
Buckingham Barn
Slonk Hill
Market Gardens
Kingston New Barn
A27
BY-PASS
CHANCTONBURY
DRIVE
SAXON
SLONK
HILL
ROAD
TRULEIGH WY.
Slonk Hill
TOTTINGTON
MILL HILL CL.
WESTMORELAND WK.
CISSBURY
DOWNSIDE CL.
SHILLINGS WY.
NEW BRN. CL.
24
Thun
M
RD.

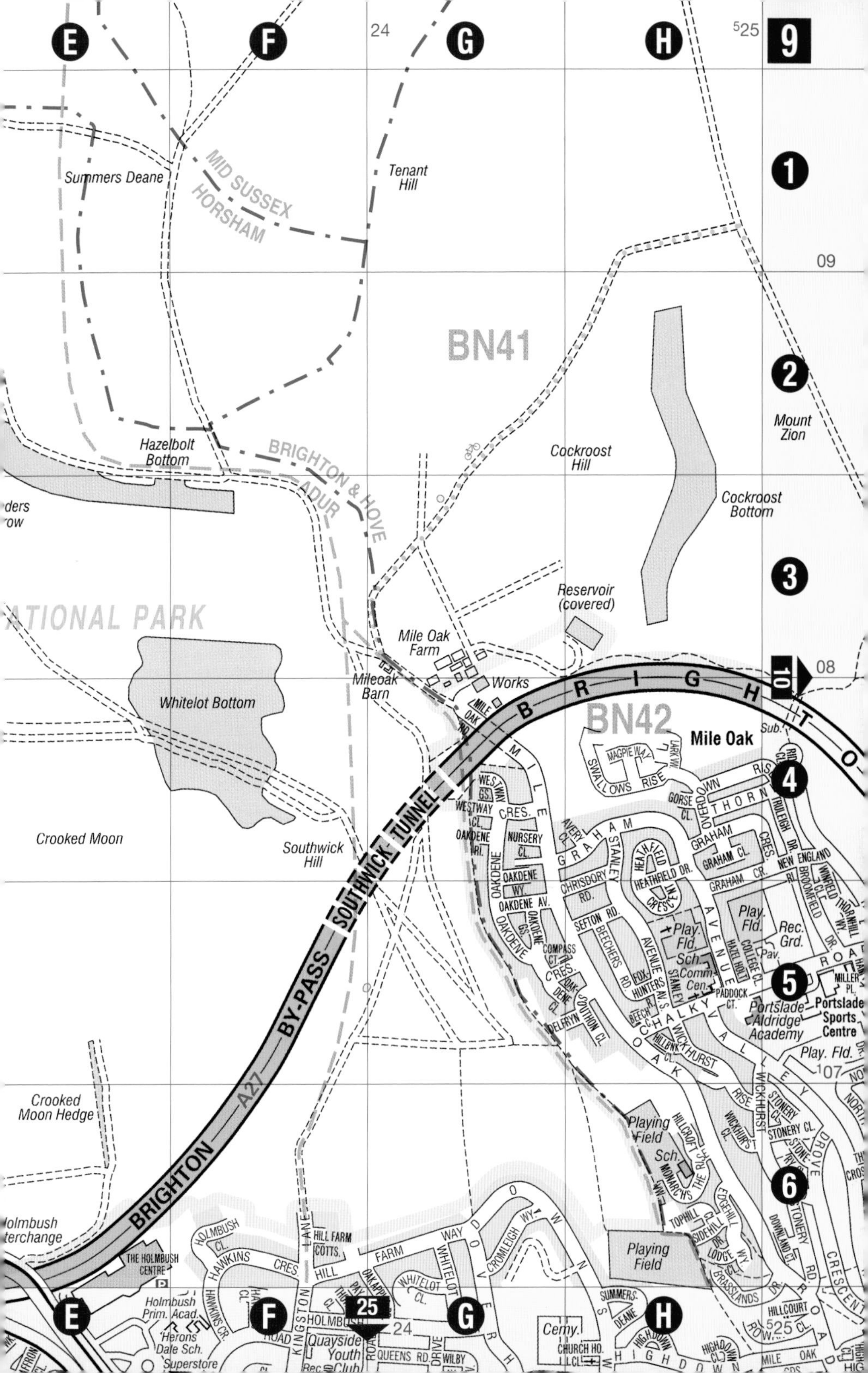

E
F
G
H
24
525
Summers Deane
MID SUSSEX
HORSHAM
Tenant Hill
BN41
Mount Zion
Hazelbolt Bottom
BRIGHTON & HOVE
ADUR
Cockroost Hill
Cockroost Bottom
ATIONAL PARK
Reservoir (covered)
Mile Oak Farm
Mileoak Barn
Works
BRIGHTON
BN42
Mile Oak
Whitelot Bottom
Crooked Moon
Southwick Hill
SOUTHWICK TUNNEL
BY-PASS
A27
BRIGHTON
Crooked Moon Hedge
Holmbush Interchange
THE HOLMBUSH CENTRE
Holmbush Prim. Acad.
Herons Dale Sch.
Superstore
Quayside Youth Club
Playing Field
Sch.
Playing Field
Play. Fld.
Sch.
Comm. Cen.
Play. Fld.
Rec. Grd.
Portslade Aldridge Academy
Portslade Sports Centre
Play. Fld.
Cemy.
GRAHAM AVENUE
CHALKY
OAK VALLEY
OAKDENE AV.
HILL FARM WAY
DOWNSWAY
HIGHDOWN
WHITELOT DR.
HOLMBUSH CL.
HAWKINS CRES.
KINGSTON LANE
STONERY RD.
DROVE ROAD

10
25

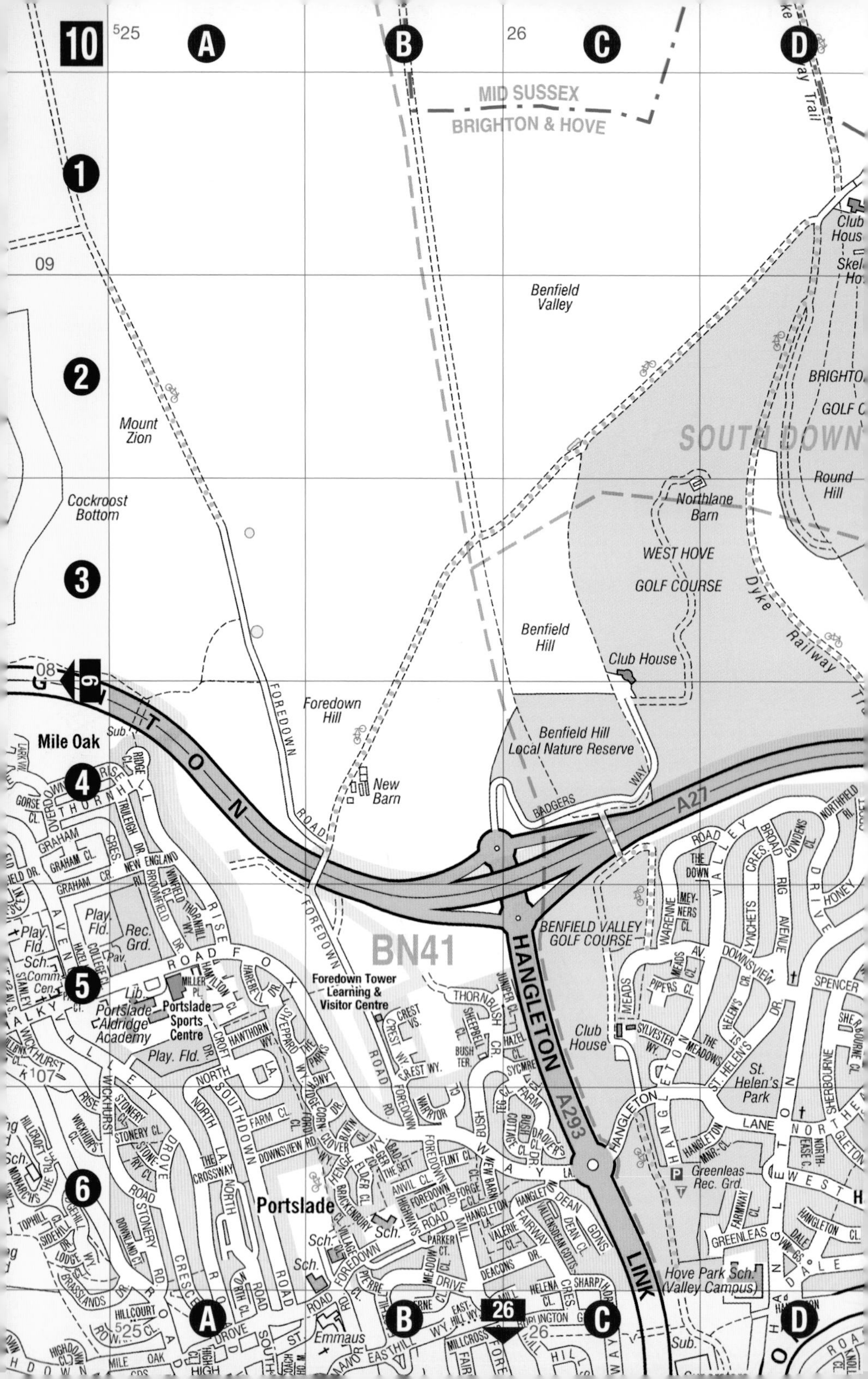
MID SUSSEX
BRIGHTON & HOVE
Benfield Valley
Mount Zion
Cockroost Bottom
SOUTH DOWNS
Round Hill
Northlane Barn
WEST HOVE GOLF COURSE
Dyke Railway Trail
Benfield Hill
Club House
Foredown Hill
Benfield Hill Local Nature Reserve
New Barn
Mile Oak
BADGERS WAY
A27
BN41
HANGLETON LINK
A293
BENFIELD VALLEY GOLF COURSE
Foredown Tower Learning & Visitor Centre
Portslade Aldridge Academy
Portslade Sports Centre
Play. Fld.
Rec. Grd.
Portslade
St. Helen's Park
Greenleas Rec. Grd.
Hove Park Sch. (Valley Campus)
Emmaus
FOREDOWN ROAD
THORNHILL RISE
FOX WAY
VALLEY DRIVE
HANGLETON LANE
STONERY ROAD
NORTH LANE
SOUTHDOWN ROAD
MILE OAK ROAD
HIGHDOWN ROAD
NEVILL ROAD
Sch.
Sub.
9
26

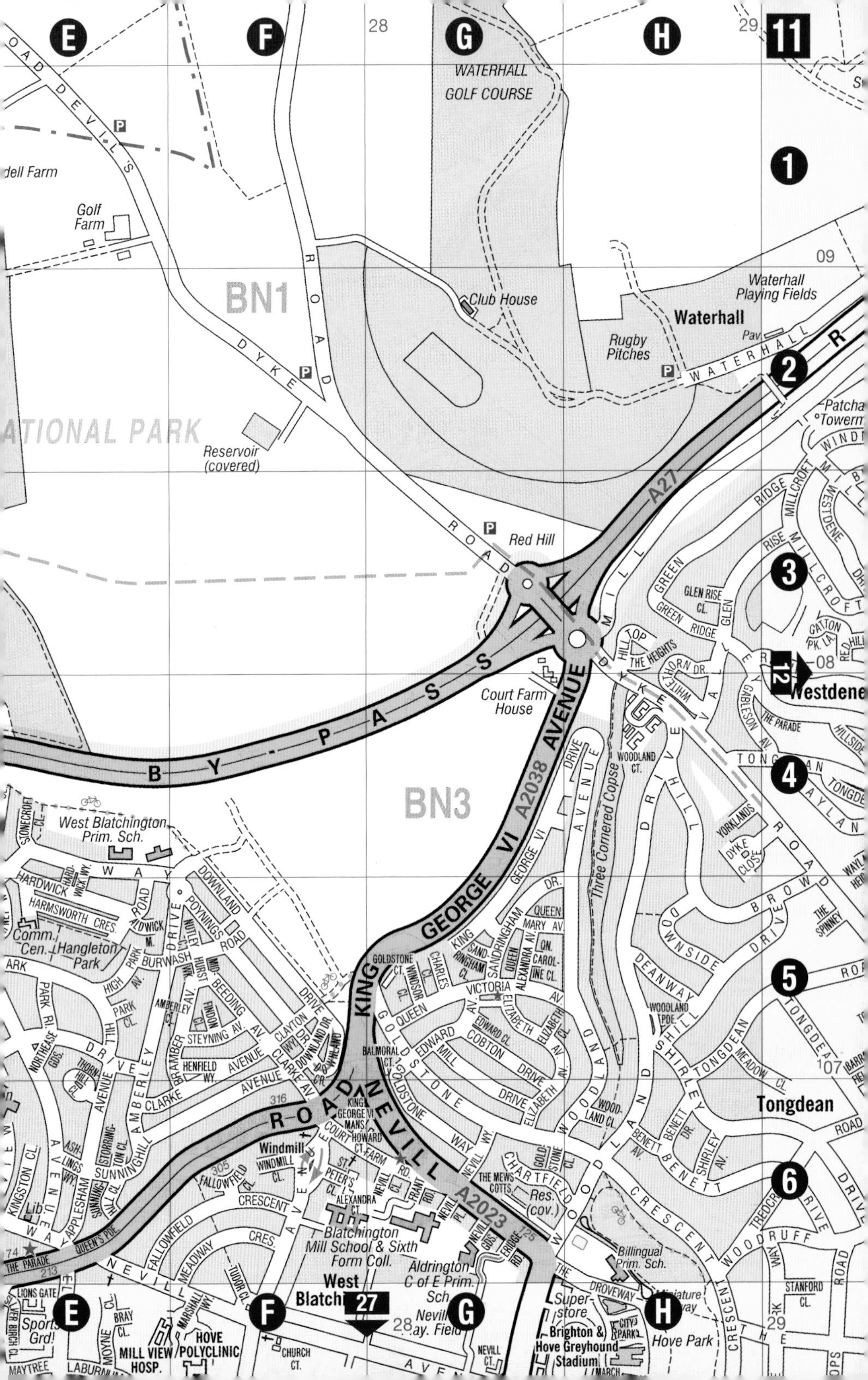

11
E
F
G
H
28
29
WATERHALL GOLF COURSE
Golf Farm
dell Farm
DEVIL'S DYKE ROAD
ROAD
BN1
Club House
Waterhall
Waterhall Playing Fields
Rugby Pitches
Pav.
WATERHALL
09
Patcham Towermill
ATIONAL PARK
Reservoir (covered)
Red Hill
A27
MILLCROFT
WESTDENE
RIDGE
RISE
GREEN RIDGE
GLEN RISE CL.
GLEN
GATTON PK. LA.
HILL TOP
THE HEIGHTS
WHITETHORN DR.
12
Westdene
08
GABLESON AV.
THE PARADE
HILLSIDE
TONGDEAN
Court Farm House
BYPASS
KING GEORGE VI AVENUE
A2038
BN3
Three Cornered Copse
WOODLAND CT.
YORKLANDS
DYKE CLOSE
DOWNSIDE
BROW
THE SPINNEY
DEANWAY
West Blatchington Prim. Sch.
STONECROFT CL.
HARDWICK
HARDWICK WY.
HARMSWORTH CRES.
Comm. Cen.
Hangleton Park
DOWNLAND
POYNINGS
ALDWICK M.
NUTLEY CL.
HURST WK.
MIDHURST
BEEDING
FINDON CL.
BURWASH
HIGH PARK AV.
PARK CL.
AMBERLEY
STEYNING AV.
HENFIELD WY.
CLAYTON WY.
DOWNLAND DR.
CLARKE AVENUE
BRAMBER
NORTHEASE GDS.
THORN HILL CL.
GOLDSTONE CT.
WINDSOR CT.
CHARLES CL.
SANDRINGHAM CL.
QUEEN MARY AV.
QN. CAROLINE CL.
ALEXANDRA AV.
VICTORIA
QUEEN
EDWARD
EDWARD CL.
COBTON
ELIZABETH AV.
ELIZABETH CL.
BALMORAL CT.
GOLDSTONE WAY
WOODLAND PDE.
SHIRLEY
TONGDEAN
MEADOW CL.
107
Tongdean
BENETT AV.
BENETT DR.
SHIRLEY AV.
TREDCROFT
WOODRUFF
STANFORD CL.
ROAD
DRIVE
316
ROAD
NEVILL
A2023
KING GEORGE VI MANS.
HOWARD CT.
COURT FARM RD.
Windmill
WINDMILL CL.
ST. PETER'S CL.
NEVILL CL.
FRANT RD.
ALEXANDRA CT.
NEVILL PL.
NEVILL GDS.
ERIDGE RD.
THE MEWS COTTS.
CHARTFIELD
GOLDSTONE CL.
Res. (cov.)
WOODLAND CL.
CRESCENT
Billingual Prim. Sch.
Blatchington Mill School & Sixth Form Coll.
Aldrington C of E Prim. Sch.
West Blatchington
27
Nevill Play. Field
FALLOWFIELD CL.
FALLOWFIELD
CRESCENT
MEADWAY CRES.
305
SUNNINGHILL
STORRINGTON CL.
ASHLINGS WY.
APPLESHAM
KINGSTON CL.
Lib.
THE PARADE
QUEEN'S PDE.
213
74
LIONS GATE
Sports Grd.
MOYNE CL.
BRAY CL.
MARSHALL WY.
TUDOR CL.
MILL VIEW HOSP.
HOVE POLYCLINIC
CHURCH CT.
NEVILL CT.
MAYTREE
LABURNUM
THE DROVEWAY
Superstore
Brighton & Hove Greyhound Stadium
CITY PARK
Miniature Railway
Hove Park
CRESCENT
125

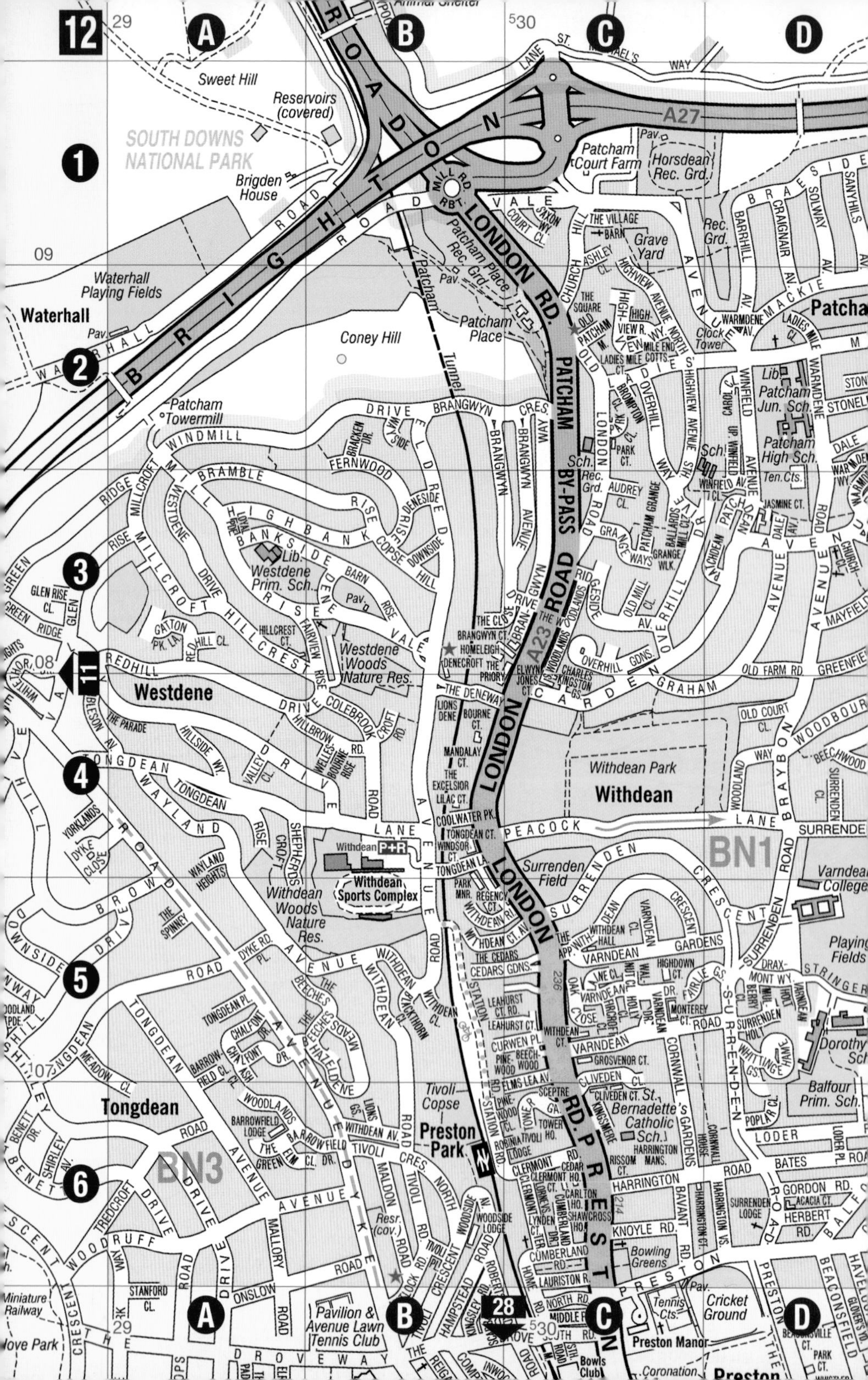

12
A
B
C
D
1
2
3
4
5
6
29
530
09
08
107
Sweet Hill
Reservoirs (covered)
SOUTH DOWNS NATIONAL PARK
Brigden House
Waterhall Playing Fields
Waterhall
Pav.
BRIGHTON ROAD
A27
ST. MICHAEL'S WAY
MILL RD. RBT.
LONDON RD.
VALE
Patcham Court Farm
Horsdean Rec. Grd.
Patcham Place Rec. Grd.
Patcham Place
Patcham Tunnel
Coney Hill
Patcham Towermill
THE VILLAGE BARN
Grave Yard
Rec. Grd.
Clock Tower
Patcham
Lib.
Patcham Jun. Sch.
Patcham High Sch.
Ten. Cts.
Sch.
Rec. Grd.
PATCHAM BY-PASS
A23
DRIVE
BRANGWYN
WINDMILL
BRAMBLE
FERNWOOD
HIGHBANK
Lib.
Westdene Prim. Sch.
Westdene Woods Nature Res.
Westdene
REDHILL
11
TONGDEAN
WAYLAND
PEACOCK LANE
Withdean Park
Withdean
Withdean P+R
Withdean Sports Complex
Withdean Woods Nature Res.
Surrenden Field
BN1
Varndean College
Playing Fields
Dorothy Sch.
Balfour Prim. Sch.
St. Bernadette's Catholic Sch.
Tivoli Copse
Preston Park
Tongdean
BN3
Resr. (cov.)
Bowling Greens
Tennis Cts.
Cricket Ground
Preston Manor
Pavilion & Avenue Lawn Tennis Club
Miniature Railway
Hove Park
DROVEWAY
Bowls Club
28
PRESTON RD.
DYKE ROAD AVENUE
LONDON ROAD
Preston

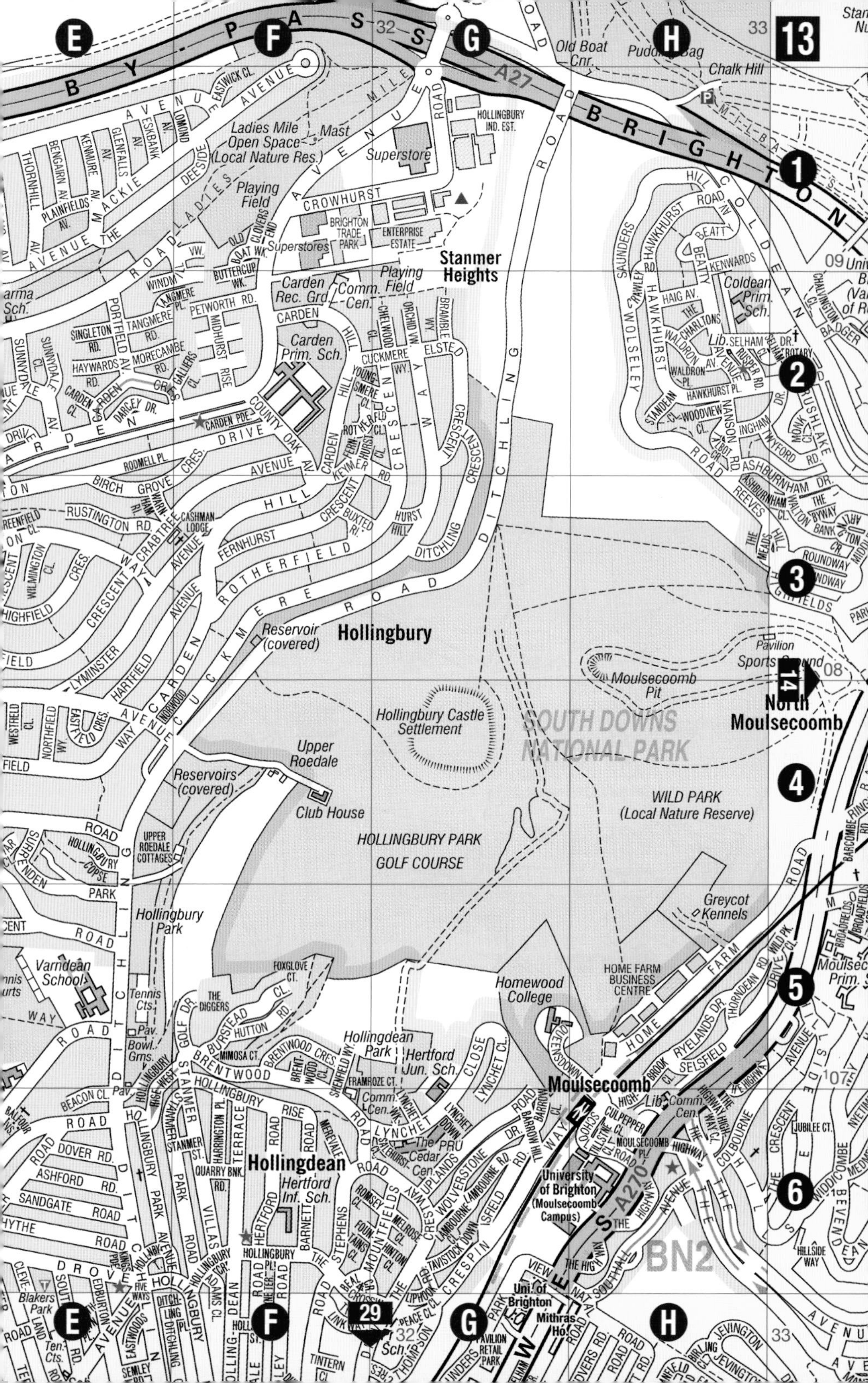

13
E
F
G
H
32
33
BY-PASS
A27
BRIGHTON
Old Boat Cnr.
Pudding Bag
Chalk Hill
Ladies Mile Open Space (Local Nature Res.)
Mast
Superstore
HOLLINGBURY IND. EST.
Playing Field
CROWHURST
BRIGHTON TRADE PARK
ENTERPRISE ESTATE
Superstores
Stanmer Heights
Carden Rec. Grd.
Comm. Cen.
Playing Field
Carden Prim. Sch.
MACKIE AVENUE
THE AVENUE
LADIES MILE ROAD
CARDEN AVENUE
DITCHLING ROAD
CARDEN HILL
CARDEN CRESCENT
CUCKMERE WAY
ELSTED CRESCENT
ROTHERFIELD CRESCENT
FERNHURST CRESCENT
BIRCH GROVE CRES.
CRABTREE AVENUE
HIGHFIELD CRES.
LYMINSTER AVENUE
CASHMAN LODGE
CARDEN PDE.
Coldean Prim. Sch.
Lib.
HAWKHURST ROAD
COLDEAN LANE
WOLSELEY ROAD
SAUNDERS HILL
HIGHFIELDS
ROUNDWAY
1
2
3
4
5
6
Hollingbury
Reservoir (covered)
Hollingbury Castle Settlement
Upper Roedale
Club House
Reservoirs (covered)
SOUTH DOWNS NATIONAL PARK
Moulsecoomb Pit
Pavilion
Sports Ground
14
08
North Moulsecoomb
WILD PARK (Local Nature Reserve)
HOLLINGBURY PARK GOLF COURSE
UPPER ROEDALE COTTAGES
Hollingbury Park
Greycot Kennels
HOME FARM BUSINESS CENTRE
HOME FARM ROAD
Homewood College
Varndean School
Tennis Cts.
Bowl. Grns.
Hollingdean Park
Hertford Jun. Sch.
Moulsecoomb
Lib.
Comm. Cen.
University of Brighton (Moulsecoomb Campus)
A270
LEWES ROAD
Hollingdean
Hertford Inf. Sch.
The Cedar Cen.
PRU
BN2
Uni. of Brighton Mithras Ho.
Moulsecoomb Prim. Sch.
Blakers Park
FIVE WAYS
29
PAVILION RETAIL PARK
107
HOLLINGBURY PARK AVENUE
STANMER VILLAS
BRENTWOOD ROAD
LYNCHET CLOSE
UPLANDS ROAD
THE HIGHWAY
COLBOURNE AVENUE
THE CRESCENT
WIDDICOMBE WAY
BEVENDEAN AVENUE
HILLSIDE WAY
JUBILEE CT.
JEVINGTON

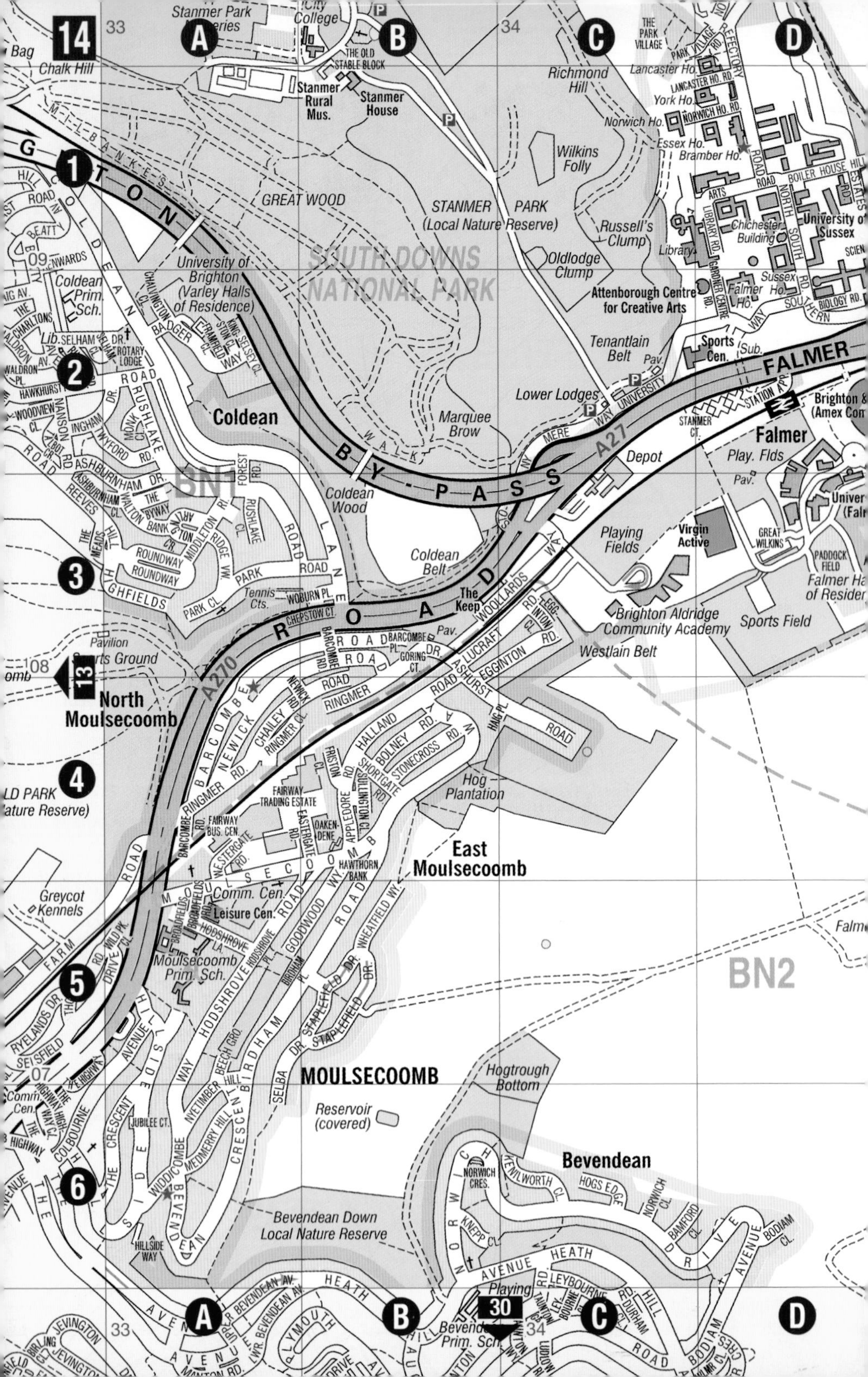

14
Chalk Hill
Stanmer Park Nurseries
City College
THE OLD STABLE BLOCK
Stanmer Rural Mus.
Stanmer House
Richmond Hill
THE PARK VILLAGE
PARK VILLAGE RD.
REFECTORY RD.
Lancaster Ho.
LANCASTER HO. RD.
York Ho.
NORWICH HO. RD.
Norwich Ho.
Essex Ho.
Bramber Ho.
Wilkins Folly
BOILER HOUSE HILL
ARTS ROAD
LIBRARY RD.
NORTH SOUTH RD.
University of Sussex
Chichester Building
Library
GARDNER CENTRE RD.
Sussex Ho.
Falmer Ho.
SOUTHERN WAY
BIOLOGY RD.
MILLBANKES
GREAT WOOD
STANMER PARK (Local Nature Reserve)
Russell's Clump
Oldlodge Clump
SOUTH DOWNS NATIONAL PARK
Attenborough Centre for Creative Arts
Tenantlain Belt
Sports Cen.
Sub.
FALMER
Lower Lodges
UNIVERSITY WAY
MERE WAY
STATION APP.
STANMER CT.
Brighton & (Amex Com
Falmer
Play. Flds
Pav.
Depot
A27
COLDEAN LANE
University of Brighton (Varley Halls of Residence)
Coldean Prim. Sch.
Lib.
SELHAM DR.
ROTARY LODGE
CHALVINGTON CL.
BADGER WAY
KING'S CL.
SELSEY CL.
Coldean
Marquee Brow
WALK
BY-PASS
Coldean Wood
Coldean Belt
BN1
RUSHLAKE ROAD
RUSHLAKE CL.
FOREST RD.
Playing Fields
Virgin Active
GREAT WILKINS
PADDOCK FIELD
Falmer Halls of Residence
Brighton Aldridge Community Academy
Sports Field
Westlain Belt
WOOLLARDS WAY
The Keep
WOBURN PL.
CHEPSTOW CT.
A270 ROAD
Tennis Cts.
PARK CL.
PARK ROAD
HIGHFIELDS
ROUNDWAY
MIDDLETON RI.
ARLINGTON CR.
THE BYWAY
WALTON BANK
ASHBURNHAM DR.
REEVES HILL
THE MEADS
HAWKHURST
WOODVIEW
NANSON RD.
INGHAM DR.
WYFORD
MONK CL.
Pavilion
Sports Ground
13
North Moulsecoomb
BARCOMBE RD.
BARCOMBE PL.
GORING CT.
NEWICK RD.
RINGMER ROAD
CHAILEY
RINGMER CL.
LUCRAFT RD.
EGGINTON RD.
ASHURST ROAD
HAIG PL.
Hog Plantation
HALLAND
BOLNEY RD.
STONECROSS RD.
SHORTGATE RD.
FRISTON CL.
SULLINGTON CL.
APPLEDORE RD.
FAIRWAY TRADING ESTATE
FAIRWAY BUS. CEN.
WESTERGATE RD.
EASTERGATE RD.
OAKENDENE
HAWTHORN BANK
East Moulsecoomb
MOULSECOOMB WAY
Comm. Cen.
Leisure Cen.
Greycot Kennels
BROADFIELDS
HODSHROVE LA.
HODSHROVE PL.
GOODWOOD WY.
WHEATFIELD WY.
Moulsecoomb Prim. Sch.
WILD PK. DRIVE
RYELANDS DR.
SELSFIELD
HIGHWAY
STAPLEFIELD DR.
BIRDHAM PL.
BN2
MOULSECOOMB
Reservoir (covered)
Hogtrough Bottom
Bevendean
HILLSIDE
JUBILEE CT.
NYETIMBER HILL
MEDMERRY HILL
BEECH GRO.
CRESCENT
BEVENDEAN
WIDDICOMBE WAY
HILLSIDE WAY
Bevendean Down Local Nature Reserve
NORWICH CRES.
KENILWORTH CL.
HOGS EDGE
NORWICH CL.
BAMFORD CL.
DRIVE
BODIAM AVENUE
BODIAM CL.
KNEPP CL.
HEATH AVENUE
HEATH HILL
LEYBOURNE RD.
DURHAM
Playing
30
Bevendean Prim. Sch.
PLYMOUTH
JEVINGTON
BIRLING
UPR. BEVENDEAN AV.
LWR. BEVENDEAN AV.
COLBOURNE
THE HIGHWAY
33
34
A B C D
1 2 3 4 5 6

E
F
36
G
H
37
Housedean Farm
Housedean Cottages
Falmer Sports Complex
Old Forge Barn
Knight's Gate
Ten. Cts.
STREET
MILL
PARK
MIDDLE ST.
ROAD
Park Wall Farm
A27 BRIGHTON
HILL
FALMER
THE COURTYARD
EAST ST.
PARK ST.
STH. ST.
Court Farm
Grave Yard
Cranedean Plantation
New Barn
BN7
09
1
2
3
4
5
6
B2123
THE DROVE
FALMER
LEWES
BRIGHTON & HOVE
Loose Bottom
108
Newmarket Plantation
SOUTH DOWNS NATIONAL PARK
JUGG'S ROAD
Newmarket Hill
Falmer Bottom
JUGG'S AVENUE
TV Receiving Station
07
Newmarket Bottom
Falmer Bo
DROVE
31
Upper Bevendean
NORTON
Bullock Hill
Mast

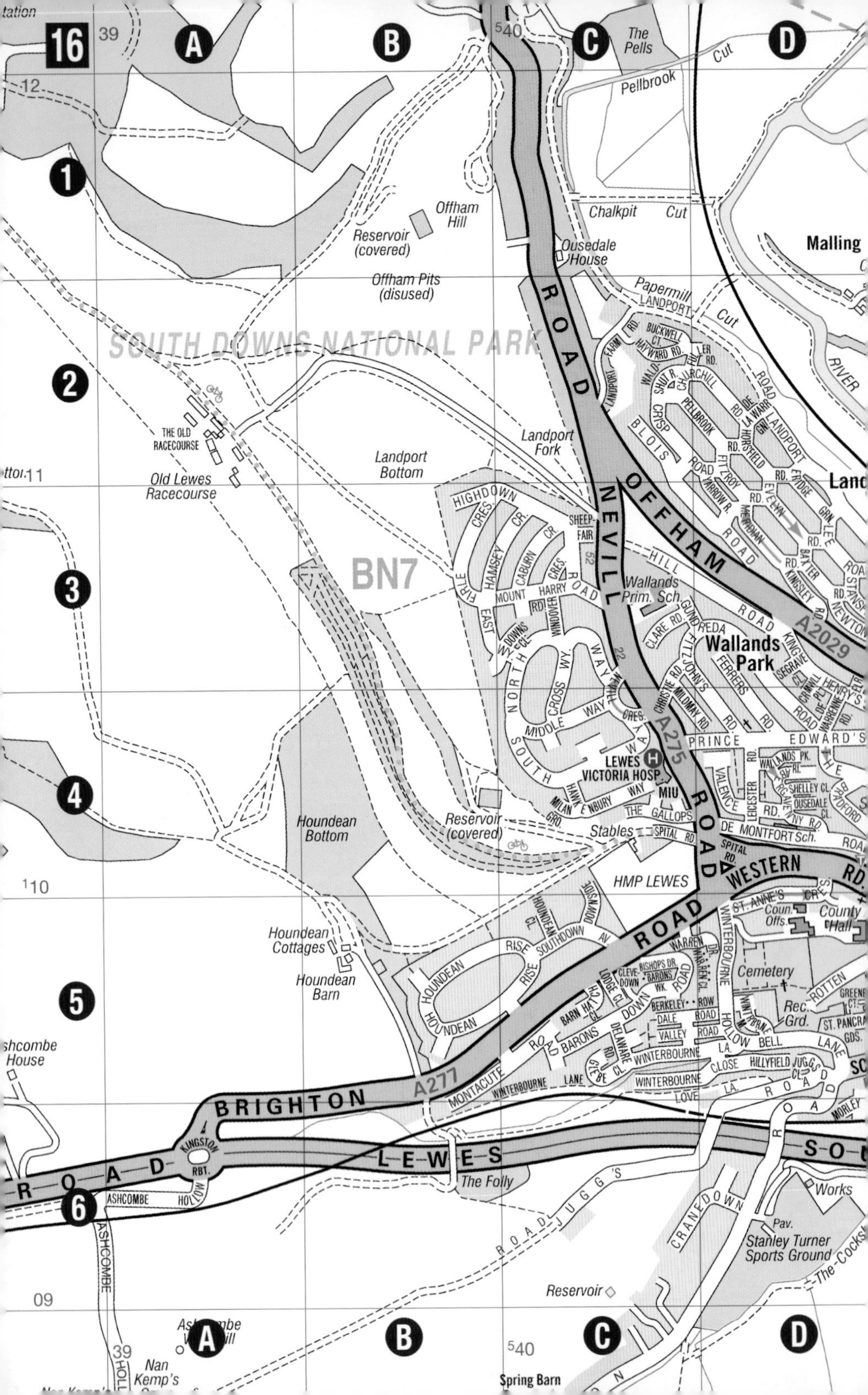

A
B
C
D
1
2
3
4
5
6
The Pells
Pellbrook
Cut
Chalkpit Cut
Offham Hill
Reservoir (covered)
Ousedale House
Malling
Offham Pits (disused)
Papermill Cut
SOUTH DOWNS NATIONAL PARK
THE OLD RACECOURSE
Old Lewes Racecourse
Landport Bottom
Landport Fork
NEVILL ROAD
OFFHAM ROAD
BN7
Wallands Prim. Sch.
Wallands Park
A2029
A275
LEWES VICTORIA HOSP.
MIU
Stables
Houndean Bottom
Reservoir (covered)
HMP LEWES
WESTERN ROAD
County Hall
Coun. Offs.
Cemetery
Rec. Grd.
Houndean Cottages
Houndean Barn
Ashcombe House
BRIGHTON ROAD
A277
KINGSTON RBT.
LEWES ROAD
The Folly
JUGG'S ROAD
Works
Pav.
Stanley Turner Sports Ground
Reservoir
Ashcombe Windmill
Nan Kemp's
Spring Barn
540
39
12
11
10
09

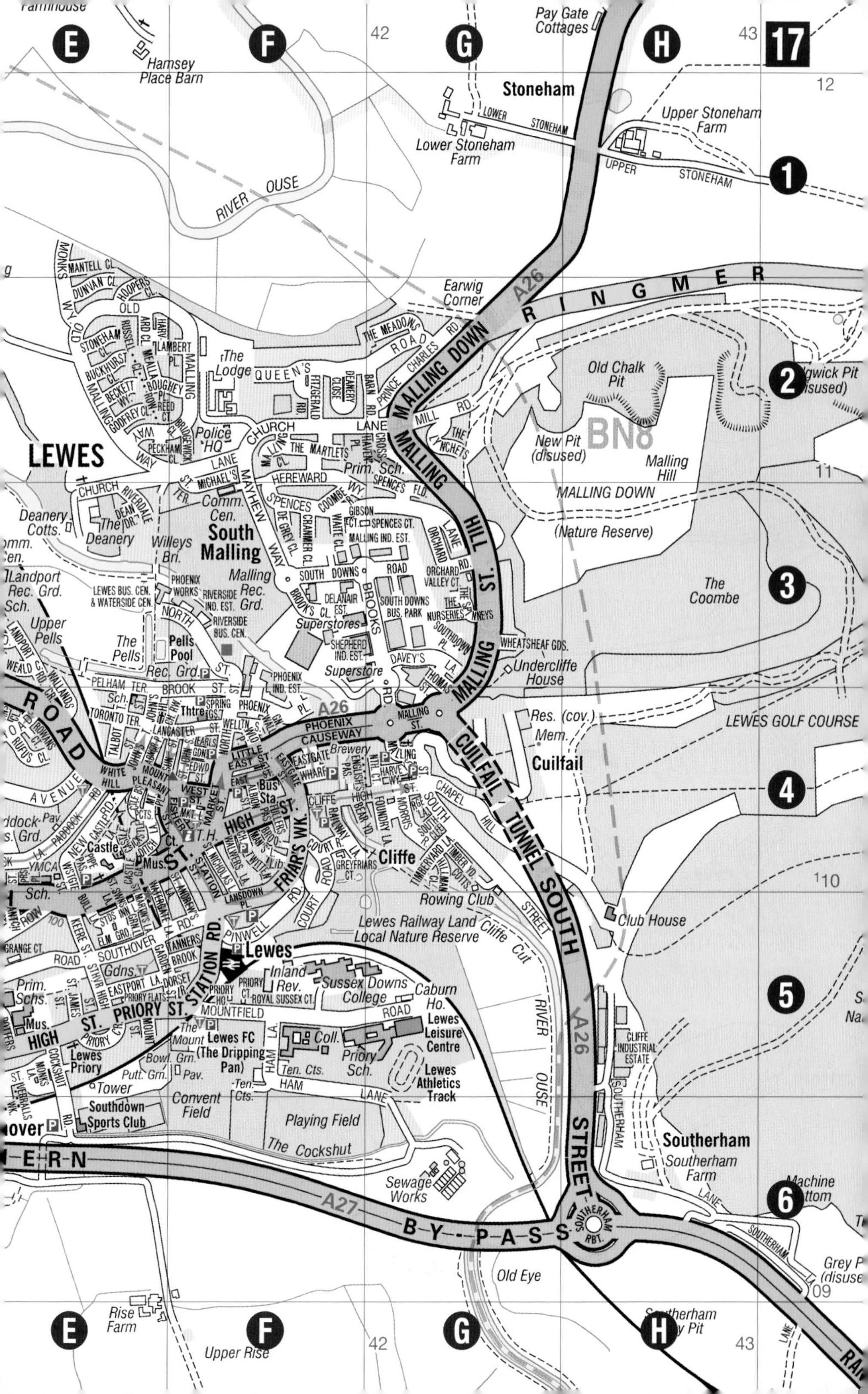
E
F
G
H
42
43
12
11
10
09
1
2
3
4
5
6
Hamsey Place Barn
Pay Gate Cottages
Stoneham
Upper Stoneham Farm
LOWER STONEHAM
Lower Stoneham Farm
UPPER STONEHAM
RIVER OUSE
Earwig Corner
A26
RINGMER
MALLING DOWN
Old Chalk Pit
BN8
New Pit (disused)
Malling Hill
MALLING DOWN (Nature Reserve)
The Coombe
LEWES
South Malling
Police HQ
The Lodge
Comm. Cen.
The Deanery
Deanery Cotts.
Willeys Bri.
Malling Rec. Grd.
Landport Rec. Grd.
Upper Pells
The Pells
Pells Pool
Superstores
Superstore
Undercliffe House
WHEATSHEAF GDS.
MALLING HILL ST.
Res. (cov.)
Mem.
Cuilfail
LEWES GOLF COURSE
CUILFAIL TUNNEL
SOUTH STREET
PHOENIX CAUSEWAY
HIGH ST.
Castle
Mus.
T.H.
Bus Sta.
Cliffe
Rowing Club
Club House
Lewes Railway Land Local Nature Reserve
Cliffe Cut
RIVER OUSE
Lewes
Inland Rev.
Sussex Downs College
Caburn Ho.
Lewes Leisure Centre
Lewes Athletics Track
Coll.
Priory Sch.
Lewes FC (The Dripping Pan)
The Mount
Lewes Priory
Tower
Bowl. Grn.
Putt. Grn.
Pav.
Southdown Sports Club
Convent Field
Playing Field
The Cockshut
Ten. Cts.
HAM LANE
Sewage Works
CLIFFE INDUSTRIAL ESTATE
Southerham
Southerham Farm
SOUTHERHAM RBT.
A27
BY-PASS
Old Eye
Rise Farm
Upper Rise
Southerham
Gdns.
SOUTHOVER
PRIORY ST.
STATION RD.
FRIAR'S WK.
WHITE HILL
ROAD
Prim. Schs.
Prim. Sch.

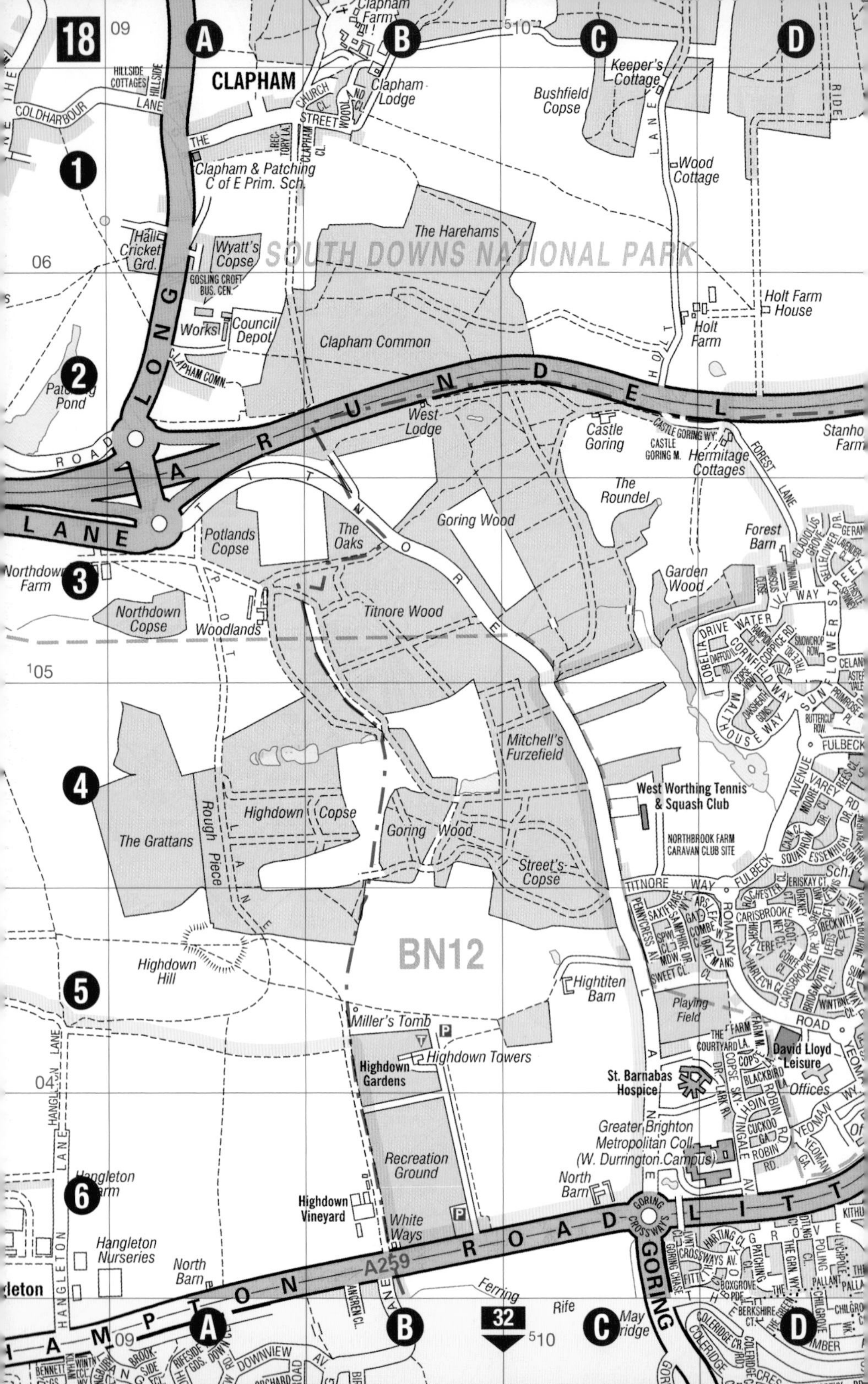
CLAPHAM
Clapham Farm
Clapham Lodge
Hillside Cottages
Coldharbour Lane
Clapham & Patching C of E Prim. Sch.
Hall Cricket Grd.
Wyatt's Copse
Gosling Croft Bus. Cen.
Works
Council Depot
Clapham Comn.
Patching Pond
Keeper's Cottage
Bushfield Copse
Wood Cottage
The Harehams
SOUTH DOWNS NATIONAL PARK
Clapham Common
Holt Farm House
Holt Farm
Holt Lane
Long Furlong
Arundel Road
Lane
West Lodge
Castle Goring
Castle Goring Wy.
Castle Goring M.
Hermitage Cottages
Forest Lane
Stanhope Farm
The Roundel
Goring Wood
Potlands Copse
The Oaks
Titnore Lane
Titnore Wood
Forest Barn
Garden Wood
Northdown Farm
Northdown Copse
Woodlands
Pottle Lane
Lily Way
Lower Street
Lobelia Drive
Water
Cornfield Way
Malthouse Way
Sunflower Way
Fulbeck
Mitchell's Furzefield
West Worthing Tennis & Squash Club
Northbrook Farm Caravan Club Site
Highdown Copse
Goring Wood
The Grattans
Rough Piece
Street's Copse
Titnore Way
Fulbeck Avenue
Romany
Carisbrooke
BN12
Highdown Hill
Hightiten Barn
Playing Field
Miller's Tomb
Highdown Towers
Highdown Gardens
The Courtyard
Farm M.
Copse La.
David Lloyd Leisure
St. Barnabas Hospice
Offices
Blackbird La.
Robin Rd.
Cuckoo
Yeoman Way
Greater Brighton Metropolitan Coll. (W. Durrington Campus)
Recreation Ground
North Barn
Goring Crossways
Highdown Vineyard
White Ways
Hangleton Lane
Hangleton Farm
Hangleton Nurseries
North Barn
Hangleton
Hampton Road
A259
Littlehampton Road
Goring
Crossways Av.
Harting Cl.
Patching
Goring Chase
Boxgrove Pde.
Berkshire Ct.
The Green
Chilgrove
Ferring Rife
May Bridge
Coleridge Cres.
Downview
Orchard
Brookside
Riffeside
Bennett
Angren Cl.
32
09
06
105
04
510
A
B
C
D
1
2
3
4
5
6

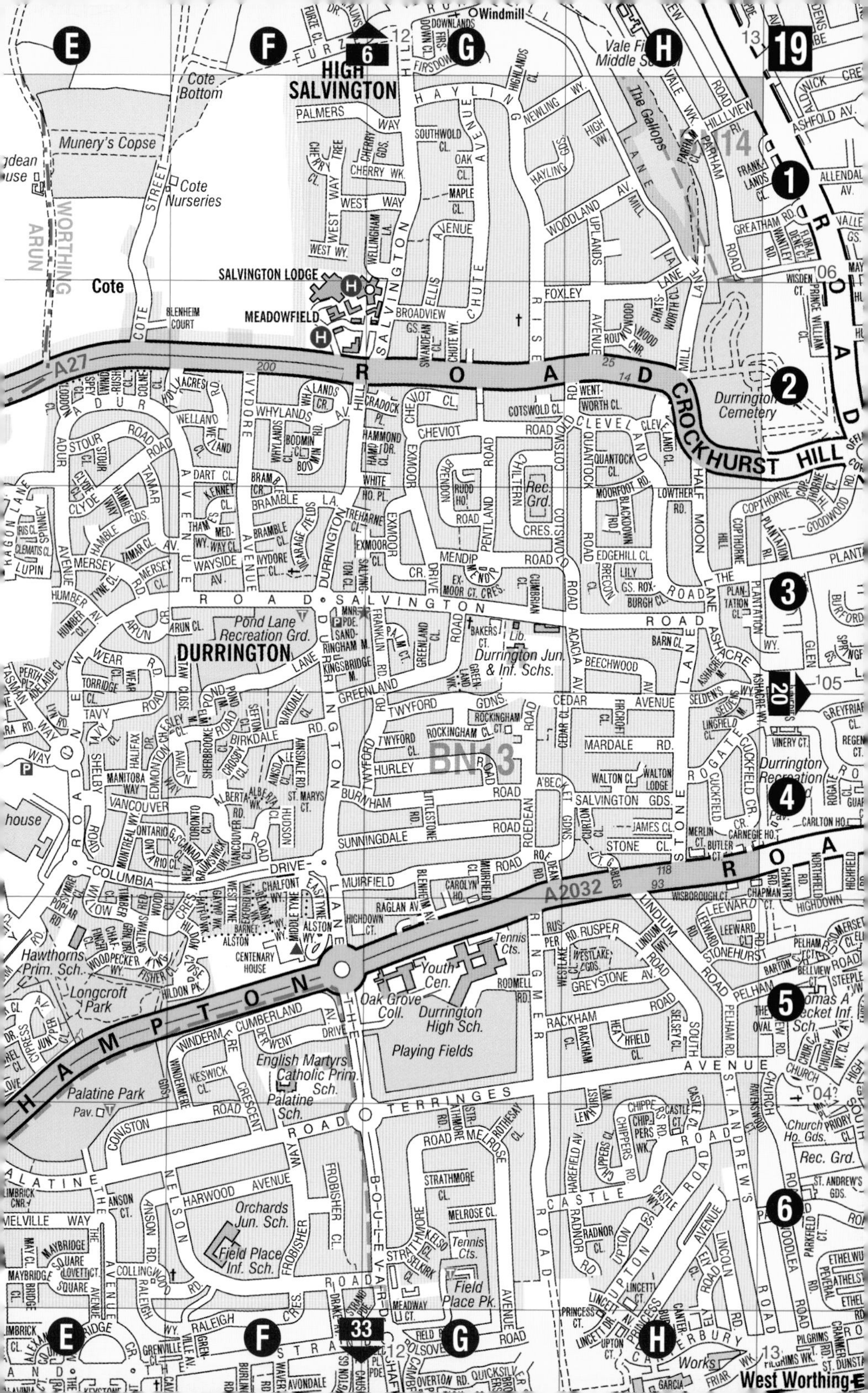
19
HIGH SALVINGTON
DURRINGTON
Cote
Windmill
Cote Bottom
Munery's Copse
Cote Nurseries
SALVINGTON LODGE
MEADOWFIELD
Vale First Middle School
The Gallops
Durrington Cemetery
CROCKHURST HILL
A27
A2032
HAMPTON
BN14
BN13
Pond Lane Recreation Grd.
Durrington Jun. & Inf. Schs.
Durrington Recreation Grd.
Hawthorns Prim. Sch.
Longcroft Park
Youth Cen.
Oak Grove Coll.
Durrington High Sch.
Playing Fields
English Martyrs Catholic Prim. Sch.
Palatine Sch.
Palatine Park
Orchards Jun. Sch.
Field Place Inf. Sch.
Field Place Pk.
Thomas A Becket Inf. Sch.
Works
West Worthing
WORTHING
ARUN
6
20
33

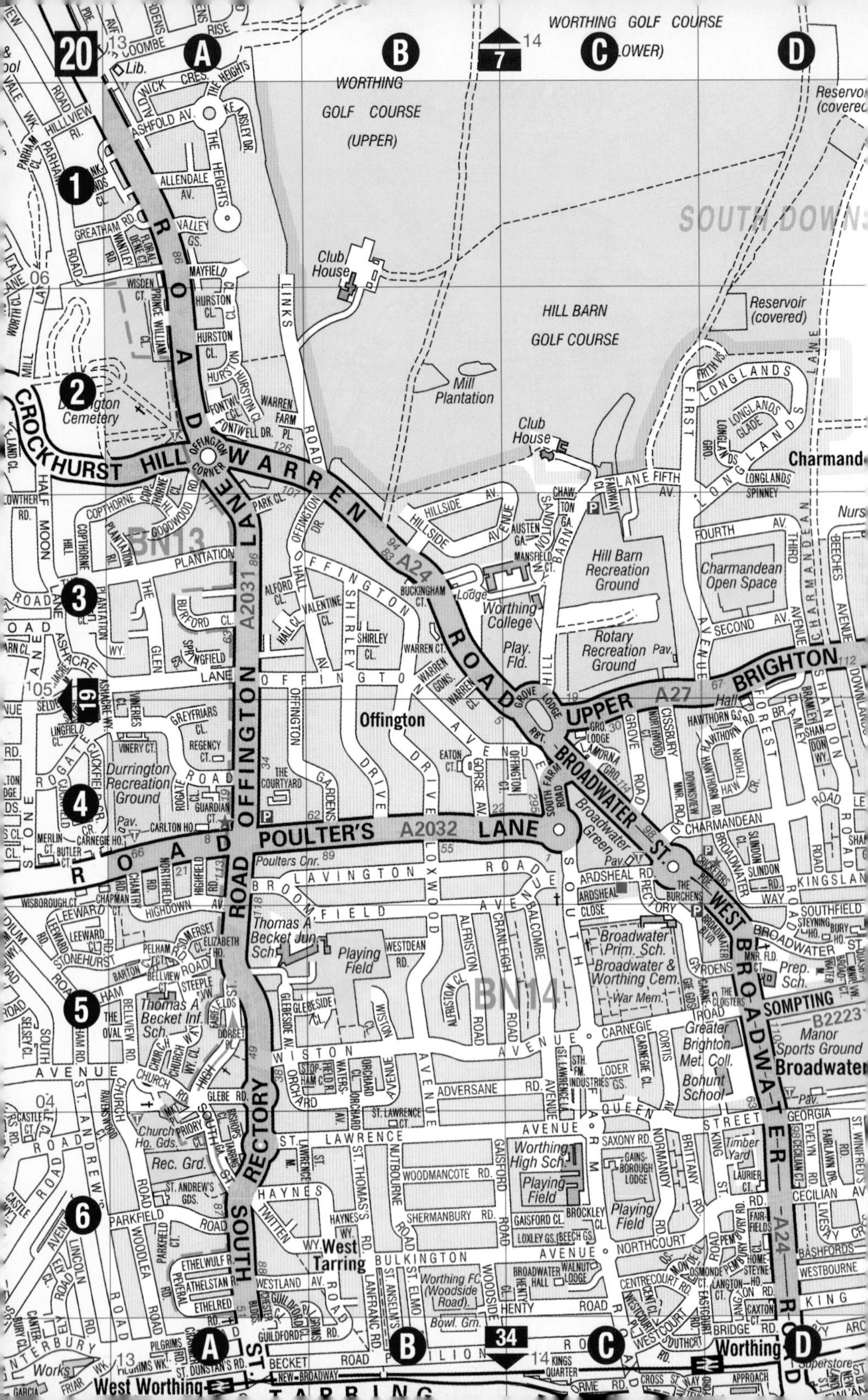
A
B
C
D
1
2
3
4
5
6
7
14
19
34
13
WORTHING GOLF COURSE (LOWER)
WORTHING GOLF COURSE (UPPER)
HILL BARN GOLF COURSE
SOUTH DOWNS
Reservoir (covered)
Club House
Mill Plantation
Durrington Cemetery
Lib.
CROCKHURST HILL
WARREN ROAD
A24
OFFINGTON LANE
A2031
OFFINGTON CORNER
BN13
BN14
Offington
Charmandean
Charmandean Open Space
Hill Barn Recreation Ground
Rotary Recreation Ground
Worthing College
Play. Fld.
UPPER BRIGHTON ROAD
A27
GROVE LODGE RBT.
BROADWATER ST. WEST
BROADWATER ST. EAST
BROADWATER ROAD
POULTER'S LANE
A2032
Poulters Cnr.
Durrington Recreation Ground
Pav.
SOUTH FARM ROAD
Broadwater Green
Broadwater Prim. Sch.
Broadwater & Worthing Cem.
War Mem.
Thomas A Becket Jun. Sch.
Thomas A Becket Inf. Sch.
Playing Field
SOMPTING ROAD
B2223
Manor Sports Ground
Broadwater
Greater Brighton Met. Coll.
Bohunt School
Prep. Sch.
Timber Yard
Worthing High Sch.
RECTORY ROAD
SOUTH STREET
West Tarring
Church Ho. Gds.
Rec. Grd.
Worthing FC (Woodside Road)
Bowl. Grn.
Worthing
West Worthing
Superstore
Works
TARRING
CLIFTON ROAD
QUEEN STREET
CARNEGIE AVENUE
HENTY ROAD
KING STREET
ST. LAWRENCE AVENUE
SEMPTING

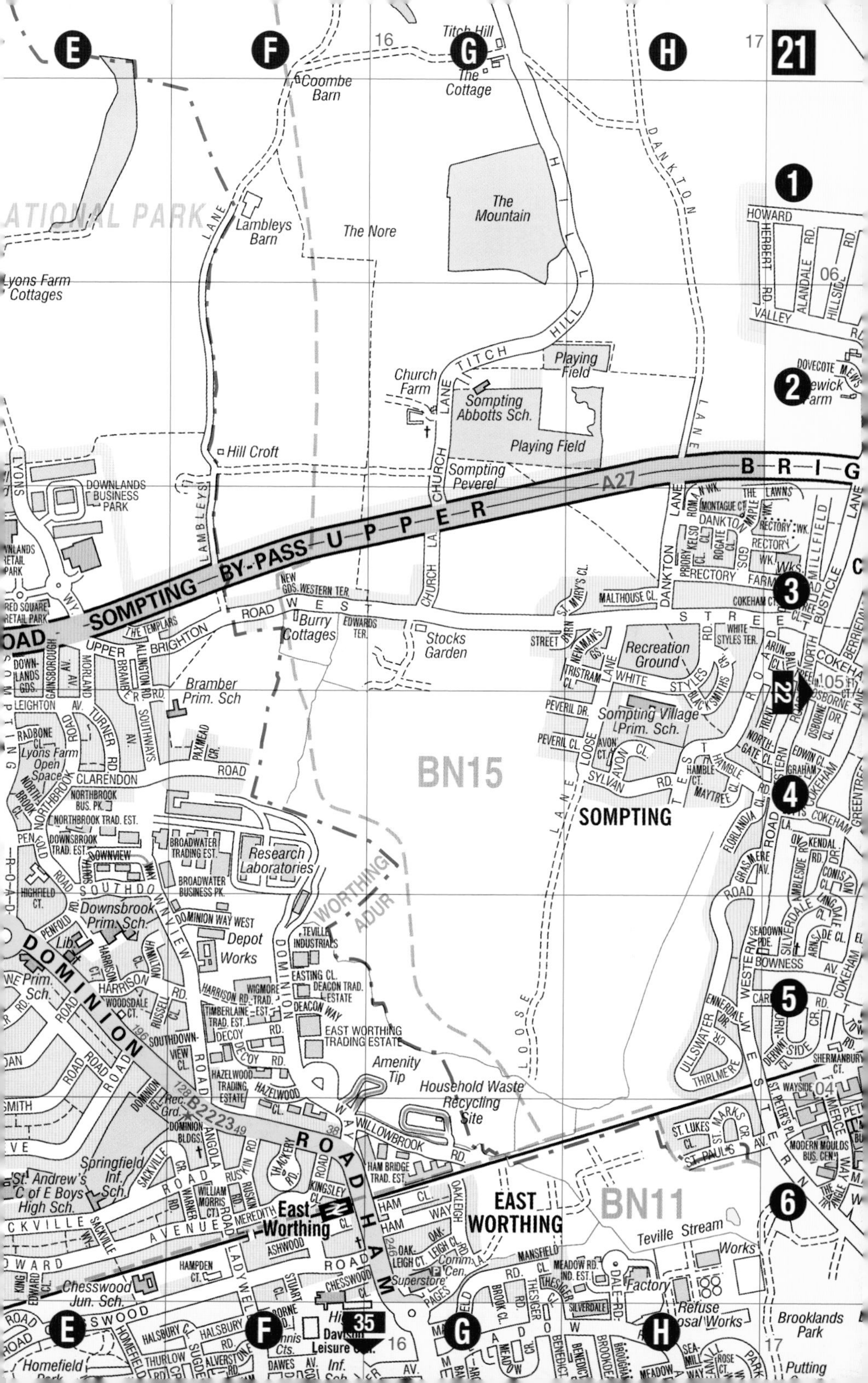
Titch Hill
The Cottage
Coombe Barn
Lambleys Barn
The Nore
The Mountain
Lyons Farm Cottages
Hill Croft
Church Farm
Sompting Abbotts Sch.
Playing Field
Sompting Peverel
DOWNLANDS BUSINESS PARK
SOMPTING BY-PASS
UPPER BRIGHTON ROAD
A27
Burry Cottages
Stocks Garden
Bramber Prim. Sch
Lyons Farm Open Space
Recreation Ground
Sompting Village Prim. Sch.
BN15
SOMPTING
Research Laboratories
WORTHING
ADUR
Downsbrook Prim. Sch.
Depot Works
EAST WORTHING TRADING ESTATE
Amenity Tip
Household Waste Recycling Site
DOMINION ROAD
B2223
HAM ROAD
Springfield Inf. Sch.
St. Andrew's C of E Boys High Sch.
East Worthing
EAST WORTHING
BN11
Teville Stream
Works
Factory
Refuse Disposal Works
Brooklands Park
Chesswood Jun. Sch.
Homefield Park
Superstore
Davison Leisure Cen.
22
35
16
17
05
06
04

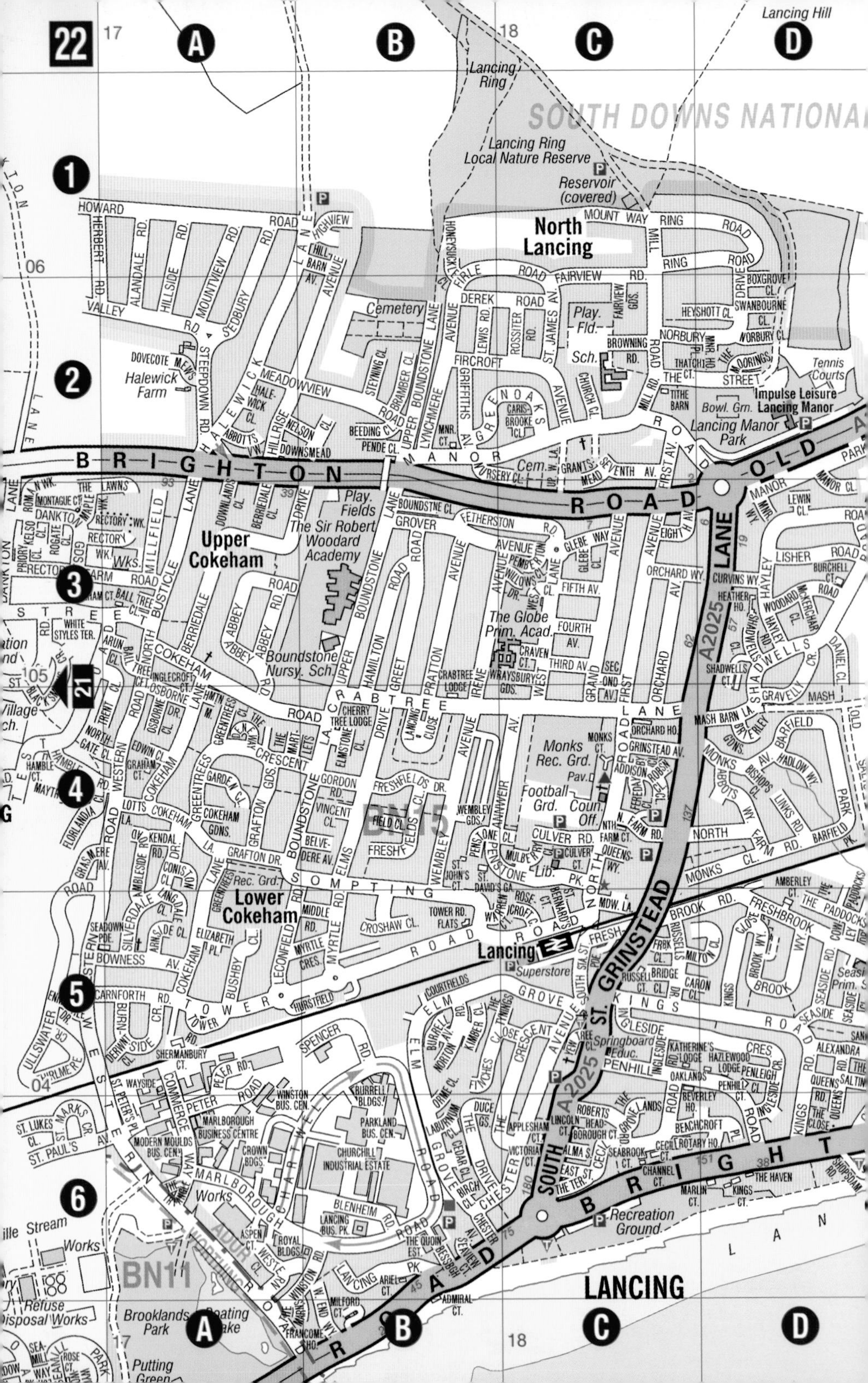
22
A
B
C
D
1
2
3
4
5
6
17
18
06
04
Lancing Hill
Lancing Ring
SOUTH DOWNS NATIONAL
Lancing Ring Local Nature Reserve
Reservoir (covered)
North Lancing
MOUNT WAY
RING ROAD
FAIRVIEW RD.
FIRLE ROAD
DEREK ROAD
Cemetery
Play. Fld.
Sch.
BROWNING RD.
NORBURY
HEYSHOTT CL.
BOXGROVE CL.
SWANBOURNE CL.
THE MOORINGS
THE STREET
Tennis Courts
Impulse Leisure Lancing Manor
Bowl. Grn.
Lancing Manor Park
TITHE BARN
MILL RD.
HOWARD ROAD
HERBERT RD.
ALANDALE RD.
HILLSIDE RD.
MOUNTVIEW RD.
SEDBURY RD.
VALLEY RD.
STEEPDOWN RD.
DOVECOTE MEWS
Halewick Farm
HALEWICK LANE
MEADOWVIEW ROAD
HIGHVIEW
HILL BARN AV.
STEYNING CL.
BRAMBER CL.
UPPER BOUNDSTONE LANE
LYNCHMERE AVENUE
HONEYSUCKLE CL.
LEWIS RD.
ROSSITER RD.
ST. JAMES AV.
FAIRVIEW GDS.
FIRCROFT
GRIFFITHS AV.
GREENOAKS
CARISBROOKE CL.
CHURCH CL.
BEEDING CL.
PENDE CL.
DOWNSMEAD
NELSON CL.
HILLRISE
ABBOTTS VW.
HALEWICK CL.
MNR. CT.
BRIGHTON ROAD
MANOR ROAD
OLD
Cem.
NURSERY CL.
GRANTS MEAD
SEVENTH AV.
FIRST AV.
Upper Cokeham
Play. Fields
The Sir Robert Woodard Academy
BOUNDSTNE CL.
GROVER
FETHERSTON RD.
GLEBE WAY
EIGHTH AV.
ORCHARD WY.
FIFTH AV.
FOURTH AV.
THIRD AV.
The Globe Prim. Acad.
CRAVEN CT.
WRAYSBURY GDS.
CRABTREE LODGE
Boundstone Nursy. Sch.
ABBEY ROAD
BERRIEDALE DRIVE
BUSTICLE LANE
MILLFIELD
COKEHAM ROAD
INGLECROFT CT.
OSBORNE CT.
CRABTREE LANE
CHERRY TREE LODGE
ELMSTONE CL.
LANCING CLOSE
FIELD CL.
GREENTREES CRESCENT
THE MARTLETS
GORDON RD.
FRESHFIELDS DR.
VINCENT CL.
BN15
WEMBLEY GDS.
WEMBLEY AVENUE
ANNWEIR AV.
Monks Rec. Grd.
Football Grd.
Pav.
Coun. Off.
CULVER RD.
Lib.
MULBERRY CL.
PENSTONE PK.
ORCHARD HO.
GRINSTEAD AV.
GRINSTEAD LANE
A2025
NORTH FARM RD.
MONKS CL.
MONKS AV.
MASH BARN LA.
BARFIELD PK.
ABBOTS WY.
BISHOPS CL.
HADLOW WY.
LINKS RD.
CURVINS WY.
HEATHER HO.
SHADWELLS CR.
SHADWELLS CT.
HAYLEY RD.
LISHER ROAD
BURCHELL CT.
WOODARD RD.
McKERCHAR CL.
DANIEL CL.
GRAVELLY CR.
MANOR CL.
LEWIN CL.
WESTERN ROAD
KENDAL RD.
AMBLESIDE RD.
CONISTON CL.
LANGDALE CL.
COKEHAM GDNS.
GRAFTON GDS.
GRAFTON DR.
Rec. Grd.
SOMPTING ROAD
Lower Cokeham
MIDDLE RD.
MYRTLE RD.
MYRTLE CRES.
CROSHAW CL.
TOWER RD. FLATS
ST. JOHN'S CT.
ST. DAVID'S GA.
ROSE CT.
ST. BERNARD'S CT.
MDW. LA.
Lancing
Superstore
BROOK RD.
FRESHBROOK
RUSSELLS CL.
MILTON CL.
BROOK WY.
KINGS
GROVE
SEADOWN PDE.
SILVERDALE
BOWNESS AV.
ELIZABETH PL.
BUSHBY CL.
LECONFIELD RD.
CARNFORTH RD.
DERWENTSIDE
BURNSIDE CR.
TOWER ROAD
HURSTFIELD
ULLSWATER
COURTFIELDS
ELM GROVE
CRESCENT
SOUTH STREET
ST. GRINSTEAD
KINGS ROAD
Springboard Educ.
PENHILL
INGLESIDE
KATHERINE'S LODGE
HAZLEWOOD LODGE
OAKLANDS
BEVERLEY HO.
BEACHCROFT
ROTARY HO.
SEASIDE ROAD
ALEXANDRA
QUEENS RD.
THE CLOSE
SHERMANBURY CT.
PETER RD.
SPENCER RD.
WINSTON BUS. CEN.
BURRELL BLDGS.
PARKLAND BUS. CEN.
CHURCHILL INDUSTRIAL ESTATE
MARLBOROUGH BUSINESS CENTRE
MODERN MOULDS BUS. CEN.
CROWN BLDGS.
COMMERCE WAY
MARLBOROUGH
CHARTWELL ROAD
Works
BLENHEIM RD.
LANCING BUS. PK.
ROYAL BLDGS.
THE QUOIN EST.
ST. LUKES CL.
ST. MARKS CR.
ST. PAUL'S AV.
WESTERN
ADUR
WORTHING ROAD
BN11
Brooklands Park
Boating Lake
Putting Green
Stream
Refuse Disposal Works
LANCING PK.
ARIEL CT.
MILFORD CT.
ADMIRAL CT.
FRANCOME HO.
LABURNUM GROVE
CEDAR CL.
BIRCH CL.
THE DRIVE
CHESTER AV.
APPLESHAM CT.
VICTORIA CT.
LINCOLN CT.
ROBERTS HEAD
BOROUGH CT.
ALMA ST.
EAST ST.
THE TER.
SEABROOK CT.
CHANNEL CT.
MARLIN CT.
KINGS CT.
THE HAVEN
SOUTH
Recreation Ground
LANCING
ROAD
BRIGHTON

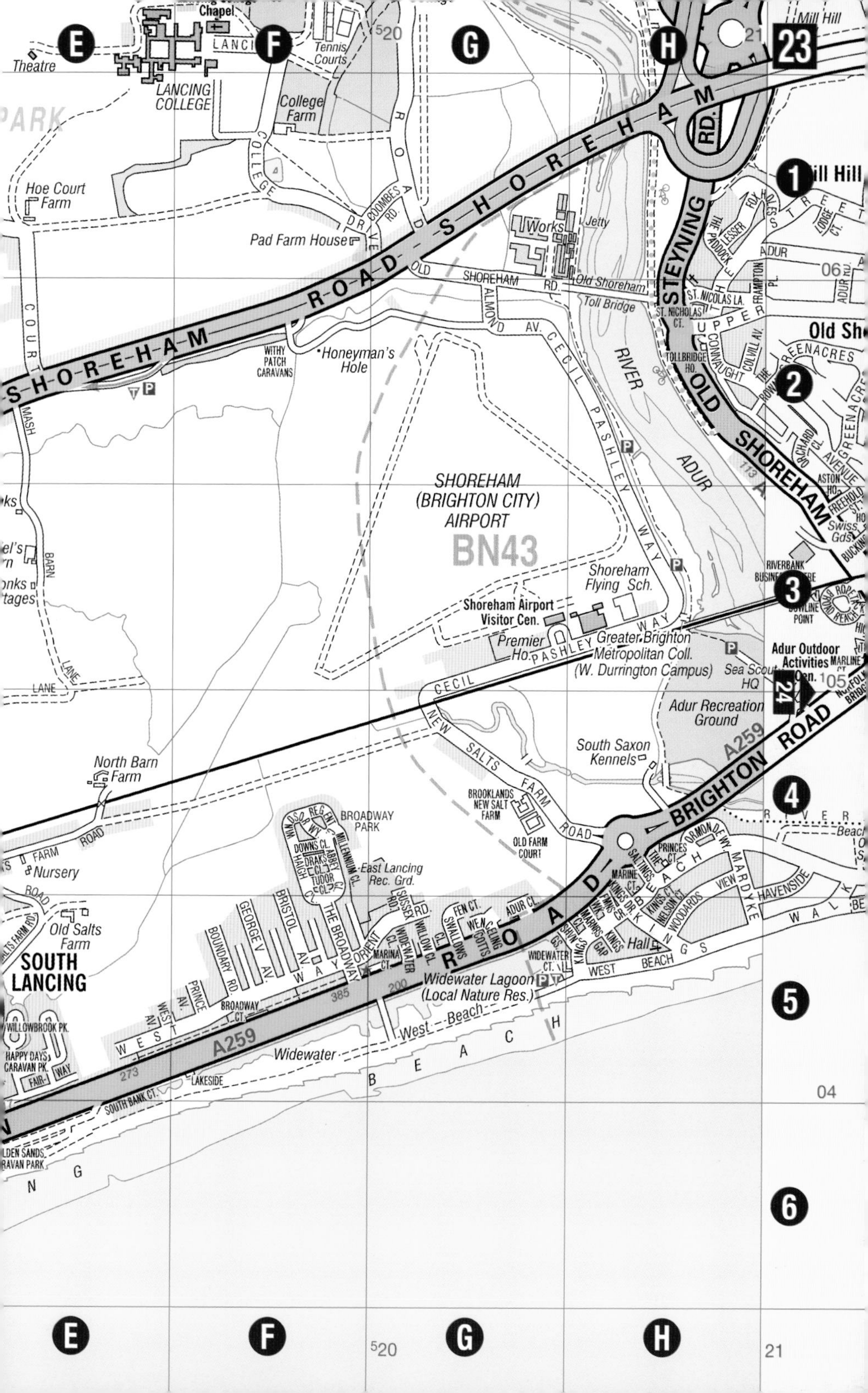

23
E
F
G
H
Chapel
Theatre
LANCING COLLEGE
College Farm
Tennis Courts
Mill Hill
Hoe Court Farm
Pad Farm House
COOMBES RD.
SHOREHAM ROAD
OLD SHOREHAM RD.
Works
Jetty
Old Shoreham Toll Bridge
STEYNING RD.
ST. NICOLAS LA.
ST. NICHOLAS CT.
TOLLBRIDGE HO.
UPPER SHOREHAM RD.
CONNAUGHT
COLVILL AV.
GREENACRES
Old Shoreham
WITHY PATCH CARAVANS
Honeyman's Hole
ALMOND AV.
CECIL PASHLEY WAY
RIVER ADUR
SHOREHAM (BRIGHTON CITY) AIRPORT
BN43
Shoreham Flying Sch.
Shoreham Airport Visitor Cen.
Premier Ho.
Greater Brighton Metropolitan Coll. (W. Durrington Campus)
RIVERBANK BUSINESS CENTRE
BOWLINE POINT
Adur Outdoor Activities Cen.
Sea Scouts HQ
24
Adur Recreation Ground
South Saxon Kennels
A259
BRIGHTON ROAD
NEW SALTS FARM ROAD
BROOKLANDS NEW SALT FARM
OLD FARM COURT
North Barn Farm
Nursery
Old Salts Farm
SOUTH LANCING
BROADWAY PARK
East Lancing Rec. Grd.
THE BROADWAY
BRISTOL AV.
GEORGE V AV.
BOUNDARY RD.
PRINCE AV.
WEST AV.
WEST WAY
BROADWAY CT.
MARINA CT.
Widewater Lagoon (Local Nature Res.)
West Beach
Widewater
BEACH
WEST BEACH
KINGS WALK
MARDYKE
HAVENSIDE
WOODARDS VIEW
Hall
WILLOWBROOK PK.
HAPPY DAYS CARAVAN PK.
LAKESIDE
SOUTH BANK CT.
GOLDEN SANDS CARAVAN PARK
1
2
3
4
5
6
520
21
06
04
105
E
F
G
H
520
21

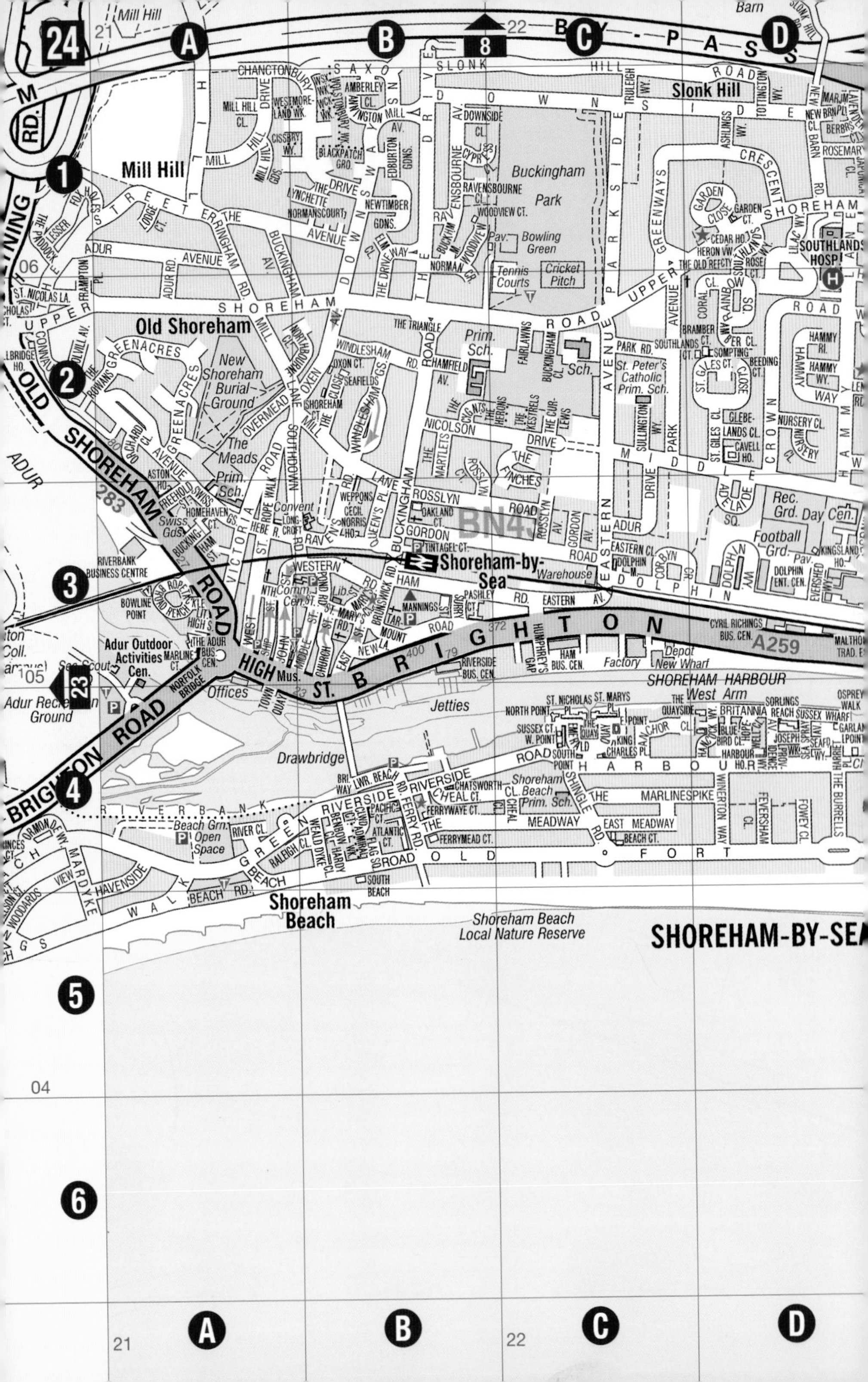
Mill Hill
Old Shoreham
New Shoreham Burial Ground
Buckingham Park
Bowling Green
Tennis Courts
Cricket Pitch
Slonk Hill
Southlands Hosp.
St. Peter's Catholic Prim. Sch.
Shoreham-by-Sea
BN43
Rec. Grd.
Day Cen.
Football Grd.
Adur Outdoor Activities Cen.
Adur Recreation Ground
Riverbank Business Centre
Bowline Point
Shoreham Harbour
West Arm
Jetties
Drawbridge
Shoreham Beach
Shoreham Beach Local Nature Reserve
Shoreham Beach Prim. Sch.
Beach Grn. Open Space
SHOREHAM-BY-SEA
BY-PASS
A259
Old Shoreham Road
Brighton Road
Upper Shoreham Road
Middle Road
High St.
Brighton Road
Harbour Road
Old Fort Road
Riverbank
Beach Green
Riverside Road
Victoria Road
Buckingham Road
Eastern Avenue
Rosslyn Road
Dolphin Road
Ham Road
Downside Road
Upper Shoreham Road
Greenways Crescent
Mill Hill
Erringham Road
Mill Lane
Southdown Road
Warehouse
Factory
Depot
New Wharf
Offices
Mus.
Sch.
Prim. Sch.
23
8
1
2
3
4
5
6
A
B
C
D
21
22
04
05
06

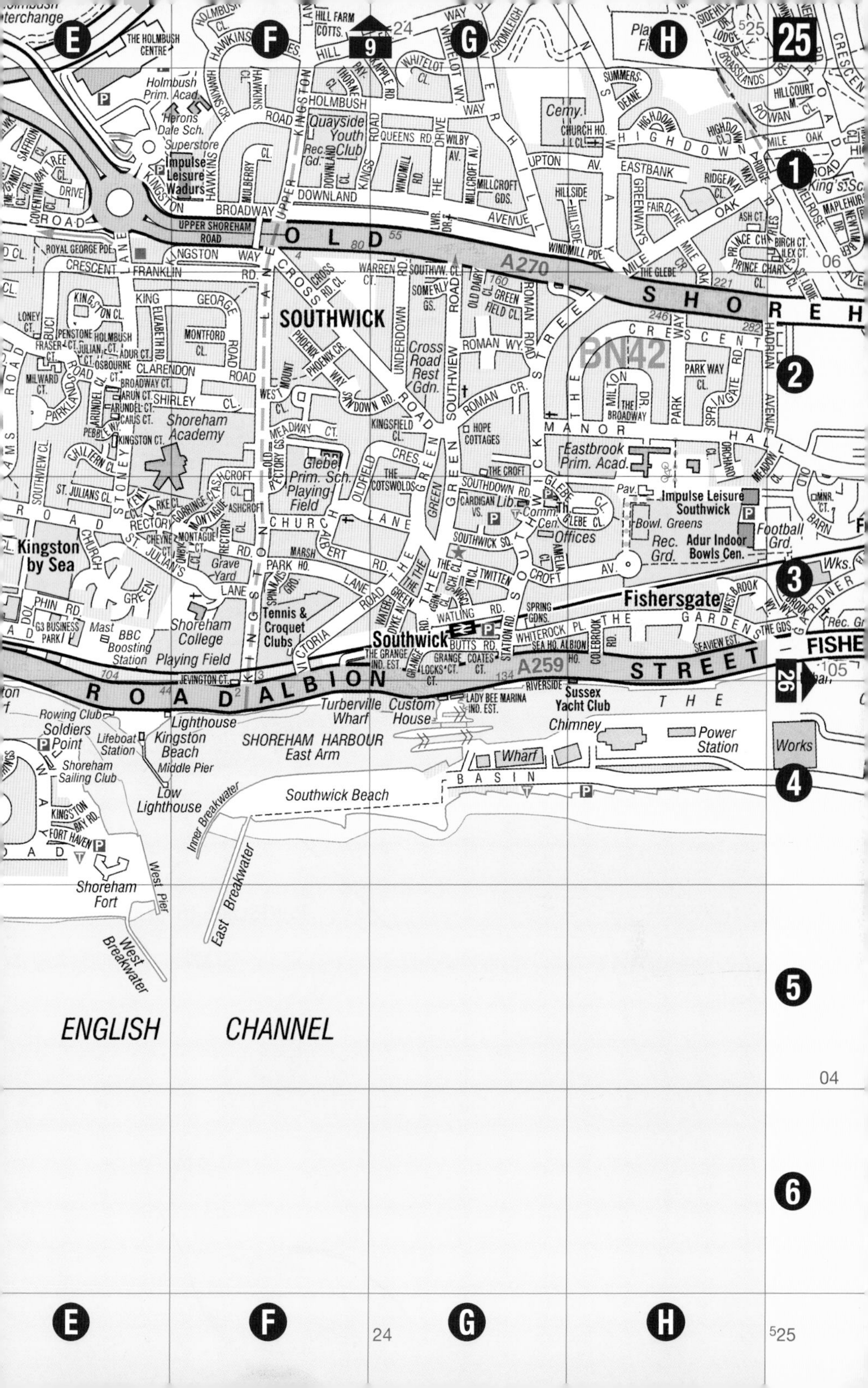
E
F
G
H
9
24
25
1
2
3
4
5
6
04
05
06
26
THE HOLMBUSH CENTRE
Holmbush Prim. Acad.
Herons Dale Sch.
Superstore
Impulse Leisure Wadurs
Quayside Youth Club
Rec. Gd.
HOLMBUSH
KINGSTON
QUEENS RD.
WILBY AV.
MILLCROFT AV.
MILLCROFT GDS.
UPTON AV.
EASTBANK
HIGHDOWN
Cemy.
CHURCH HO.
SUMMERSDEANE
HILLCOURT M.
ROWAN CL.
MILE OAK
RIDGEWAY
HILLSIDE
FAIRDENE
GREENWAYS
DOWNLAND
BROADWAY
UPPER SHOREHAM ROAD
OLD
A270
SHOREHAM
WINDMILL PDE.
THE GLEBE
PRINCE CHARLES
KING'S SCH.
KINGSTON WAY
ROYAL GEORGE PDE.
CRESCENT
FRANKLIN RD.
KING GEORGE ROAD
MONTFORD CL.
CLARENDON ROAD
SHIRLEY CL.
SOUTHWICK
WARREN CT.
SOUTHVIEW CL.
SOMERLY GS.
OLD DAIRY CL.
GREEN FIELD CL.
ROMAN ROAD
BN42
CRESCENT
PARK WAY CL.
SPRINGATE RD.
HADRIAN AVENUE
Cross Road Rest Gdn.
ROMAN WY.
ROMAN CR.
MILTON DR.
THE BROADWAY
PHOENIX WAY
SANDOWN RD.
UNDERDOWN ROAD
MANOR HALL
HOPE COTTAGES
Eastbrook Prim. Acad.
Shoreham Academy
Glebe Prim. Sch. Playing Field
KINGSFIELD CL.
OLDFIELD CRES.
THE COTSWOLDS
THE GREEN
THE CROFT
SOUTHDOWN RD.
Lib.
Comm. Cen.
Th.
GLEBE CL.
Offices
Pav.
Impulse Leisure Southwick
Bowl. Greens
Rec. Grd.
Adur Indoor Bowls Cen.
Football Grd.
Kingston by Sea
CHURCH LANE
SOUTHWICK SQ.
ALBERT RD.
PARK HO.
TWITTEN
CROFT AV.
Grave Yard
Tennis & Croquet Clubs
Shoreham College Playing Field
G3 BUSINESS PARK
Mast
BBC Boosting Station
VICTORIA ROAD
Fishersgate
THE GARDENS
WHITEROCK PL.
SEA HO.
ALBION HO.
SPRING GDNS.
WATLING RD.
Southwick
BUTTS RD.
STATION RD.
THE GRANGE IND. EST.
GRANGE CT.
COATES CT.
LOCKS CT.
SEAVIEW EST.
A259
ALBION STREET
FISHERSGATE
JEVINGTON CT.
RIVERSIDE
Sussex Yacht Club
LADY BEE MARINA IND. EST.
Turberville Wharf
Custom House
Lighthouse
Rowing Club
Soldiers Point
Lifeboat Station
Kingston Beach
Middle Pier
Shoreham Sailing Club
SHOREHAM HARBOUR
East Arm
Chimney
Power Station
Works
Wharf
BASIN
Southwick Beach
Low Lighthouse
Inner Breakwater
KINGSTON BAY RD.
FORT HAVEN
Shoreham Fort
West Pier
East Breakwater
West Breakwater
ENGLISH CHANNEL

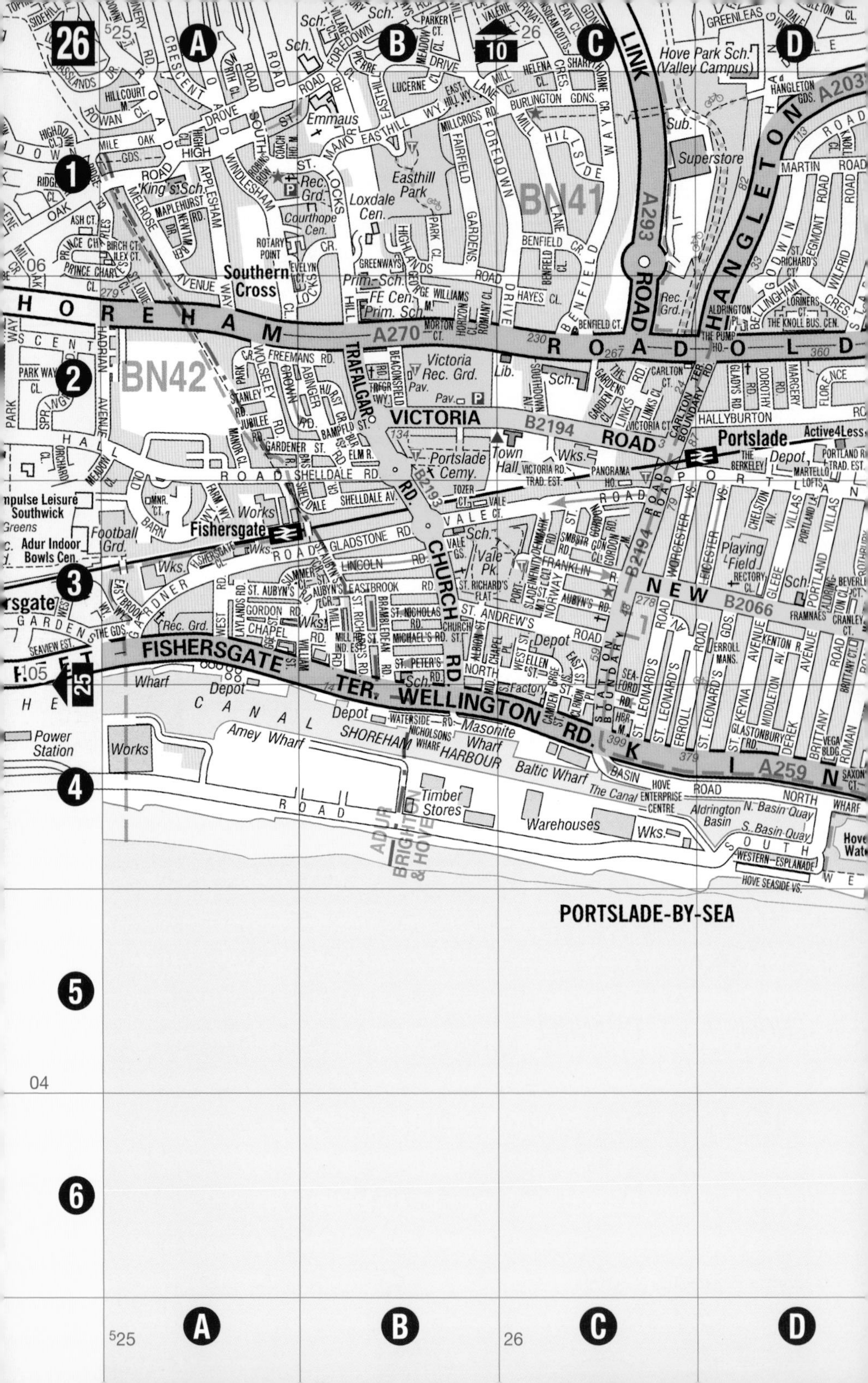

A
B
C
D
10
1
2
3
4
5
6
BN41
BN42
Southern Cross
Fishersgate
Portslade
PORTSLADE-BY-SEA
HOREHAM ROAD
A270
OLD SHOREHAM ROAD
VICTORIA ROAD
B2194
NEW CHURCH RD.
B2066
FISHERSGATE TER.
WELLINGTON RD.
KINGSWAY
A259
LINK ROAD
A293
HANGLETON ROAD
TRAFALGAR RD.
B2193
CHURCH RD.
STATION ROAD
BOUNDARY ROAD
Emmaus
Easthill Park
Loxdale Cen.
Courthope Cen.
Hove Park Sch. (Valley Campus)
Superstore
Victoria Rec. Grd.
Portslade Cemy.
Town Hall
Vale Pk.
Playing Field
Football Grd.
Adur Indoor Bowls Cen.
Power Station
CANAL
SHOREHAM HARBOUR
Amey Wharf
Baltic Wharf
Masonite Wharf
Timber Stores
Warehouses
Aldrington Basin
N. Basin Quay
S. Basin Quay
ADUR
BRIGHTON & HOVE
25
04
06
525
26

27
E
F
G
H
11
West Blatchington
Blatchington Mill School & Form
Aldrington C of E Prim. Sch.
Nevill Play. Field
Billingham Prim. S
Miniature Railway
Hove Park
Brighton & Hove Greyhound Stadium
Super-store
Hlth. Club
Riptide
Pav.
Bowl. Grn.
Ten. Cts.
Hove Rec.
Sports Grd.
MILL VIEW HOSP.
HOVE POLYCLINIC
Hospice
Sch.
Hove Park School & Sixth Form Cen.
Play Fld.
Hove Cemetery
War Mem.
ENGLISH BUS. PK.
A270
SHOREHAM
NEVILL AVENUE
THE DROVEWAY
ORCHARD
ORCHARD GDNS.
CRANMER AV.
ELM DRIVE
LABURNUM AV.
WAYFIELD AV.
HOLMES AV.
OLD SHOREHAM ROAD
SACKVILLE TRAD. EST.
GOLDSTONE RETAIL PK.
Wks.
THE CHROME WORKS
CLARKS IND. EST.
Aldrington
The Lioncare Sch.
ST. JOSEPH'S TRAD. EST.
ST. JOSEPH'S BUS. PK.
SUSSEX HO. BUS. PK.
Hove
HOVE BUS. CEN.
Bus Depot
KINGS GATE
Sch.
Ten. Cts.
Drive Bri.
CROMWELL
A2023
SACKVILLE ROAD
PORTLAND RD.
STONEHAM
YMCA
MARMION
BYRON
WORDSWORTH
COWPER
LIVINGSTONE
SHIRLEY
GOLDSTONE
CLARENDON
BLATCHINGTON
Davis Park
BN3
Rec. Grd.
NEW CHURCH ROAD
Aldrington Rec. Grd.
Pav.
ALDRINGTON HO.
Syn. Sch.
Hove Mus.
Adult Educ. Cen.
Super-store
Lib.
B2066
CHURCH ROAD
GRAND AV.
KINGSWAY
Skate Pk.
Miniature Golf Course
Western Lawns
Bowling Greens
ESPLANADE
Cheetahs Gym
King Alfred Leis. Cen.
King's Lawns
HOVE
Pier
1
2
3
4
5
6
28
105
04
06
28
29
E
F
G
H

28
A
B
C
D
12
1
2
3
4
5
6
27
44
29
530
04
06
105
Pavilion & Avenue Lawn Tennis Club
Prep. Sch. at Hove
Play. Fld.
Hove Rec. Grd.
Bowling Greens
Cricket Ground
Preston Manor
Preston
Coronation Garden
Clock Tower
Preston Park
Tennis Court
Bowls Club
The Rookery
Cardinal Newman RC Sch.
Playing Field
Dyke Road Park
Stanford Jun. Sch.
Brighton Tech. Coll.
Depot
Hove
Sussex County Cricket Ground
St. Ann's Well Gardens
Court
Town Ho.
British Airways i360
Norfolk Groyne
The Brighton Cen.
Odeon
Churchill Sq. Shop. Cen.
Clock Twr.
Riptide
DROVEWAY
THE DROVEWAY
HOVE PARK
OLD SHOREHAM ROAD
UPPER DRIVE
THE DRIVE
CROMWELL ROAD
DAVIGDOR RD.
DYKE ROAD
DYKE RD.
PRESTON ROAD
A23
A270
A259
B2120
B2185
B2121
B2122
NEW ENGLAND
CHATHAM PL.
BUCKINGHAM PLACE
WESTERN ROAD
CHURCH RD.
KINGS ESPLANADE
KINGSWAY
HOVE ESPLANADE
Brunswick Lawns
King's Lawns
SEA WALL
KINGS RD.
MONTPELIER RD.
VERNON TER.
LANSDOWNE PL.
GRAND AV.
PALMEIRA SQUARE
ADELAIDE CR.
BRUNSWICK PL.
SEVEN DIALS
STANFORD AVENUE
HIGHDOWN RD.
ADDISON RD.
WEST ST.
QUEEN'S RD.

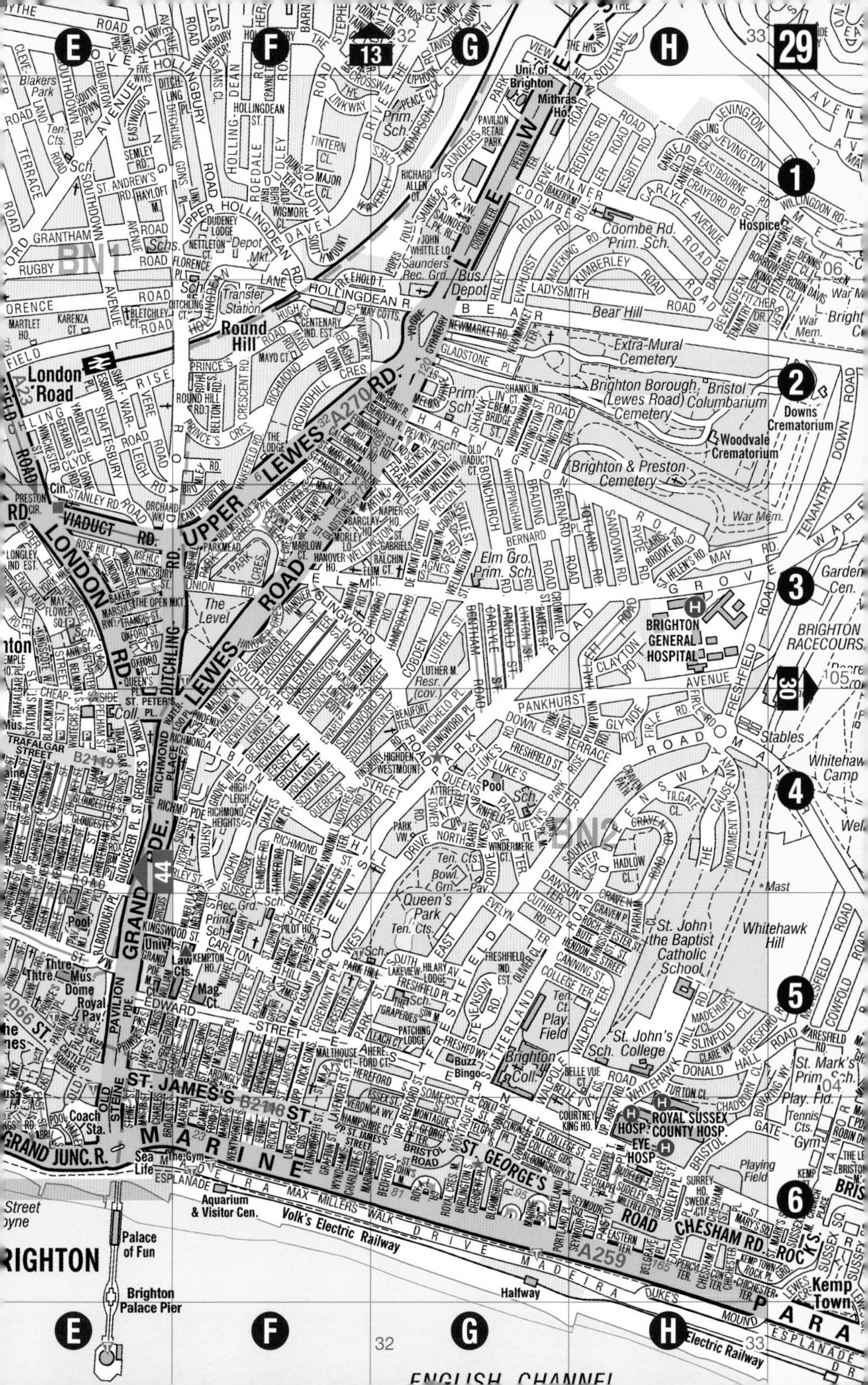
E
F
G
H
13
32
33
1
2
3
4
5
6
30
44
BN1
BN2
A23
A270
B2119
B2118
A259
Blakers Park
London Road
Round Hill
Transfer Station
Depot Mkt.
Uni. of Brighton
Mithras Ho.
Pavilion Retail Park
Saunders Rec. Grd.
Bus Depot
Coombe Rd. Prim. Sch.
Hospice
Bear Hill
Extra-Mural Cemetery
Brighton Borough (Lewes Road) Cemetery
Bristol Columbarium
Downs Crematorium
Woodvale Crematorium
Brighton & Preston Cemetery
War Mem.
Elm Gro. Prim. Sch.
Garden Cen.
Brighton General Hospital
Brighton Racecourse
The Level
Luther M. Resr. (cov.)
Stables
Whitehawk Camp
Queen's Park
Ten. Cts.
Bowl. Grn.
Pool
Mast
Whitehawk Hill
St. John the Baptist Catholic School
St. John's College
Play Field
Brighton Coll.
Buzz Bingo
Royal Sussex County Hosp.
Eye Hosp.
St. Mark's Prim. Sch.
Play. Fld.
Playing Field
Gym
Thtre.
Mus.
Dome
Royal Pav.
Law Cts.
Mag. Ct.
Univ.
Coach Sta.
Sea Life
The Gym
Aquarium & Visitor Cen.
Palace of Fun
Brighton Palace Pier
Volk's Electric Railway
Halfway
Kemp Town
BRIGHTON
LEWES ROAD
UPPER LEWES RD.
LONDON RD.
DITCHLING RD.
GRAND PDE.
MARINE PARADE
MADEIRA DRIVE
EDWARD STREET
EASTERN ROAD
CHESHAM RD.
ST. JAMES'S ST.
ELM GROVE
QUEEN'S PARK RD.
FRESHFIELD RD.
HOLLINGDEAN RD.
HARTINGTON ROAD
MANOR ROAD
ENGLISH CHANNEL

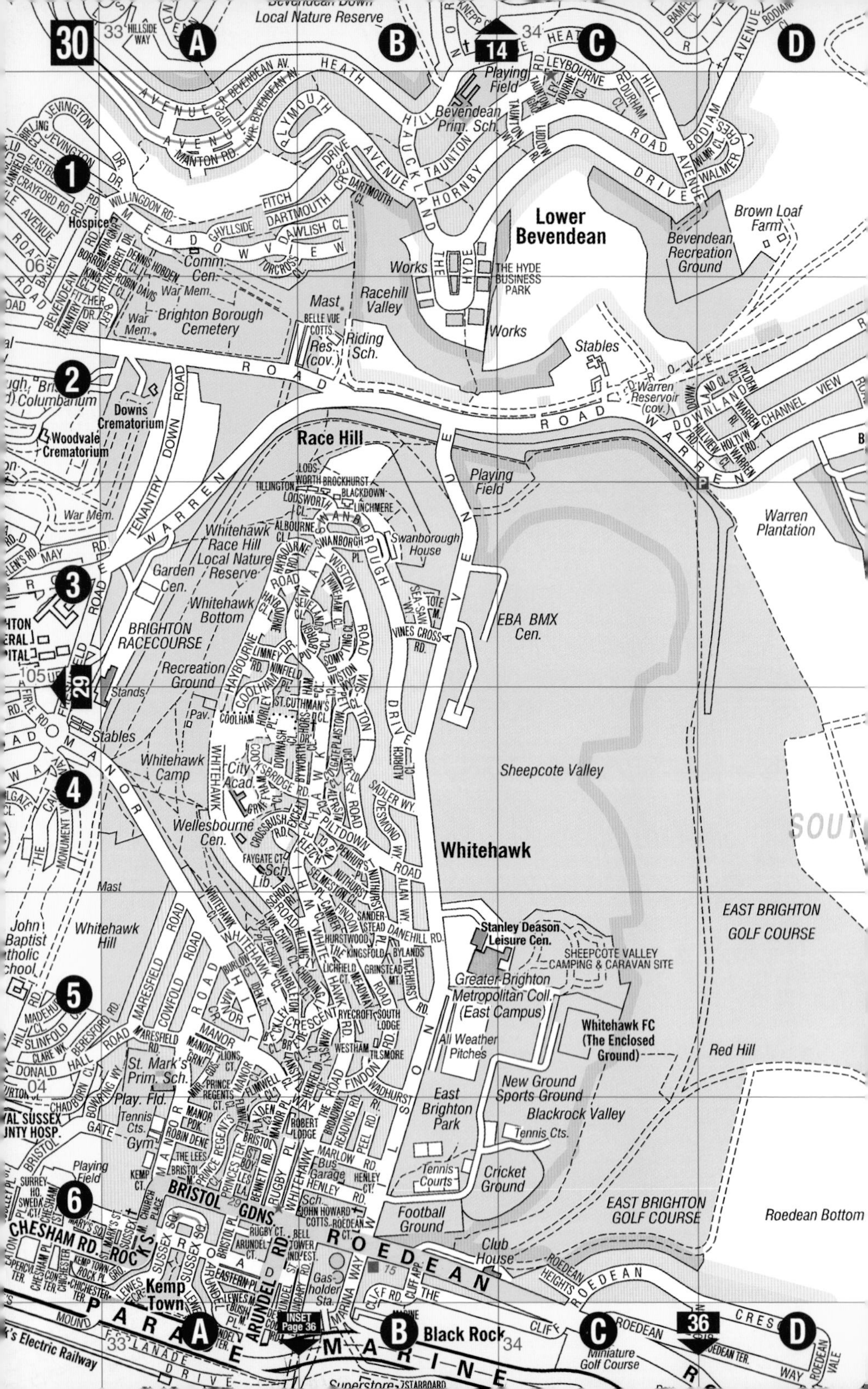

A 33 HILLSIDE WAY • Bevendean Down
Local Nature Reserve **B** 14 Playing Field **C** 34 HEATH **D**

LWR BEVENDEAN AV.

Lower Bevendean

Bevendean Prim. Sch.

Brown Loaf Farm

1

Hospice

Comm. Cen.

War Mem.

Ghyllside • Torcross • Dawlish Cl.

Works

THE HYDE BUSINESS PARK

THE HYDE

Bevendean Recreation Ground

Brighton Borough Cemetery

Mast.

BELLE VUE COTTS.

Res. (cov.)

Racehill Valley

Riding Sch.

Works

Stables

War Mem.

2

Columbarium

Downs Crematorium

Woodvale Crematorium

Warren Reservoir (cov.)

WARREN ROAD

Channel View

War Mem.

Race Hill

Playing Field

Warren Plantation

3

Whitehawk Race Hill Local Nature Reserve

Garden Cen.

BRIGHTON RACECOURSE

Whitehawk Bottom

LOOSWORTH • BROCKHURST • TILLINGTON • BLACKDOWN • LINCHMERE • ALBOURNE CL. • SWANBOROUGH PL.

Swanborough House

TOTE M.

EBA BMX Cen.

Recreation Ground

29 105

Stands

Pav.

COOLHAM

Whitehawk Camp

Stables

City Acad.

ST. CUTHMAN'S CL.

CROSSBUSH RD.

Sheepcote Valley

4

Wellesbourne Cen.

Whitehawk

SADLER WY. • DESMOND W. ROAD

SOU

Mast.

Sch. Lib.

FAYGATE CT.

EAST BRIGHTON GOLF COURSE

John Baptist Catholic School

Whitehawk Hill

SANDERSTEAD • HURSTWOOD • KINGSFOLD • LICHFIELD CT. • GRINSTEAD MT.

DANEHILL RD.

Stanley Deason Leisure Cen.

SHEEPCOTE VALLEY CAMPING & CARAVAN SITE

5

MADEIRA CT. • SLINFOLD • CLARE MK.

St. Mark's Prim. Sch.

Play. Fld.

MARESFIELD ROAD • CONFOLD ROAD

BYLANDS • RYECROFT CL.

SOUTH LODGE • WESTHAM • TILSMORE

Greater Brighton Metropolitan Coll. (East Campus)

All Weather Pitches

Whitehawk FC (The Enclosed Ground)

Red Hill

RL SUSSEX NTY HOSP.

DONALD HALL

Tennis Cts. Gym

MANOR RD. • LIONS • BRISTOL

New Ground Sports Ground

Blackrock Valley

Tennis Cts.

6

Playing Field

CHESHAM RD. • ROC

BRISTOL GDNS.

Robin Dene • The Lees • KEMP CT.

PRINCES TER. • PRINCE REGENTS

John Howard Cotts.

BELL TOWER INDEST.

East Brighton Park

Tennis Courts

Cricket Ground

Club House

EAST BRIGHTON GOLF COURSE

Kemp Town

Football Ground

Roedean Bottom

ROEDEAN HEIGHTS

ROEDEAN TER.

's Electric Railway **A** 33 PLANADE DRIVE • Gasholder Sta. • INSET Page 36 **B** Black Rock 34 **C** 36 **D**

MARINE

ROEDEAN

Miniature Golf Course

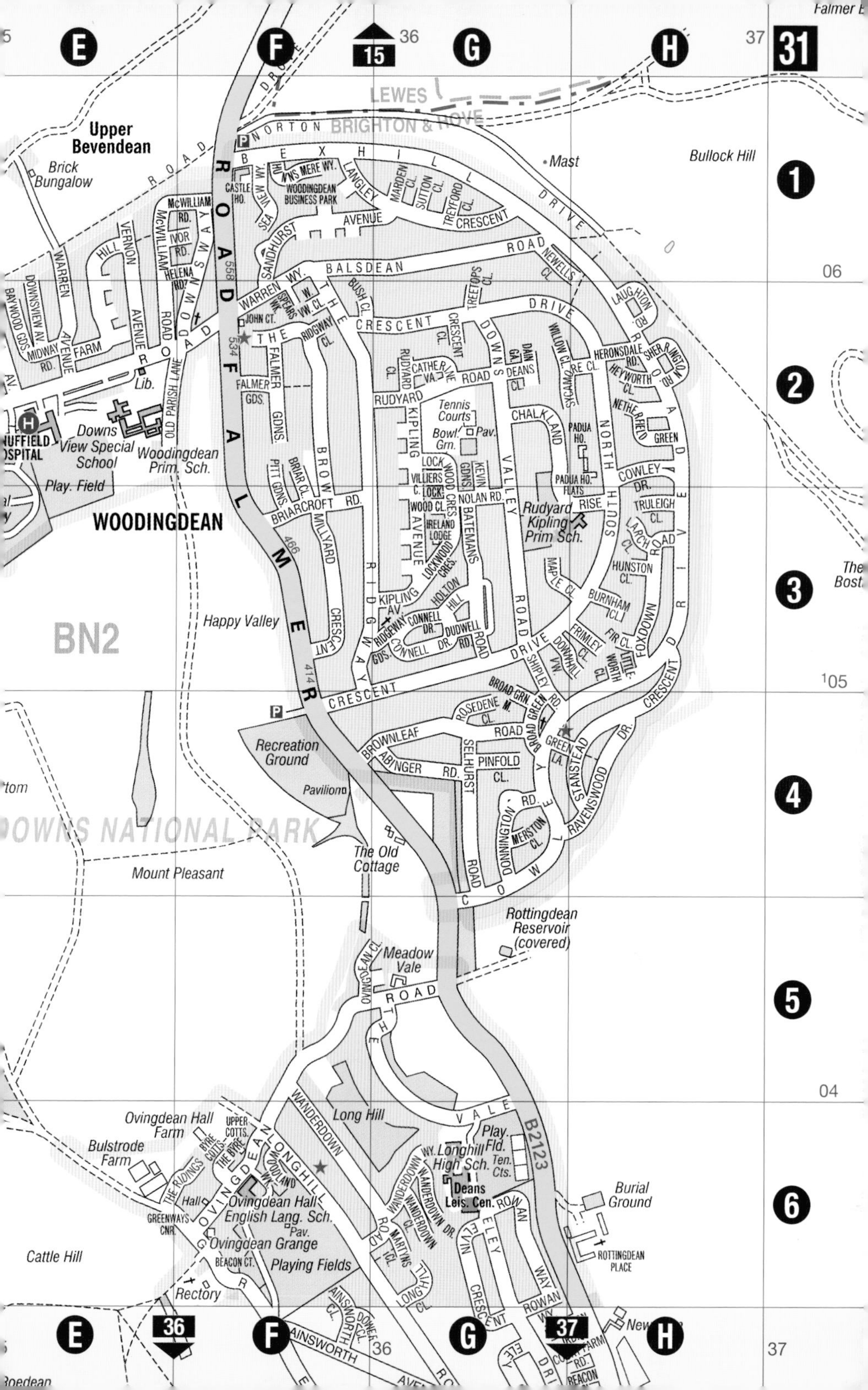
E
F
G
H
15
36
37
Falmer
Upper Bevendean
Brick Bungalow
Bullock Hill
Mast
WOODINGDEAN
BN2
Happy Valley
Recreation Ground
Pavilion
The Old Cottage
Mount Pleasant
DOWNS NATIONAL PARK
Rottingdean Reservoir (covered)
Meadow Vale
Long Hill
Ovingdean Hall Farm
Bulstrode Farm
Cattle Hill
Ovingdean Hall English Lang. Sch.
Ovingdean Grange
Playing Fields
Rectory
Longhill High Sch.
Deans Leis. Cen.
Play. Fld.
Ten. Cts.
Burial Ground
ROTTINGDEAN PLACE
Nuffield Hospital
Downs View Special School
Woodingdean Prim. Sch.
Play. Field
Lib.
Rudyard Kipling Prim Sch.
Tennis Courts
Bowl. Grn.
Pav.
WOODINGDEAN BUSINESS PARK
LEWES
BRIGHTON & HOVE
FALMER ROAD
NORTON
BEXHILL
DRIVE
BALSDEAN ROAD
WARREN ROAD
THE CRESCENT
DOWNS VALLEY ROAD
SOUTH
NORTH
CRESCENT DRIVE
COWLEY DR.
HERONSDALE RD.
HEYWORTH CL.
LAUGHTON RD.
SHERRINGTON RD.
NETHERFIELD GREEN
TRULEIGH CL.
HUNSTON CL.
LARCH CL.
BURNHAM CL.
FOXDOWN
LITTLEWORTH CL.
FIR CL.
FRIMLEY CL.
DOWNHILL VW.
SHIPLEY RD.
MAPLE CL.
PADUA HO.
PADUA HO. FLATS
CHALKLAND RISE
SYCAMORE CL.
WILLOW CL.
DAIN GA.
DEANS CL.
TREETOPS CL.
NEWELLS CL.
TREYFORD CL.
SUTTON CL.
MARDEN CL.
LANGLEY CRESCENT
AVENUE
SANDHURST
SEA VIEW WY.
CASTLE HO.
MCWILLIAM RD.
IVOR RD.
HELENA RD.
VERNON AVENUE
HILL
DOWNSVIEW AV.
BAYWOOD GDS.
MIDWAY RD.
FARM
OLD PARISH LANE
DOWNSWAY
SPEARS WK.
W. VW. CL.
JOHN CT.
RIDGWAY CL.
FALMER GDS.
GDNS.
BUSH CL.
CATHERINE VA.
RUDYARD CL.
RUDYARD ROAD
KIPLING AVENUE
LOCKWOOD CRES.
VILLIERS C.
KEVIN GDNS.
NOLAN RD.
BATEMANS
IRELAND LODGE
HOLTON HILL
KIPLING AV.
CONNELL DR.
DUDWELL RD.
RIDGEWAY GDS.
THE RIDGWAY
BRIARCROFT RD.
BRIAR CL.
PITT GDNS.
THE BROW
MILLYARD CRESCENT
BROADGRN.
ROSEDENE CL.
BROAD GREEN
GREEN LA.
STANSTEAD
RAVENSWOOD DR.
BROWNLEAF ROAD
ABINGER RD.
SELHURST ROAD
PINFOLD CL.
DONNINGTON RD.
MERSTON CL.
COWLEY
OVINGDEAN CL.
OVINGDEAN ROAD
THE VALE
B2123
WANDERDOWN ROAD
WANDERDOWN CL.
WANDERDOWN DR.
WANDERDOWN WY.
MARTINS CL.
LONGHILL CL.
ROWAN WAY
ELEY CRESCENT
UPPER COTTS.
BYRE COTTS.
THE BYRE
THE RIDINGS
Hall
WOODLAND
GREENWAYS CNR.
BEACON CT.
AINSWORTH CL.
AINSWORTH
DOWER CL.
COURT FARM RD.
BEACON
558
534
466
414
06
105
04
1
2
3
4
5
6
36
37

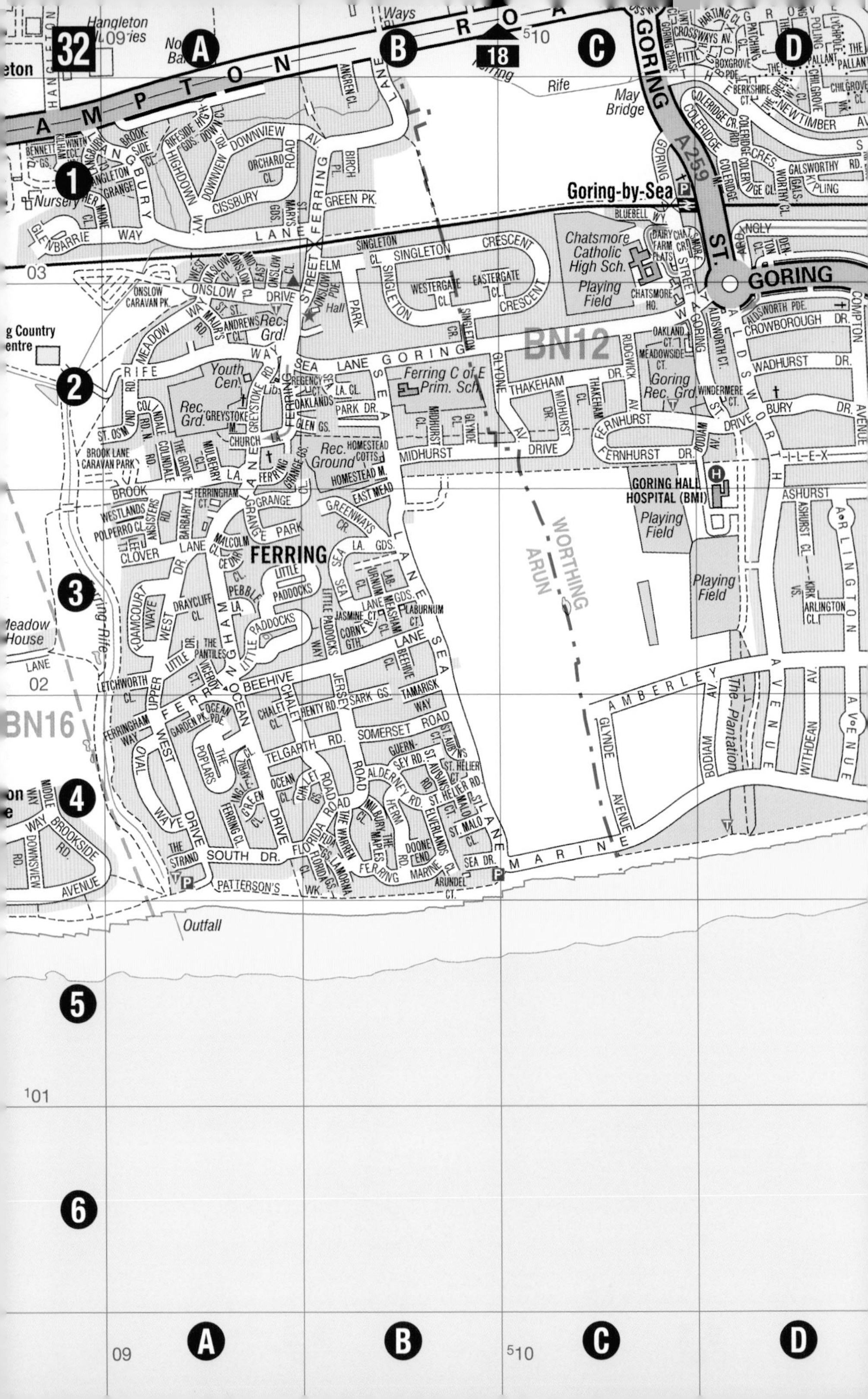

18
A B C D
1 2 3 4 5 6
HAMPTON ROAD
GORING ST.
A259
Goring-by-Sea
GORING
FERRING
BN12
BN16
Chatsmore Catholic High Sch.
Ferring C of E Prim. Sch.
GORING HALL HOSPITAL (BMI)
Goring Rec. Grd.
Playing Field
Rec. Grd.
Rec. Ground
Youth Cen.
Hall
WORTHING
ARUN
Rife
May Bridge
Nursery
Meadow House
Outfall
MARINE
SEA LANE
FERRING LANE
FERRING STREET
GORING WAY
ALDSWORTH AVENUE
AMBERLEY
The Plantation
GLYNDE AVENUE
SOUTH DR.
PATTERSON'S WK.
09
510
101
02
03

33
19
34
E
F
G
H
1
2
3
4
5
6
12
13
101
03
02
BN13
BN11
West Worthing
WEST WORTHING
Durrington-on-Sea
GORING-BY-SEA
GORING ROAD
MILL ROAD
MULBERRY LA.
MARINE CRESCENT
WEST ST.
Field Place Inf. Sch.
Place Pk.
Works
Gasholder
Government Offices
Worthing Leis. Cen.
West Park Rec. Grd.
RSPCA Clinic
West Pk. School
Goring Prim. Sch.
Lib.
Sch.
Sea Place Marine
HOLM OAK BUS. CEN.
GORING BUS. PK.
MARTLETS TRAD. EST.
GARCIA TRAD. EST.
OAKLANDS BUS. CEN.
STRAND
SHAFTESBURY AVENUE
CHESTERFIELD RD.
CANTERBURY RD.
TARRING RD.
RUGBY RD.
MARLBOROUGH RD.
ROBSON RD.
WEST PARK LA.
TRENT RD.
BARRINGTON RD.
ROSEBERY AV.
ELGIN RD.
WALPOLE AV.
WELLESLEY AV.
CLIVE AV.
MELBOURNE RD.
ALINORA CRESCENT
NUTLEY CRESCENT
COWDRAY DRIVE
PARKLANDS AVENUE
SOUTHSEA AV.
SEA PLACE
GEORGE V AVENUE
COURTLANDS WAY
GERALD ROAD
PHROSSO RD.
AGLAIA ROAD
WALLACE AVENUE
PEVENSEY RD.
HYTHE RD.
SANDOWN AV.
FAIRVIEW AV.
BROOK BARN WAY
MOAT WAY
WEST PDE.
ESPLANADE

34
A
B
C
D
13
14
20
West Tarring
Worthing FC (Woodside Road).
Bowl. Grn.
BN14
Worthing
Superstore
West Worthing
TARRING ROAD
A2031
TEVILLE RD.
TEVILLE GATE
1
WEST WORTHING
Heene
Victoria Rec. Grd.
COWPER ROAD
WYKEHAM RD.
RICHMOND ROAD
MILL ROAD
A259
2
3
4
5
6
HOSP.
Bingo
Bowling Alley
The Lido
Pavilion Theatre
MARINE PARADE
ESPLANADE
Marine Gds.
33
ENGLISH CHANNEL
101
02
03
A
B
C
D
13
14

35
E
F
G
H
1
2
3
4
5
6
03
02
101
16
17
WORTHING
WORTHING HOSPITAL
Homefield Park
Physiotherapy Centre
Chesswood Jun. Sch.
High Sch.
Davison Leisure Cen.
Inf. Sch.
Tennis Cts.
Superstore
Beach House Park
Seadown Sch.
Splashpoint
Beach Ho. Grds.
Denton Gds.
Coach Sta.
Refuse Disposal Works
Brooklands Park
Putting Green
Warehouse
Works
CHESSWOOD ROAD
LYNDHURST ROAD
BROUGHAM ROAD
MEADOW ROAD
CHURCH WALK
BRIGHTON ROAD
HIGH ST.
B2223
A259
LADYWELL
HOMEFIELD
THURLOW RD.
SUGDEN RD.
CRANWORTH RD.
HALSBURY CL.
HALSBURY RD.
ALVERSTONE RD.
COTTENHAM RD.
ELDON RD.
SELBORNE RD.
DAWES AV.
DAWES CL.
COLEBROOK CL.
COLEBROOK CT.
CHESTER AV.
TEN ACRES
WINDSOR ROAD
GANNON RD.
ST. GEORGE'S RD.
ALEXANDRA RD.
PENDINE AV.
NAVARINO RD.
CHATHAM RD.
DEVONPORT RD.
DEVONPORT PL.
OPHIR ROAD
HEATHERSTONE RD.
MALVERN CL.
NEWPORT M.
THALASSA RD.
BROUGHAM CT.
PEARSONS RETREAT
CORONATION HOMELETS
SEAMILL PK. AV.
SEAMILL PARK CR.
ONSLOW CT.
BROOKDEAN RD.
BENEDICT DR.
BENEDICT CL.
MEADOW CL.
MEADOW CR.
MANSFIELD RD.
BROOK CL.
THESIGER RD.
SILVERDALE
MEADOW RD. IND. EST.
DALE RD.
MADEIRA AV.
FARNCOMBE RD.
SANDITON CT.
SELDEN RD.
SELDEN LA.
HORTON CT.
WAKEHURST CT.
TRASLYN CT.
WESTMINSTER CT.
LUDLOW CT.
MERTON RD.
NEW PDE.
THE ESPLANADE
BEACH PARADE
MARINE PARADE
WINDSOR CT.
PARK AV.
PARK LODGE
BIRCH TREE CT.
PARKSIDE M.
PROVIDENCE TER.
MARKWICK M.
WARWICK RD.
WARWICK PL.
ALFRED PL.
YORK RD.
STEINE GDS.
WARNES
KINGS M.
ASH GRO.
ELM RD.
CHARLECOTE RD.
HAMPDEN CT.
ASHWOOD
STUART CL.
PAGES

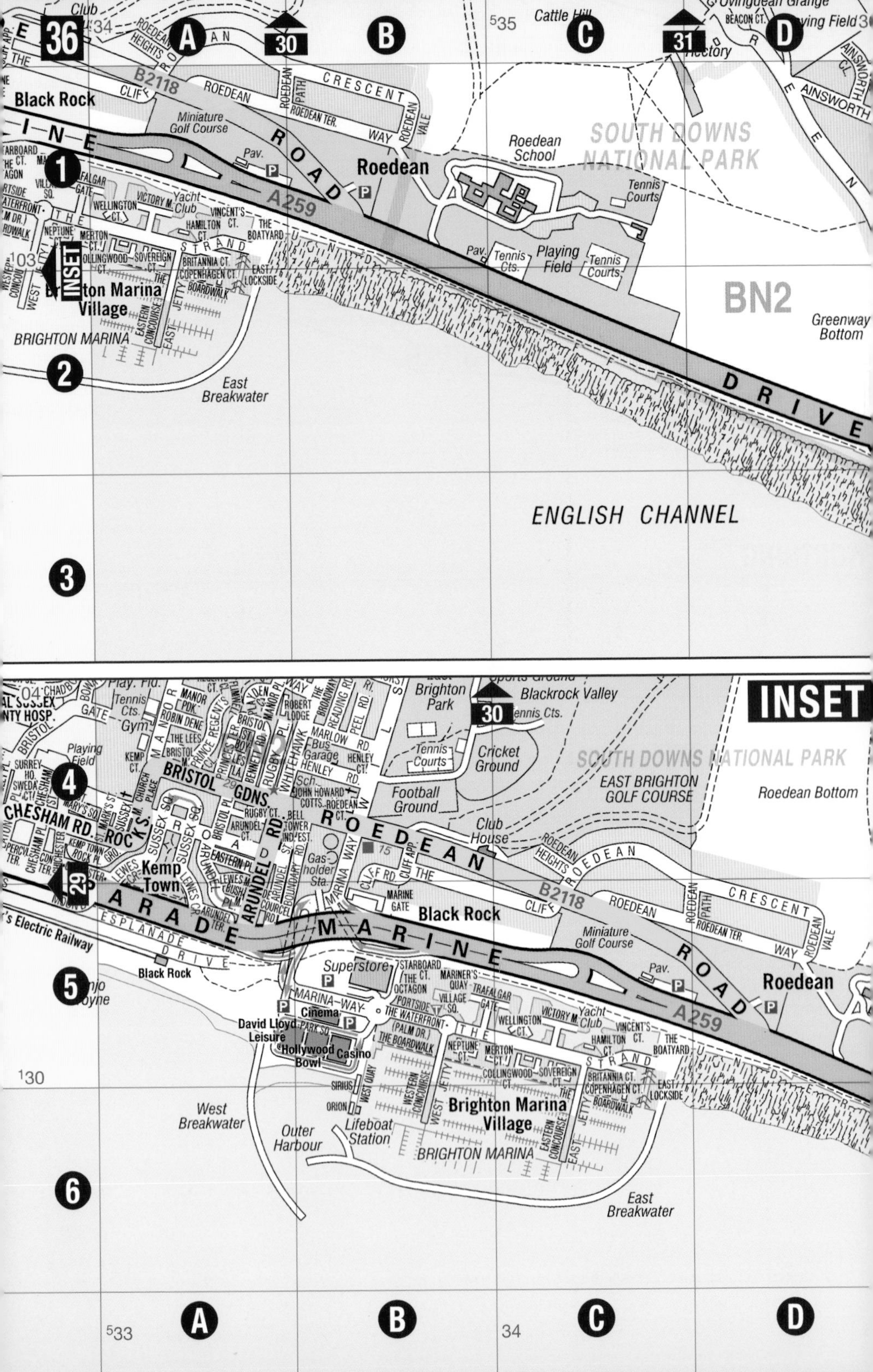

A
B
C
D
30
31
Cattle Hill
Ovingdean Grange
Rectory
AINSWORTH
Black Rock
B2118
CLIFF
ROEDEAN CRESCENT
ROEDEAN TER.
ROEDEAN PATH
ROEDEAN VALE
WAY
Miniature Golf Course
ROAD
Roedean
Roedean School
SOUTH DOWNS NATIONAL PARK
Tennis Courts
Pav.
A259
Yacht Club
VINCENT'S CT.
THE BOATYARD
STRAND
Playing Field
Tennis Cts.
BN2
Greenway Bottom
INSET
Brighton Marina Village
BRIGHTON MARINA
East Breakwater
DRIVE
ENGLISH CHANNEL
1
2
3
4
5
6
INSET
Blackrock Valley
East Brighton Park
Cricket Ground
Football Ground
EAST BRIGHTON GOLF COURSE
Roedean Bottom
Club House
BRISTOL GDNS.
CHESHAM RD.
Kemp Town
ARUNDEL RD.
MARINE PARADE
Black Rock
Superstore
Cinema
David Lloyd Leisure
Hollywood Bowl
Casino
West Breakwater
Outer Harbour
Lifeboat Station
Volk's Electric Railway
29

E · 31 · ROTTINGDEAN PLACE · F · 37 · G · H · 38 · 37

New Barn

SOUTH DOWNS NATIONAL PARK

1

NEW BARN WY.
NEW BARN 3RD RD.
COURT FARM RD.
BEACON CL.
ELEY CRES.
ELEY DRIVE
MOWBRAY
COURT ORD RD.
COURT ORD COTTS.
ROWAN WY.
AVENUE
ROAD
JN HILL
SHEEP
WALK

WINGDEAN

Pavilion
Cricket Ground

Playing Field
Tennis Court
War Mem.
ROTYNGS
Play. Fld.
Bowling Green
BURNES VA.
CHALLONERS

Beacon Hill
(Local Nature Reserve)

St. Dunstan's
Training Centre
& Holiday Home

Miniature
Golf Course

Beacon
Mill

Pav.
NEVILL
THE CAPE
PARK CRES.
WEST ST.

MARINE

A259

Our Lady of
Lourdes RC
Prim. Sch.

THE GREEN
HIGH ST.
THE GREEN
DEAN
BAZEHILL GATE
NORTH CL.
GORHAM CL.
NORTHFIELD RI.
CHALLONERS RI.
ROYS CL.
GORHAM
ROYS CL.
COURT
LANE
WELLESMERE RD.
AVENUE
USTRELLS RD.

Tudor
CL. Prim. Sch.
Dean Hall
The
Granger
Lib.
WHITEWAY
Vicarage
OLDE PLACE M.
VICARAGE LA.
SQ. RD.
M.
STEYNING War
Mem.
Pav. Play. Fld.
CASPIAN CL.
CONWY CT.
DENES M.
ST.
AUBYN'S MEAD
KIPLING CT.
OCEAN REACH
ST. MARGARETS CT.
AZURE
HIGHCLIFF CT.

LANE
WHITEWAY
CHALEY
ROAD
Hall

ROTTINGDEAN

LANE
NEWLANDS ROAD

KNOLE
CRESCENT
GRAND
RD.
THE PARK
AVENUE
CRANLEIGH
ROAD EAST
WEST CR. LENHAM
CRESCENT
LITTLE
ROMNEY RD.
GREENWAY CT.
LENHAM
AVENUE

WESTMESTON
AVENUE
CHORLEY
AVENUE
FOUNTHILL RD.
ASHDOWN RD.
FOUNTHILL
DRIVE
EILEEN AV.
MARINE CL.
ABBOT SBURY CL.

BISHOPSTONE
FALMER
WIVELSFIELD
SAXON CL.
FALMER AV.
UMULU
03
DRIVE
LINDFIELD CL.
LUSTRELLS CL.
LUSTRELLS AV.
TREMOLA LA.
GLYNDE
BOURNE
WEST
DRIVE
LUSTRELLS
CRESCENT

2

ACCINGTON VA.
Salte
Prim.
MAYFIEW CT.

Bowl. Grn.
Saltdean Park
WEST
LYDEAN DRIVE
CHICHESTER
ARUNDEL DRIVE
SALTDEAN PARK RD.
SALTDEAN VALE
Lib.

3

101
02 ENDEL
NORWENDI CT.
38
MARINE CT.
DRIVE

4

5

101

6

E · F · 37 · G · H · 38

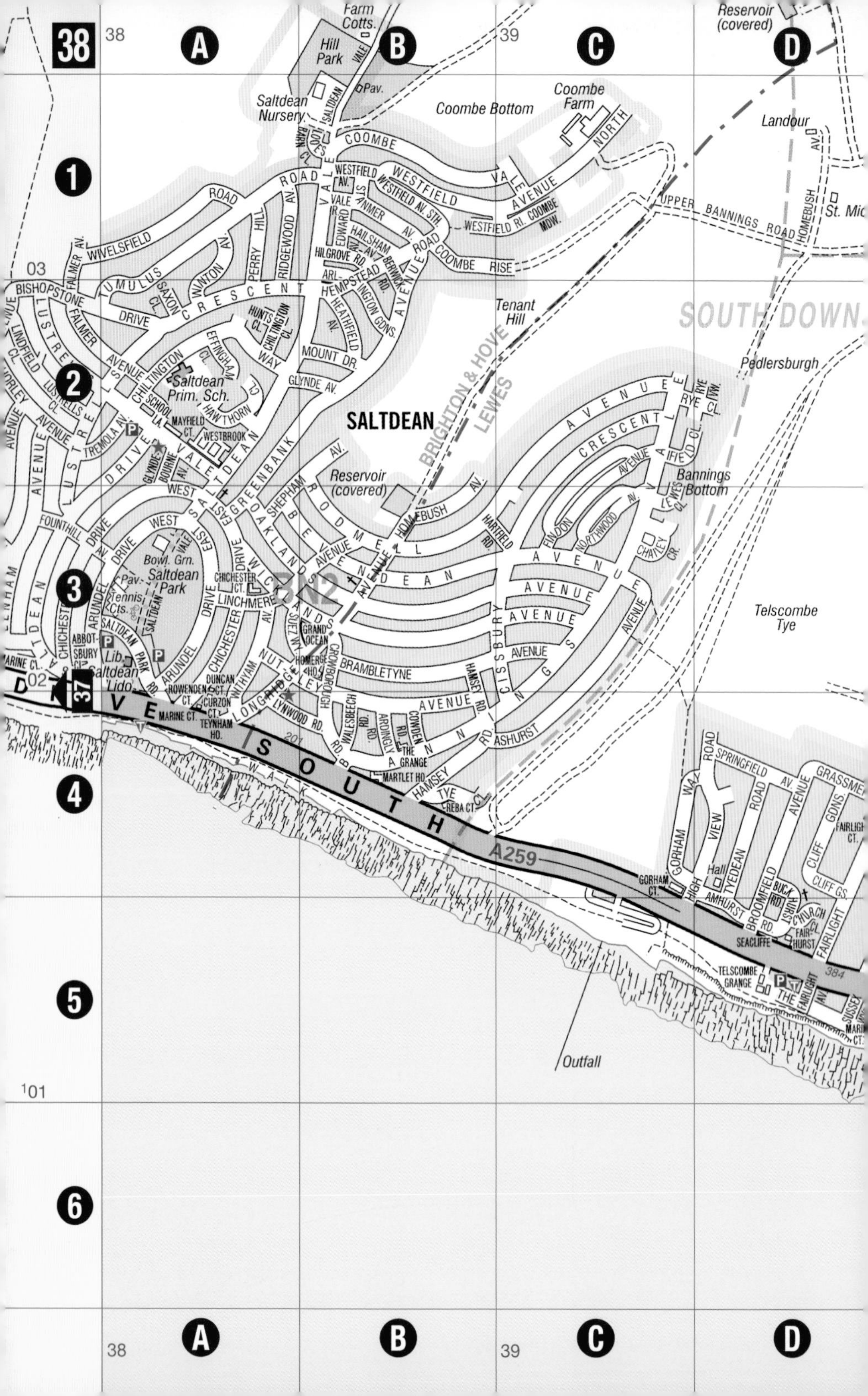
SALTDEAN
Saltdean Nursery
Farm Cotts.
Hill Park
Coombe Bottom
Coombe Farm
Reservoir (covered)
Landour
Tenant Hill
SOUTH DOWN
Pedlersburgh
BRIGHTON & HOVE
LEWES
Saltdean Prim. Sch.
Reservoir (covered)
Bannings Bottom
Telscombe Tye
Bowl. Grn.
Saltdean Park
Tennis Cts.
Saltdean Lido
BN2
A259
SOUTH
Outfall
Hall
TELSCOMBE GRANGE
COOMBE ROAD
WESTFIELD AVENUE
UPPER BANNINGS ROAD
COOMBE RISE
TUMULUS ROAD
CRESCENT DRIVE
BISHOPSTONE DRIVE
CHILTINGTON WAY
MOUNT DR.
GLYNDE AV.
SALTDEAN VALE
GREENBANK AV.
RODMELL AVENUE
WICKLANDS AVENUE
SHEPHAM AV.
BEVENDEAN AVENUE
LINCHMERE AV.
BRAMBLETYNE AVENUE
LONGRIDGE AV.
NUTLEY AV.
CISSBURY AVENUE
ASHURST RD.
HAMSEY RD.
TYE CL.
GORHAM AV.
HIGHVIEW WAY
TYEDEAN ROAD
SPRINGFIELD AV.
BROOMFIELD AVENUE
FAIRLIGHT AV.
MARINE CT.
MARTLET HO.
THE GRANGE
TEYNHAM HO.
GRAND OCEAN
101
201
384
02
03
38
39
37

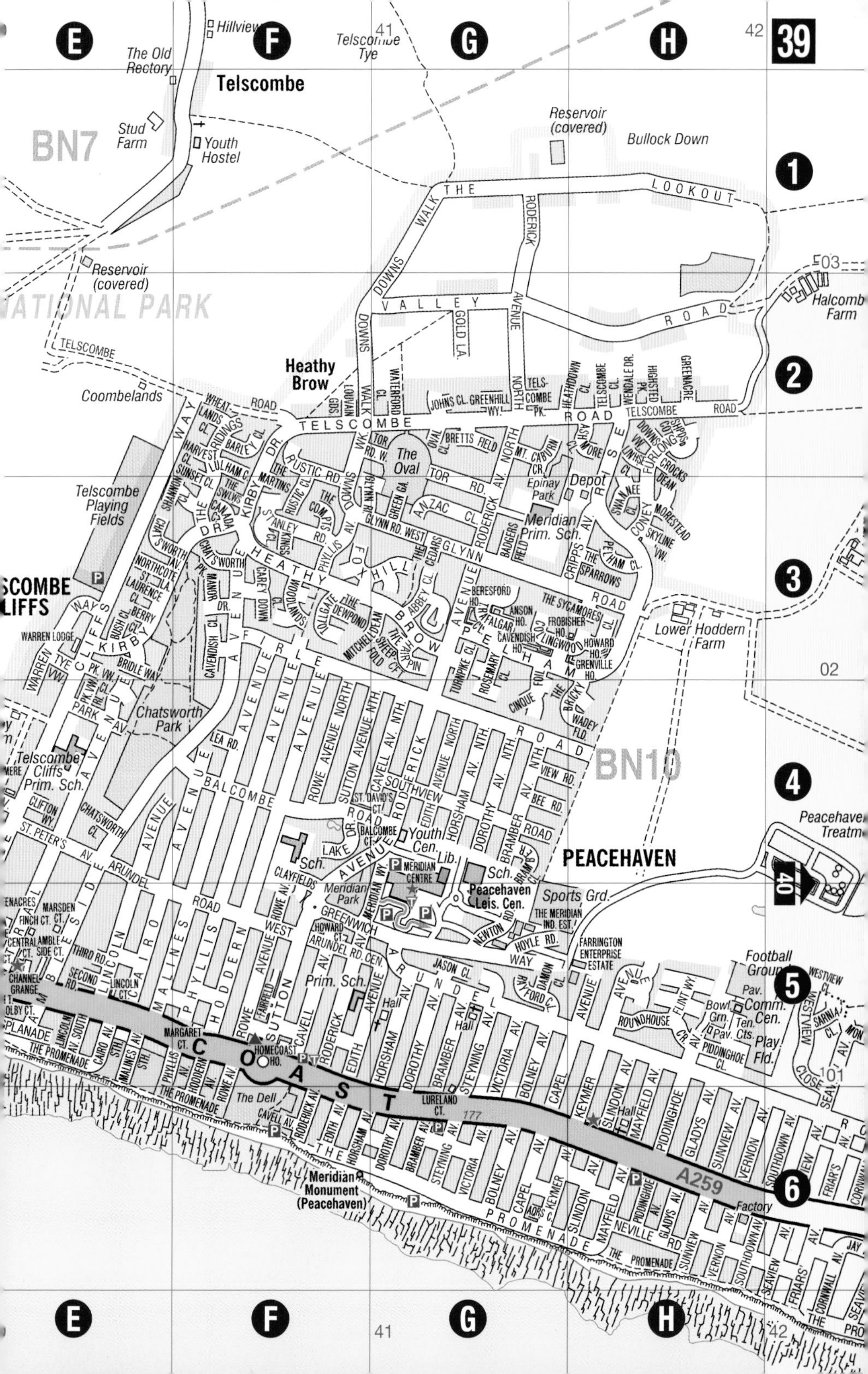

E
F
G
H
41
42
1
2
3
4
5
6
Telscombe
The Old Rectory
Hillview
Telscombe Tye
Stud Farm
Youth Hostel
BN7
Reservoir (covered)
Bullock Down
THE LOOKOUT
RODERICK AVENUE
DOWNS WALK
VALLEY ROAD
GOLD LA.
NATIONAL PARK
Halcombe Farm
TELSCOMBE
Coombelands
Heathy Brow
TELSCOMBE ROAD
WHEATLANDS CL.
RIDINGS
BARLEY CL.
HARVEST CL.
SUNSET CL.
LULHAM C.
THE SWLWS
THE MARTINS
RUSTIC RD.
RUSTIC CL.
THE COMPTS
STANLEY CL.
KINGS RD.
PHYLLIS AV.
DOWNS WK.
TOR RD. W.
The Oval
OVAL CL.
BRETTS FIELD
TOR RD.
GLYNN RD.
GREEN GA.
ANZAC CL.
GLYNN RD. WEST
RODERICK AV. NORTH
MT. CABURN CR.
Epinay Park
Depot
Meridian Prim. Sch.
BADGERS FIELD
CRIPPS AV.
THE SPARROWS
PELHAM CL.
SWANNEE CL.
CONEY RISE
MORESTEAD
SKYLINE VW.
CROCKS DEAN
FURLONG
DOWNS VW.
LINHSEY CL.
JOHNS CL.
GREENHILL WY.
TELSCOMBE PK.
HEATHDOWN CL.
TELSCOMBE CL.
WENDALE DR.
HIGHSTED PK.
GREENACRE
WATERFORD CL.
LOUVAIN GDS.
Telscombe Playing Fields
SHANNON CL.
CHATSWORTH AV.
CANADA CL.
KIRBY DR.
HEATHY BROW
FOXHILL
THE CEDARS
GLYNN
THE SYCAMORES
ROAD
SCOMBE CLIFFS
NORTHCOTE LA.
LAURENCE CL.
BERRY CL.
BUSH CL.
KIRBY
WARREN LODGE
WARREN VW.
TYE VW.
CLIFFS WAY
PK. VW.
BRIDLE WAY
CHATSWORTH PK.
MANOR DR.
CAREY DOWN
WOODLANDS CL.
TOLLGATE
THE DEWPOND
MITCHELLDEAN
THE SHEEPFOLD
THE HAIRPIN
ABBEY CL.
BERESFORD HO.
TRAFALGAR
ANSON HO.
FROBISHER HO.
CAVENDISH HO.
COLLINGWOOD
HOWARD HO.
GRENVILLE HO.
PELHAM RISE
TURNPIKE CL.
ROSEMARY CL.
CINQUE FOIL
THE BRICKY
WADEY FLD.
Lower Hoddern Farm
02
CAVENDISH CL.
FIRLE ROAD
Chatsworth Park
PARK AV.
Telscombe Cliffs Prim. Sch.
LEA RD.
BALCOMBE
CLIFTON WY.
ST. PETER'S AV.
CHATSWORTH CL.
BN10
VIEW RD.
BEE RD.
BRAMBER AV. NTH.
DOROTHY AV. NTH.
HORSHAM AV. NTH.
EDITH AV. NTH.
SOUTHVIEW
CAVELL AV. NTH.
SUTTON AVENUE NTH.
ROWE AVENUE NORTH
RODERICK AVENUE NORTH
ST. DAVID'S CT.
LAKE DR.
BALCOMBE CT.
Youth Cen.
Lib.
Sch.
MERIDIAN CENTRE
Meridian Park
MERIDIAN WY.
CLAYFIELDS
Peacehaven Leis. Cen.
PEACEHAVEN
Sports Grd.
THE MERIDIAN IND. EST.
NEWTON RD.
HOYLE RD.
GREENWICH
HOWARD CT.
ARUNDEL RD. CEN.
ARUNDEL ROAD WEST
FARRINGTON ENTERPRISE ESTATE
JASON CL.
WAY
DAMON CL.
RAYFORD CL.
Peacehaven Treatm
40
Football Ground
WESTVIEW CL.
Pav.
Comm. Cen.
Bowl. Grn.
Ten. Cts.
Play. Fld.
SARNIA CL.
WESTVIEW CLOSE
PIDDINGHOE CL.
FLINT WY.
ROUNDHOUSE CR.
MARSDEN CT.
FINCH CT.
CENTRAL CT.
AMBLESIDE CT.
THIRD RD.
SECOND RD.
CHANNEL GRANGE
LINCOLN CT.
LINCOLN
CAIRO
MALINES
PHYLLIS
HODDERN
ROWE AV.
SUTTON
CAVELL
RODERICK
FAIRFIELD
Prim. Sch.
Hall
MARGARET CT.
HOMECOAST HO.
COAST
LINCOLN AV. SOUTH
CAIRO AV.
MALINES AV. STH.
THE PROMENADE
The Dell
CAVELL AV.
RODERICK AV.
EDITH AV.
HORSHAM AV.
DOROTHY AV.
BRAMBER AV.
STEYNING AV.
VICTORIA AV.
BOLNEY AV.
CAPEL AV.
KEYMER AV.
SLINDON AV.
MAYFIELD AV.
PIDDINGHOE AV.
GLADYS AV.
SUNVIEW AV.
VERNON AV.
SOUTHDOWN AV.
SEAVIEW AV.
FRIARS' AV.
CORNWALL AV.
LURELAND CT.
177
A259
Meridian Monument (Peacehaven)
PROMENADE
NEVILLE RD.
Factory
101
JAY

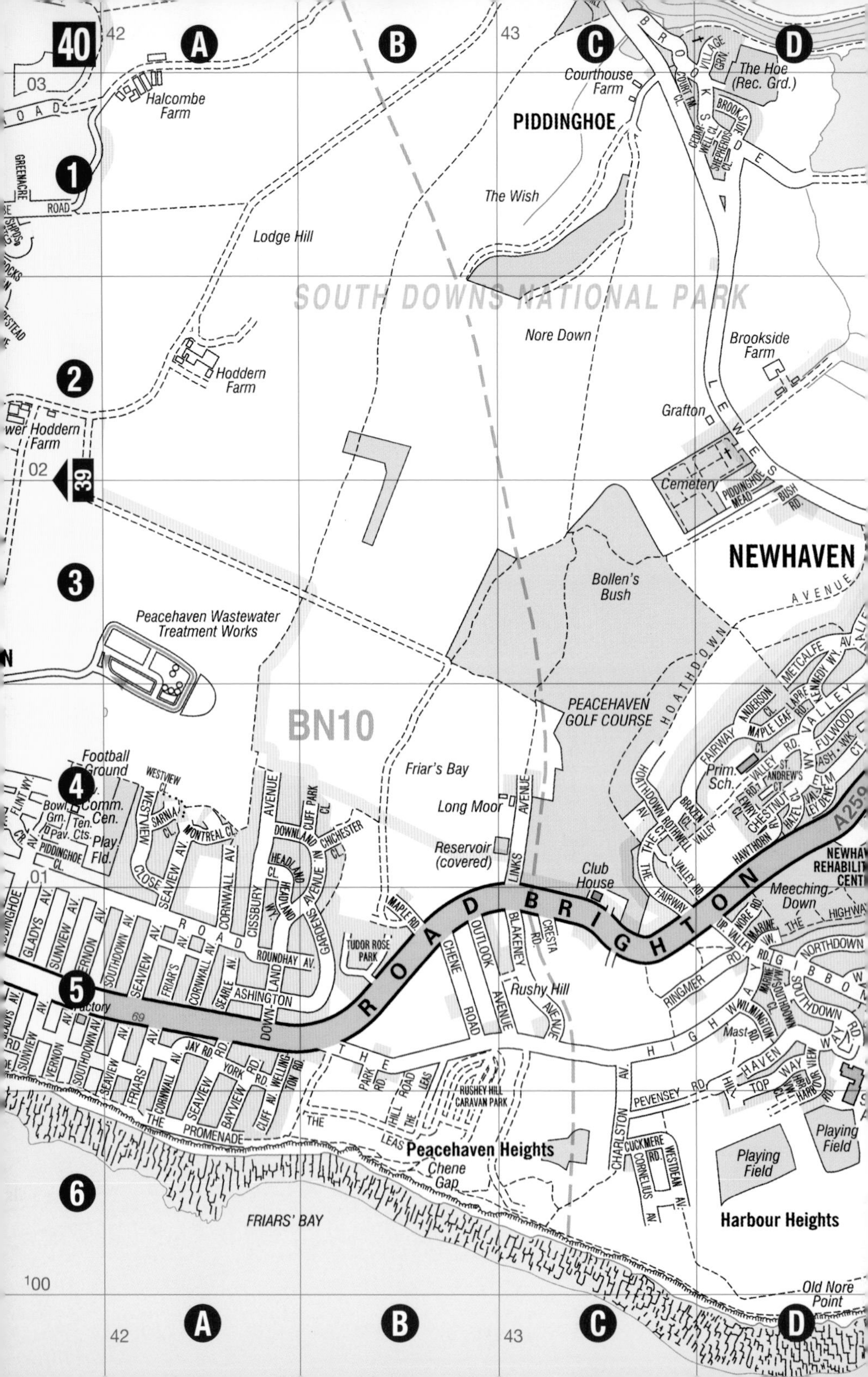

PIDDINGHOE
NEWHAVEN
SOUTH DOWNS NATIONAL PARK
BN10
Halcombe Farm
Courthouse Farm
The Hoe (Rec. Grd.)
The Wish
Lodge Hill
Nore Down
Brookside Farm
Hoddern Farm
Grafton
Cemetery
Bollen's Bush
Peacehaven Wastewater Treatment Works
PEACEHAVEN GOLF COURSE
Football Ground
Friar's Bay
Long Moor
Reservoir (covered)
Club House
Prim. Sch.
Meeching Down
Rushy Hill
TUDOR ROSE PARK
RUSHEY HILL CARAVAN PARK
Peacehaven Heights
Chene Gap
FRIARS' BAY
Harbour Heights
Playing Field
Old Nore Point
BRIGHTON ROAD
LEWES ROAD
A259
HIGHWAY
THE PROMENADE
Factory
69

39

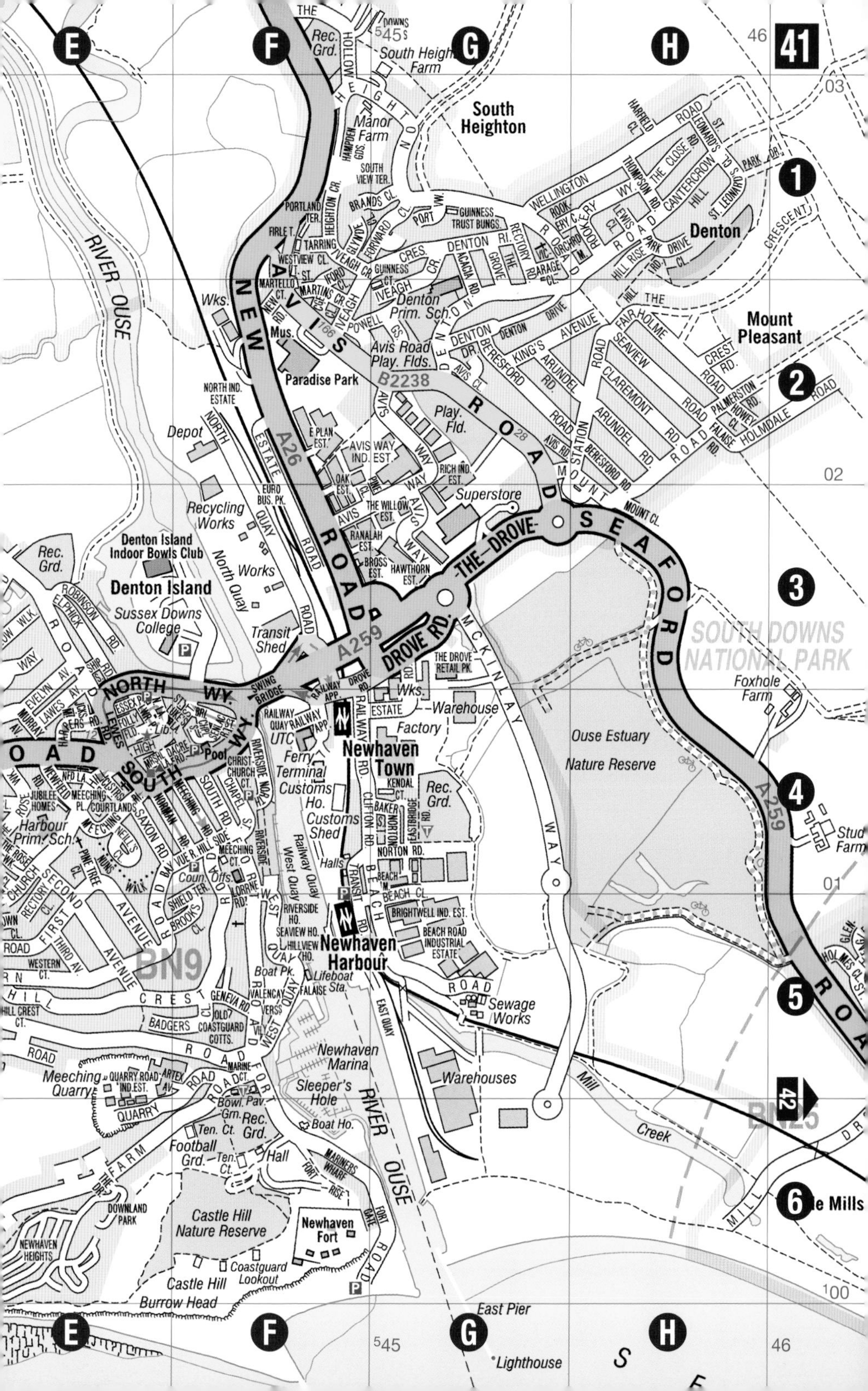
E
F
G
H
1
2
3
4
5
6
545
46
03
02
01
100
South Heighton
Manor Farm
South Heighton Farm
Denton
Mount Pleasant
Denton Prim. Sch.
Avis Road Play. Flds.
Paradise Park
Mus.
Wks.
NEW ROAD
AVIS ROAD
A26
B2238
A259
SEAFORD ROAD
THE DROVE
DROVE RD.
NORTH WY.
SOUTH WY.
RIVER OUSE
Depot
Recycling Works
Denton Island Indoor Bowls Club
Denton Island
Sussex Downs College
North Quay
Works
Transit Shed
Superstore
Play. Fld.
SOUTH DOWNS NATIONAL PARK
Foxhole Farm
Ouse Estuary Nature Reserve
Warehouse
Factory
Newhaven Town
UTC
Ferry Terminal
Customs Ho.
Customs Shed
Railway Quay
West Quay
Halls
Rec. Grd.
Newhaven Harbour
Boat Pk.
Lifeboat Sta.
Sewage Works
Harbour Prim. Sch.
Coun. Offs.
Pool
BN9
Meeching Quarry
Newhaven Marina
Sleeper's Hole
Boat Ho.
Warehouses
Mill Creek
BN25
42
Football Grd.
Hall
Castle Hill Nature Reserve
Newhaven Fort
Coastguard Lookout
Castle Hill
Burrow Head
East Pier
Lighthouse
Mills

Bishopstone
The Rookery
Hall
Rookery Hill
SOUTH DOWNS NATIONAL PARK
East Blatchington
St. John's Sch.
BUCKLE HOLIDAY PARK
Newhaven & Seaford Sailing Club
Bishopstone
SUNNYSIDE PARK
NEW COASTGUARD COTTS.
BEACH COTTAGES
HIGH BEACH HO.
COOMBE LODGE
Pavs.
Salts Recreation Ground
Tennis Cts.
Seaford
DANNFIELDS HO.
SEAFORD
Seaford Museum (Martello Tower no.
NEWHAVEN ROAD
BUCKLE BY-PASS
A259
CLAREMONT RD.
STATION APPROACH
GRAND AVENUE
PROMENADE
PARADE
DORD
BA
41

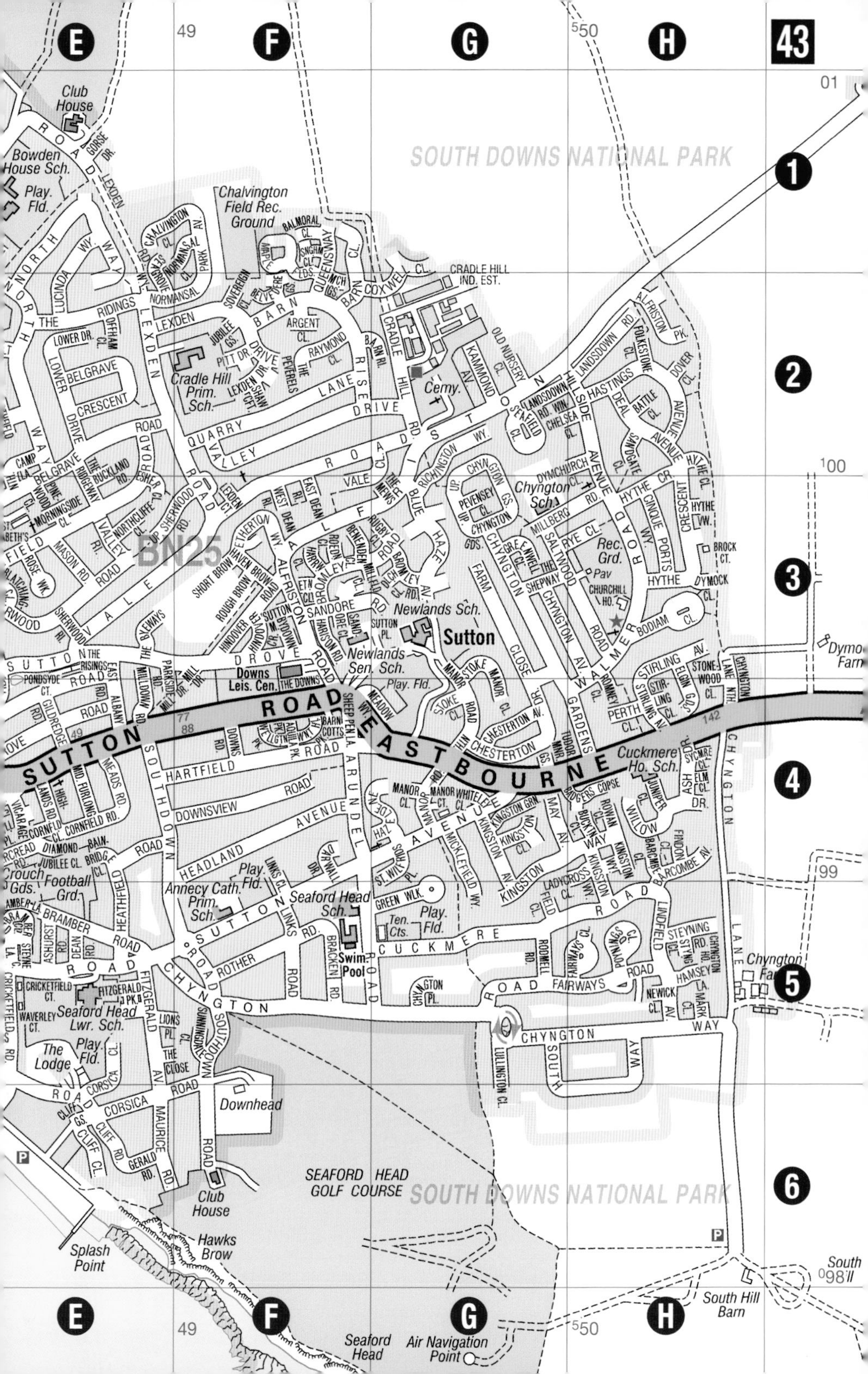
SOUTH DOWNS NATIONAL PARK
Club House
Bowden House Sch.
Play. Fld.
Chalvington Field Rec. Ground
CRADLE HILL IND. EST.
Cradle Hill Prim. Sch.
Cemy.
BN25
Chyngton Sch.
Rec. Grd.
Pav
CHURCHILL HO.
Newlands Sch.
Sutton
Newlands Sen. Sch.
Play. Fld.
Downs Leis. Cen.
SUTTON ROAD
EASTBOURNE ROAD
Cuckmere Ho. Sch.
Dymock Farm
Crouch Gds.
Football Grd.
Annecy Cath. Prim. Sch.
Seaford Head Sch.
Ten. Cts.
Swim. Pool
Seaford Head Lwr. Sch.
The Lodge
Chyngton Farm
Downhead
SEAFORD HEAD GOLF COURSE
Club House
Hawks Brow
Splash Point
Seaford Head
Air Navigation Point
South Hill Barn
South Hill

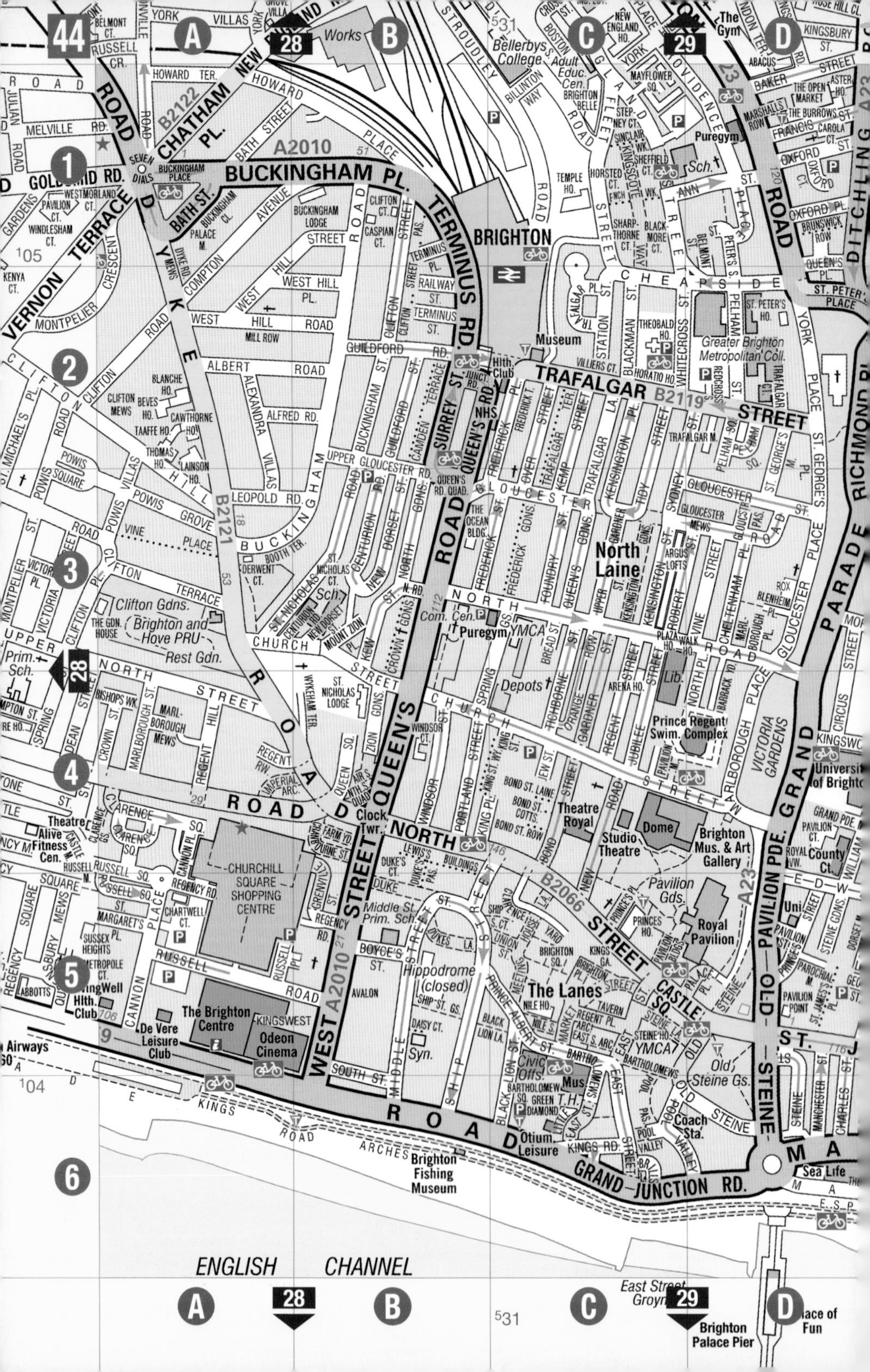

44
A
B
C
D
1
2
3
4
5
6
28
29
Works
Bellerbys College
Adult Educ. Cen.
The Gym
CHATHAM PL.
NEW ENGLAND RD.
B2122
A2010
BUCKINGHAM PL.
TERMINUS RD.
DYKE ROAD
B2121
VERNON TERRACE
MONTPELIER CRESCENT
GOLDSMID RD.
SEVEN DIALS
BRIGHTON
Museum
Greater Brighton Metropolitan Coll.
TRAFALGAR STREET
B2119
North Laine
QUEEN'S ROAD
SURREY ST.
GLOUCESTER RD.
NORTH ROAD
Puregym
YMCA
Depots
Lib.
Prince Regent Swim. Complex
VICTORIA GARDENS
GRAND PARADE
RICHMOND
DITCHLING ROAD
University of Brighton
Clifton Gdns.
Brighton and Hove PRU
Rest Gdn.
CHURCH STREET
NORTH STREET
WESTERN ROAD
Clock Twr.
CHURCHILL SQUARE SHOPPING CENTRE
Theatre Royal
Studio Theatre
Dome
Brighton Mus. & Art Gallery
Pavilion Gds.
Royal Pavilion
B2066
EAST STREET
CASTLE SQ.
The Lanes
Hippodrome (closed)
Middle St. Prim. Sch.
WEST STREET
The Brighton Centre
Odeon Cinema
De Vere Leisure Club
Syn.
Civic Offs.
Mus.
T.H.
Otium Leisure
Coach Sta.
Old Steine Gs.
OLD STEINE
PAVILION PDE.
A23
KINGS ROAD
GRAND JUNCTION RD.
Brighton Fishing Museum
Sea Life
ENGLISH CHANNEL
East Street Groyne
Brighton Palace Pier
Palace of Fun
531
104
105

INDEX

Including Streets, Places & Areas, Hospitals etc., Industrial Estates,
Selected Flats & Walkways, Service Areas, Stations and Selected Places of Interest.

HOW TO USE THIS INDEX

1. Each street name is followed by its Postcode District, then by its Locality abbreviation(s) and then by its map reference; e.g. **Abbey Cl.** BN10: Peace..........3G **39** is in the BN10 Postcode District and the Peacehaven Locality and is to be found in square 3G on page **39**. The page number is shown in bold type.

2. A strict alphabetical order is followed in which Av., Rd., St., etc. (though abbreviated) are read in full and as part of the street name; e.g. **Ashcombe Hollow** appears after **Ash Cl.** but before **Ash Ct.**

3. Streets and a selection of flats and walkways that cannot be shown on the mapping, appear in the index with the thoroughfare to which they are connected shown in brackets; e.g. **Abergavenny Ho.** BN3: Hove..........4B **28** (off Holland Rd.)

4. Addresses that are in more than one part are referred to as not continuous.

5. Places and areas are shown in the index in BLUE TYPE and the map reference is to the actual map square in which the town centre or area is located and not to the place name shown on the map; e.g. ALDRINGTON..........3F **27**

6. An example of a selected place of interest is **Beacon Mill Rottingdean**..........3F **37**

7. An example of a station is **Aldrington Station (Rail)**..........2G **27**

8. An example of a junction name or service area is **GROVE LODGE RDBT.**..........3C **20**

9. An example of a Hospital, Hospice or selected Healthcare facility is **ACRE DAY HOSPITAL**..........3C **34**

10. Map references for entries that appear on large scale page **44** are shown first, with small scale map references shown in brackets; e.g. **Abacus** BN1: Brig..........1D **44** (3E **29**)

GENERAL ABBREVIATIONS

App. : Approach	**Dr.** : Drive	**La.** : Lane	**Rdbt.** : Roundabout
Arc. : Arcade	**E.** : East	**Lit.** : Little	**Shop.** : Shopping
Av. : Avenue	**Ent.** : Enterprise	**Lwr.** : Lower	**Sth.** : South
Blvd. : Boulevard	**Est.** : Estate	**Mnr.** : Manor	**Sq.** : Square
Bri. : Bridge	**Fld.** : Field	**Mkt.** : Market	**St.** : Street
Bldgs. : Buildings	**Flds.** : Fields	**Mdw.** : Meadow	**Ter.** : Terrace
Bus. : Business	**Gdn.** : Garden	**Mdws.** : Meadows	**Trad.** : Trading
Cvn. : Caravan	**Gdns.** : Gardens	**M.** : Mews	**Up.** : Upper
Cen. : Centre	**Gth.** : Garth	**Mt.** : Mount	**Vw.** : View
Circ. : Circle	**Ga.** : Gate	**Mus.** : Museum	**Vs.** : Villas
Cl. : Close	**Gt.** : Great	**Nth.** : North	**Vis.** : Visitors
Cnr. : Corner	**Grn.** : Green	**Pde.** : Parade	**Wlk.** : Walk
Cott. : Cottage	**Gro.** : Grove	**Pk.** : Park	**W.** : West
Cotts. : Cottages	**Hgts.** : Heights	**Pas.** : Passage	**Yd.** : Yard
Ct. : Court	**Ho.** : House	**Pl.** : Place	
Cres. : Crescent	**Ind.** : Industrial	**Ri.** : Rise	
Cft. : Croft	**Info.** : Information	**Rd.** : Road	

LOCALITY ABBREVIATIONS

Bishopston: BN25 ....Bishop	**Goring-by-Sea**: BN12, BN13..........Gor S	**Peacehaven**: BN9, BN10 ....Peace	**South Heighton**: BN9..........S Heig
Bramber: BN44..........Bramb	**High Salvington**: BN13..........High S	**Piddinghoe**: BN9..........Pidd	**South Lancing**: BN15..........S Lan
Brighton: BN1, BN2, BN3..........Brig	**Hove**: BN3..........Hove	**Portslade**: BN41, BN42..........Ports	**Southwick**: BN42..........S'wick
Broadwater: BN14..........Broadw	**Kingston Gorse**: BN16..........King G	**Ringmer**: BN8..........Ring	**Stanmer**: BN1..........Stan
Charman Dean: BN14..........Char D	**Kingston near Lewes**: BN2, BN7..........King L	**Rottingdean**: BN2..........Rott	**Steyning**: BN44..........Stey
Clapham: BN13..........Clap	**Lancing**: BN15..........Lan	**Saltdean**: BN2, BN10..........Salt	**Telscombe Cliffs**: BN7, BN10..........Tels C
Durrington: BN13..........Durr	**Lewes**: BN7, BN8..........Lewes	**Salvington**: BN13, BN14..........Salv	**Upper Beeding**: BN44..........Up B
Falmer: BN1, BN2, BN3..........Falm	**Newhaven**: BN9..........Newh	**Seaford**: BN25..........Sea	**West Tarring**: BN13, BN14..........W Tar
Ferring: BN12..........Fer	**North Lancing**: BN15..........N Lan	**Shoreham Beach**: BN43..........Shor B	**Woodingdean**: BN2..........W'dean
Findon Valley: BN13, BN14..........Fin V	**Offham**: BN7..........Off	**Shoreham-by-Sea**: BN15, BN43..........Shor S	**Worthing**: BN11, BN12, BN13, BN14......Worth
Findon: BN13, BN14..........Fin	**Ovingdean**: BN2..........O'dean	**Small Dole**: BN5..........Small D	
Glynde: BN8..........Glyn	**Patching**: BN12, BN13..........Pat	**Sompting**: BN15..........Somp	

A

Abacus BN1: Brig 1D **44** (3E **29**)
....(off London Ter.)
Abbey Cl. BN10: Peace..........3G **39**
Abbey Cl. BN15: S Lan 4F **23**
Abbey Rd. BN11: Worth 3B **34**
Abbey Rd. BN15: Somp 3A **22**
Abbey Rd. BN2: Brig 6H **29**
Abbey Rd. BN44: Stey 2D **4**
Abbotsbury Cl. BN2: Salt..........3H **37**
Abbots Way BN15: Lan 4D **22**
Abbotts BN1: Brig.......... 5A **44** (5C **28**)
Abbotts Cl. BN11: Worth..........2D **34**
Abbotts Vw. BN15: Somp 2A **22**
A'Becket Gdns. BN13: Durr 4G **19**
Aberdeen Rd. BN2: Brig 2G **29**
Abergavenny Ho. BN3: Hove..........4B **28**
....(off Holland Rd.)
Abergavenny Rd. BN7: Lewes..........4D **16**
Abingdon Wlk. BN13: Durr 5F **19**
....(off Middle Tyne)
Abinger Ct. BN41: Ports 2B **26**
....(off Abinger Rd.)
Abinger Pl. BN7: Lewes..........4E **17**
Abinger Rd. BN2: W'dean..........4G **31**
Abinger Rd. BN41: Ports..........2B **26**
Acacia Av. BN13: Durr 3H **19**
Acacia Av. BN3: Hove 1F **27**
Acacia Ct. BN1: Brig..........6D **12**
Acacia Rd. BN9: Newh 1G **41**
Acre Cl., The BN11: Worth..........3B **34**
ACRE DAY HOSPITAL..........3C **34**
Active4Less Hove 2D **26**

Adams Cl. BN1: Brig..........6F **13**
Addison Cl. BN15: Lan 4C **22**
Addison Rd. BN3: Hove 3C **28**
Adelaide Cl. BN13: Durr 3E **19**
Adelaide Cl. BN25: Sea 2D **42**
Adelaide Cres. BN3: Hove 5A **28**
Adelaide Mans. BN3: Hove..........5A **28**
Adelaide M. BN3: Hove..........4G **27**
Adelaide Sq. BN43: Shor S..........3D **24**
Admiral Ct. BN15: Lan..........6B **22**
Admirals Wlk. BN43: Shor B 4B **24**
Adur Av. BN13: Durr 2E **19**
Adur Av. BN43: Shor S..........1A **24**
Adur Bus. Cen., The
....3A **24**
Adur Cl. BN15: S Lan..........5G **23**
Adur Cl. BN43: Shor S 2E **25**
Adur Dr. BN43: Shor S..........3C **24**
Adur Indoor Bowls Cen...........3H **25**
Adur Outdoor Activities Cen...........3A **24**
Adur Rd. BN43: Shor S..........2A **24**
Adur Valley Ct. BN44: Up B..........4G **5**
Adur Vw. BN44: Up B..........4F **5**
Adversane Rd. BN14: Worth..........5B **20**
Aglaia Rd. BN11: Worth..........3H **33**
Agnes St. BN2: Brig..........3G **29**
Ainsdale Cl. BN13: Durr 4F **19**
Ainsdale Rd. BN13: Durr 4F **19**
Ainsworth Cl. BN2: O'dean..........1D **36**
Ainsworth Cl. BN2: O'dean..........6F **31**
Airedale Ct. BN11: Worth 2B **34**
Airlie Ho. BN3: Hove 4A **28**
....(off Grand Av.)

Air St. BN1: Brig 4B **44** (5D **28**)
Alandale Rd. BN15: Somp..........2A **22**
Alan Way BN2: Brig 4B **30**
Albany Cl. BN11: Worth..........3A **34**
Albany M. BN3: Hove..........4H **27**
Albany Rd. BN25: Sea..........4B **42**
Albany Towers BN3: Hove..........5H **27**
....(off St Catherine's Ter.)
Albany Vs. BN3: Hove..........5H **27**
Albemarle, The BN2: Brig... 6D **44** (6E **29**)
....(off Marine Pde.)
Albemarle Ho. BN11: Worth 2A **34**
....(off Southview Dr.)
Albemarle Mans. BN3: Hove..........5H **27**
....(off Medina Ter.)
Alberta Rd. BN13: Durr 4F **19**
Alberta Wlk. BN13: Durr..........4F **19**
Albert Mans. BN11: Worth 4A **28**
....(off Church Rd.)
Albert M. BN3: Hove..........4A **28**
Albert Rd. BN1: Brig..........2A **44** (4D **28**)
Albert Rd. BN42: S'wick 3F **25**
Albion Cl. BN2: Brig..........5F **29**
....(off George St.)
Albion Hill BN2: Brig..........4F **29**
Albion Ho. BN2: Brig..........4F **29**
....(off Albion St.)
Albion Ho. BN42: S'wick..........3H **25**
Albion St. BN2: Brig..........4F **29**
Albion St. BN41: Ports..........3B **26**
Albion St. BN42: S'wick..........4F **25**
Albion St. BN7: Lewes..........4F **17**
Albourne Cl. BN2: Brig..........3A **30**
Alces Pl. BN25: Sea..........2D **42**

Alder Cl. BN13: Durr..........5E **19**
Alderney Rd. BN12: Fer..........4B **32**
Aldrich Cl. BN2: Brig..........4B **30**
ALDRINGTON..........3F **27**
Aldrington Av. BN3: Hove..........2G **27**
Aldrington Cl. BN3: Hove..........3D **26**
ALDRINGTON HOUSE..........3F **27**
Aldrington Pl. BN3: Hove..........2D **26**
Aldrington Station (Rail)..........2G **27**
Aldsworth Av. BN12: Gor S 2D **32**
Aldsworth Ct. BN12: Gor S..........2D **32**
Aldsworth Pde. BN12: Gor S 2D **32**
Aldwick Cres. BN14: Fin V 1A **20**
Aldwick M. BN3: Hove..........5E **11**
Alexander Ter. BN11: Worth 2A **34**
....(off Liverpool Gdns.)
Alexandra Cl. BN25: Sea..........2D **42**
Alexandra Cl. BN12: Gor S..........1E **33**
Alexandra Cl. BN3: Hove..........6F **11**
Alexandra Rd. BN11: Worth 2F **35**
Alexandra Rd. BN15: S Lan..........5D **22**
Alexandra Vs. BN1: Brig..........2A **44** (4D **28**)
Alfa Ct. BN10: Tels C 5E **39**
Alford Cl. BN14: Salv..........3B **20**
Alfred Davey Ct.
BN1: Brig 3C **44** (4E **29**)
....(off Tichbourne St.)
Alfred Pl. BN11: Worth..........2F **35**
Alfred Rd. BN11: Worth 2A **44** (4D **28**)
Alfriston Cl. BN14: Worth..........5B **20**
Alfriston Cl. BN2: Brig..........4B **30**
Alfriston Ho. BN14: Broadw..........5D **20**
....(off Broadwater St. E.)
Alfriston Pk. BN25: Sea..........2H **43**

Alfriston Rd. – Beacon Ct.

Alfriston Rd. BN14: Worth 5B **20**
Alfriston Rd. BN25: Sea 3F **43**
Alice Cl. BN3: Hove 5B **28**
Alice St. BN3: Hove 5B **28**
Alinora Av. BN12: Gor S 2F **33**
Alinora Cl. BN12: Gor S 2F **33**
Alinora Cres. BN12: Gor S 4E **33**
Alinora Dr. BN12: Gor S 3E **33**
Alive Fitness & Natural Health Cen. 4A **44** (5C **28**)
(off Castle St.)
Allendale Av. BN14: Fin V 1A **20**
Allington Rd. BN14: Broadw 3E **21**
All Saints Arts & Youth Cen. 4F **17**
(off Friar's Wlk.)
Alma St. BN15: S Lan 6C **22**
Almond Av. BN43: Shor S 2G **23**
Alpine Rd. BN3: Hove 2F **27**
Alston Way BN13: Durr 5F **19**
Alverstone Rd. BN11: Worth 1F **35**
Ambassadors, The BN3: Hove 4A **28**
(off Wilbury Rd.)
Amber Cl. BN43: Shor S 2D **24**
Amber Ct. BN3: Hove
Bell Mead 3B **28**
Amber Ct. BN3: Hove
Salisbury Rd. 4A **28**
Amber Ho. BN3: Hove 4H **27**
Amberley Cl. BN3: Hove 5E **11**
Amberley Cl. BN43: Shor S 1B **24**
Amberley Ct. BN11: Worth 2H **33**
Amberley Ct. BN15: S Lan 4D **22**
Amberley Dr. BN12: Gor S 4C **32**
Amberley Dr. BN3: Hove 6E **11**
Amberley Lodge BN2: Brig 4B **30**
(off Whitehawk Way)
Ambleside Av. BN10: Tels C 5E **39**
Ambleside Ct. BN10: Tels C 5E **39**
Ambleside Rd. BN15: Somp 4A **22**
Ambrose Pl. BN11: Worth 2D **34**
Amelia Cl. BN42: S'wick 3G **25**
Amelia Ct. BN11: Worth 2D **34**
Amelia Cres. BN11: Worth 2C **34**
(off Amelia Rd.)
Amelia Pk. 2C **34**
(off Park Crescent)
Amelia Rd. BN11: Worth 2C **34**
Amesbury Cres. BN3: Hove 3E **27**
Amex Community Stadium 2D **14**
AMF Bowling Worthing 3D **34**
Amherst Cres. BN3: Hove 2F **27**
Amhurst Rd. BN10: Tels C 5D **38**
Amo M. BN11: Worth 3C **34**
(off Montague St.)
Anchor Cl. BN43: Shor B 4C **24**
Anchor Ct. BN12: Gor S 3G **33**
Ancren Cl. BN12: Fer 6B **18**
Anderson Cl. BN9: Newh 4D **40**
Andrew Cl. BN44: Stey 4C **4**
Anglesea St. BN11: Worth 1C **34**
Angmering Ct. BN1: Brig 3B **14**
(off Newick Rd.)
Angola Rd. BN14: Broadw 6F **21**
Angus Rd. BN12: Gor S 2G **33**
Anne of Cleves House 5E **17**
Annes Path BN7: Lewes 6E **17**
Annington Commercial Cen.
BN44: Bramb 6D **4**
Annington Gdns. BN43: Shor S 1B **24**
Annington Rd. BN44: Bramb 5D **4**
(not continuous)
Ann St. BN1: Brig 1D **44** (3E **29**)
Ann St. BN11: Worth 2D **34**
Annweir Av. BN15: Lan 4B **22**
Anscombe Cl. BN11: Worth 3H **33**
Anscombe Rd. BN11: Worth 3H **33**
Ansisters Rd. BN12: Fer 3A **32**
Anson Ct. BN12: Gor S 6E **19**
Anson Ho. BN10: Peace 3G **39**
Anson Rd. BN12: Gor S 6E **19**
Ansty Cl. BN2: Brig 5A **30**
Antioch St. BN7: Lewes 5E **17**
Antony Cl. BN25: Sea 1A **42**
Anvil Cl. BN41: Ports 6B **10**
Anzac Cl. BN10: Peace 3G **39**
Appledore Rd. BN2: Brig 4B **14**
Applesham Av. BN3: Hove 6E **11**
Applesham Ct. BN15: Lan 6C **22**
Applesham Way BN41: Ports 1A **26**
Approach, The BN1: Brig 5C **12**
April Cl. BN12: Fer 4A **32**
Apsley Way BN13: Durr 5D **18**
Aqua Ct. BN10: Tels C 5D **38**
Aquarium & Visitors Cen.
Volk's Electric Railway 6F **29**
Aquarius Cl. BN10: Peace 6G **39**
Aquila Pk. BN25: Sea 4F **43**
Archibald Rd. BN11: Worth 1G **35**
Ardale Cl. BN11: Worth 2H **33**
Ardingly Ct. BN2: Brig 5F **29**
(off High St.)
Ardingly Dr. BN12: Gor S 1D **32**
Ardingly Rd. BN2: Salt 4B **38**
Ardingly St. BN2: Brig 5F **29**
Ardsheal Cl. BN14: Broadw 4C **20**
Ardsheal Rd. BN14: Broadw 4C **20**
Arena Ho. BN1: Brig 4C **44** (5E **29**)
(off Regent St.)
Argent Cl. BN25: Sea 2F **43**
Argus Lofts BN1: Brig 3C **44** (4E **29**)
(off Kensington St.)
Argyle Rd. BN1: Brig 2D **28**
Argyle Vs. BN1: Brig 2D **28**
(off Argyle Rd.)
Ariadne Rd. BN11: Worth 3B **34**
Ariel Ct. BN15: Lan 6B **22**
Arlington Av. BN12: Gor S 3D **32**
Arlington Cl. BN12: Gor S 3D **32**
Arlington Cres. BN1: Brig 3A **14**
Arlington Gdns. BN2: Salt 1B **38**
Arlington M. BN2: Brig 6H **29**
(off Eastern Rd.)
Arnold St. BN2: Brig 3G **29**
Arnside Cl. BN15: Somp 5A **22**
Artex Av. BN9: Newh 5F **41**
Arthur St. BN3: Hove 2G **27**
Arts Rd. BN1: Falm 1D **14**
Arun Cl. BN13: Durr 3F **19**
Arun Cl. BN15: Somp 3A **22**
Arun Ct. BN43: Shor S 2E **25**
Arun Cres. BN13: Durr 3E **19**
Arundel Cl. BN43: Shor S 2E **25**
Arundel Ct. BN1: Brig 3A **12**
(off Mill Ri.)
Arundel Ct. BN11: Worth 2H **33**
Arundel Ct. BN12: Fer 4B **32**
Arundel Ct. BN2: Brig 4A **36**
Arundel Ct. BN43: Shor S 2E **25**
Arundel Dr. E. BN2: Salt 3A **38**
Arundel Dr. W. BN2: Salt 3H **37**
Arundel Grn. BN7: Lewes 3D **16**
Arundel M. BN2: Brig 4A **36**
(off Arundel Pl.)
Arundel Pl. BN2: Brig 4A **36**
Arundel Rd. BN10: Peace 5G **39**
Arundel Rd. BN2: Brig 5A **36**
Arundel Rd. BN25: Sea 4F **43**
Arundel Rd. BN9: Newh 2G **41**
Arundel Rd. Central BN10: Peace 5F **39**
Arundel Rd. W. BN10: Peace 4E **39**
Arundel St. BN2: Brig 5A **36**
Arundel Ter. BN2: Brig 5A **36**
Ashacre La. BN13: Salv 3H **19**
Ashacre M. BN13: Salv 3H **19**
Ashacre Way BN13: Salv 3H **19**
Ashburnham Cl. BN1: Brig 3H **13**
Ashburnham Cl. BN13: Durr 4D **18**
Ashburnham Dr. BN1: Brig 2H **13**
Ash Cl. BN14: Fin 2C **6**
Ash Cl. BN3: Hove 5A **12**
Ashcombe Hollow BN7: King L 6A **16**
Ashcombe Hollow BN7: Lewes 6A **16**
Ash Ct. BN42: S'wick 1H **25**
Ashcroft BN43: Shor S 3F **25**
Ashcroft Cl. BN43: Shor S 3F **25**
Ashdown BN3: Hove 4A **28**
Ashdown Av. BN2: Salt 3H **37**
Ashdown Rd. BN11: Worth 1D **34**
Ashdown Rd. BN2: Brig 2F **29**
Ash Dr. BN25: Sea 4H **43**
Ashfold Av. BN14: Fin V 1A **20**
Ashford Rd. BN1: Brig 6E **13**
Ash Gro. BN11: Worth 2E **35**
Ashington Ct. BN14: Broadw 5D **20**
(off Broadway St. E.)
Ashington Ct. BN2: Brig 4B **30**
(off Whitehawk Way)
Ashington Gdns. BN10: Peace 5A **40**
Ashleigh Glegg Ho. BN25: Sea 3C **42**
(off Grosvenor Rd.)
Ashley Cl. BN1: Brig 1C **12**
Ashley Ho. BN3: Hove 5H **27**
Ashlings Way BN3: Hove 6E **11**
Ashlings Way BN43: Shor S 1D **24**
Ashmore Cl. BN10: Peace 2H **39**
Ashton Lodge BN2: Brig 4F **29**
(off Ashton Ri.)
Ashton Ri. BN2: Brig 4F **29**
Ashurst Av. BN2: Salt 4C **38**
Ashurst Cl. BN12: Gor S 3D **32**
Ashurst Dr. BN12: Gor S 3D **32**
Ashurst Rd. BN2: Brig 3B **14**
Ashurst Rd. BN25: Sea 5E **43**
Ash Wlk. BN9: Newh 4D **40**
Ashwood Cl. BN11: Worth 6F **21**
Aspen Ct. BN15: Lan 6A **22**
Assembly Hall Worthing 2D **34**
Aster Ho. BN1: Brig 1D **44** (3E **29**)
(off Ditchling Rd.)
Aston Ho. BN43: Shor S 2A **24**
Astra Ho. BN1: Brig 5C **28**
(off Kings Rd.)
Athelstan Rd. BN14: W Tar 6A **20**
Athenaeum, The
BN3: Hove Brighton 4A **28**
Atlantic Ct. BN43: Shor B 4B **24**
Atlantic Hgts. BN2: Salt 3A **38**
(off Suez Way)
Atlingworth Ct. BN2: Brig 6F **29**
(off Atlingworth St.)
Atlingworth St. BN2: Brig 6F **29**
Atrium Ho. BN1: Brig 3C **44** (4E **29**)
(off Regent St.)
Attenborough Cen. for Creative Arts 2D **14**
Attree Ct. BN2: Brig 4G **29**
Attree Dr. BN2: Brig 4G **29**
Auckland Dr. BN2: Brig 1B **30**
Audrey Cl. BN1: Brig 3C **12**
Audrey Cl. BN25: Sea 2C **42**
Augusta Ho. BN11: Worth 3D **34**
Augusta Pl. BN11: Worth 3D **34**
Austen Ga. BN14: Char D 3C **20**
Avalon BN1: Brig 5B **44** (5D **28**)
Avalon Way BN13: Durr 4F **19**
Avenue, The BN12: Gor S 6E **19**
Avenue, The BN2: Brig 6H **13**
Avenue, The BN43: Shor S 1A **24**
Avenue, The BN7: Lewes 4D **16**
Avenue Ct. BN3: Hove 4A **28**
(off Palmeira Av.)
Avery Cl. BN41: Ports 4H **9**
Avila Ho. BN11: Worth 2C **34**
(off Gratwicke Rd.)
Avis Cl. BN9: Newh 2G **41**
Avis Pde. Shops BN9: Newh 2G **41**
(off Avis Rd.)
Avis Rd. BN9: Newh 2F **41**
(not continuous)
Avis Way BN9: Newh 2G **41**
Avis Way Ind. Est. BN9: Newh 2F **41**
Avon Cl. BN15: Somp 4H **21**
Avon Ct. BN15: Somp 4H **21**
Avon Ct. BN2: Brig 5F **29**
(off Mt. Pleasant)
Avondale Cl. BN12: Gor S 1F **33**
Avondale Ct. BN25: Sea 4D **42**
(off Avondale Rd.)
Avondale Rd. BN25: Sea 4D **42**
Avondale Rd. BN3: Hove 3B **28**
Aylesbury BN3: Hove 4C **28**
Aymer Ho. BN3: Hove 4G **27**
Aymer Rd. BN3: Hove 4G **27**
Aynsley Ct. BN3: Hove 2A **28**
Azure BN2: Rott 3G **37**

B

Baden Rd. BN2: Brig 1H **29**
Badger Cl. BN41: Ports 6B **10**
Badgers Cl. BN9: Newh 5E **41**
Badgers Copse BN25: Sea 4H **43**
Badgers Fld. BN10: Peace 3G **39**
Badgers Way BN3: Hove 4C **10**
Badger Way BN1: Brig 2A **14**
Bainbridge Cl. BN25: Sea 4E **43**
Bakers Ct. BN13: Durr 3G **19**
Baker St. BN1: Brig 1D **44** (3E **29**)
Baker St. BN9: Newh 4G **41**
Bakery M. BN2: Brig 1G **29**
Balchin Ct. BN2: Brig 3G **29**
Balcombe Av. BN14: Worth 5C **20**
Balcombe Ct. BN10: Peace 4G **39**
Balcombe Ct. BN11: Worth 3B **34**
Balcombe Rd. BN10: Peace 4F **39**
Balfour Rd. BN1: Brig 6D **12**
Balfour Vs. BN1: Brig 6E **13**
Ballards Mill Cl. BN1: Brig 3C **12**
Ball Tree Cl. BN15: Somp 3A **22**
Ball Tree Cft. BN15: Somp 3A **22**
Balmoral Cl. BN25: Sea 1F **43**
Balmoral Ct. BN11: Worth 2A **34**
Balmoral Ct. BN3: Hove 5G **11**
Balsdean Rd. BN2: W'dean 1F **31**
Baltic Vw. BN2: Salt 3A **38**
(off Suez Way)
Baltimore Ct. BN3: Hove 3A **28**
Bamford Cl. BN2: Brig 6C **14**
Bampfield St. BN41: Ports 2B **26**
Bank Pas. BN11: Worth 2D **34**
(off Liverpool Rd.)
Bank Pas. BN44: Stey 3C **4**
Bankside BN1: Brig 3A **12**
Bankside Ct. BN1: Brig 3A **12**
(off Bankside)
Bannings Va. BN2: Salt 4B **38**
Banstead Cl. BN12: Gor S 4E **33**
Baranscraig Av. BN1: Brig 1E **13**
Barbary La. BN12: Fer 3A **32**
Barber Ct. BN7: Lewes 5D **16**
(off St Pancras Rd.)
Barbican House Mus. 4E **17**
Barclay Ho. BN2: Brig 3F **29**
Barcombe Av. BN25: Sea 4H **43**
Barcombe Cl. BN25: Sea 4H **43**
Barcombe Pl. BN1: Brig 3B **14**
Barcombe Rd. BN1: Brig 4A **14**
Barfield Pk. BN15: Lan 4D **22**
Barley Cl. BN10: Tels C 2F **39**
Barley Grange BN13: Clap 4D **18**
Barn Cl. BN13: Durr 3H **19**
Barn Cl. BN25: Sea 2F **43**
Barn Cotts. BN25: Sea 4F **43**
Barnes Rd. BN41: Ports 2B **26**
Barnett Rd. BN1: Brig 6F **13**
Barnet Way BN13: Durr 5F **19**
Barnet Way BN3: Hove 5E **11**
Barnfield Gdns. BN2: Brig 4G **29**
Barn Hatch Cl. BN7: Lewes 5C **16**
Barn Ho., The BN25: Sea 2D **42**
Barn Ri. BN1: Brig 3B **12**
Barn Ri. BN25: Sea 2F **43**
Barn Rd. BN7: Lewes 2G **17**
Barn Theatre Southwick, The 3G **25**
Barons Cl. BN25: Sea 2B **42**
Barons Ct. BN11: Worth 1C **34**
Barons Down Rd. BN7: Lewes 5C **16**
Barons Wlk. BN7: Lewes 5C **16**
Barrack Yd. BN1: Brig 4D **44** (4E **29**)
(off North Rd.)
Barrhill Av. BN1: Brig 1D **12**
Barrington Cl. BN12: Gor S 2E **33**
Barrington Rd. BN12: Gor S 2E **33**
(not continuous)
Barrow Cl. BN1: Brig 6G **13**
Barrowfield Cl. BN3: Hove 5A **12**
Barrowfield Dr. BN3: Hove 6A **12**
Barrowfield Lodge BN3: Hove 6A **12**
Barrow Hill BN1: Brig 6G **13**
Barry Wlk. BN2: Brig 4G **29**
Bartholomews BN1: Brig 5C **44** (5E **29**)
Bartholomew Sq.
BN1: Brig 6C **44** (5E **29**)
(off Bartholomews)
Bartletts Cotts. BN14: Broadw 5D **20**
(off Broadwater St. E.)
Barton Cl. BN13: W Tar 5A **20**
Basement, The 3C **44** (4E **29**)
(off Robert St.)
Bashfords La. BN14: Broadw 6D **20**
Basin Rd. Nth. BN41: Ports 4C **26**
Basin Rd. Sth. BN41: Ports 4A **26**
Basin Rd. Sth. BN42: Ports 4G **25**
Basin Rd. Sth. BN42: S'wick 4G **25**
Batemans Cl. BN13: Durr 5D **18**
Batemans Rd. BN2: W'dean 3G **31**
Bates Rd. BN1: Brig 6D **12**
Bath Ct. BN3: Hove 5H **27**
(off King's Esplanade)
Bath Pl. BN11: Worth 3D **34**
Bath Rd. BN11: Worth 3A **34**
Bath St. BN1: Brig 1A **44** (3D **28**)
Battle Cl. BN25: Sea 2H **43**
Bavant Rd. BN1: Brig 6C **12**
Baxter Rd. BN7: Lewes 3D **16**
Baxter St. BN2: Brig 3G **29**
Bay Tree Cl. BN43: Shor S 1E **25**
Bayview Rd. BN10: Peace 6A **40**
Bay Vue Rd. BN9: Newh 4E **41**
Baywood Gdns. BN2: W'dean 2E **31**
Bazehill Rd. BN2: Rott 2F **37**
Beach Cl. BN25: Sea 4C **42**
Beach Cl. BN9: Newh 5G **41**
Beach Cotts. BN25: Sea 3B **42**
Beach Ct. BN43: Shor B 4C **24**
Beachcroft Pl. BN15: S Lan 6C **22**
Beach Grn. BN43: Shor B 4H **23**
Beach House Pk. 2E **35**
Beach M. BN9: Newh 4G **41**
Beach Pde. BN11: Worth 3E **35**
Beach Rd. BN43: Shor B 5A **24**
Beach Rd. BN9: Newh 4G **41**
Beach Rd. Ind. Est. BN9: Newh 5G **41**
Beachside Cl. BN12: Gor S 3G **33**
Beacon Cl. BN1: Brig 6E **13**
Beacon Cl. BN2: Rott 1F **37**
Beacon Cl. BN25: Sea 2C **42**
Beacon Ct. BN2: O'dean 6F **31**

46 A-Z Brighton & Worthing

Beacon Dr. – Brighton Cen., The

Beacon Dr. BN25: Sea 2C 42
Beacon Hill BN2: O'dean 1E 37
Beacon Hill 2E 37
Beacon Ho. BN3: Hove 3D 26
(off Erroll Rd.)
Beacon Mill Rottingdean 3F 37
Beacon Rd. BN25: Sea 3C 42
(not continuous)
Beaconsfield Pde. BN1: Brig 2D 28
(off Beaconsfield Rd.)
Beaconsfield Rd. BN1: Brig 2E 29
Beaconsfield Rd. BN41: Ports 2B 26
Beaconsfield Vs. BN1: Brig 6D 12
Beaconsville Ct. BN1: Brig 1D 28
Beal Cres. BN1: Brig 6F 13
Beame Ct. BN25: Sea 4C 42
Bear Rd. BN2: Brig 2G 29
Bear Yd. BN7: Lewes 4F 17
Beatty Av. BN1: Brig 1H 13
Beaufort Ter. BN2: Brig 4G 29
Beau Ho. BN1: Brig 1A 44 (3D 28)
(off Bath St.)
Beaumont Rd. BN14: Broadw 5D 20
Beccles Rd. BN11: Worth 2B 34
Becket Rd. BN14: Worth 1A 34
Beckett Way BN7: Lewes 2E 17
Beckley Cl. BN2: Brig 5A 30
Beckworth Cl. BN13: Durr 5D 18
Bedford Ct. BN1: Brig 5C 28
(off Bedford Pl.)
Bedford Pl. BN1: Brig 5C 28
Bedford Row BN11: Worth 2E 35
Bedford Sq. BN1: Brig 5C 28
Bedford St. BN2: Brig 6G 29
Bedford Towers BN1: Brig 5C 28
(off Kings Rd.)
Beech Cl. BN14: Fin 1C 6
Beech Cl. BN41: Ports 5H 9
Beechers Rd. BN41: Ports 5H 9
Beeches, The BN1: Brig 5B 12
Beeches Av. BN14: Char D 3D 20
Beech Gdns. BN14: Worth 6C 20
Beech Gro. BN15: S Lan 5E 23
Beech Gro. BN2: Brig 5A 14
Beech Rd. BN14: Fin 1C 6
Beechwood BN1: Brig 5C 12
Beechwood Av. BN1: Brig 4D 12
Beechwood Av. BN13: Durr 3H 19
Beechwood Cl. BN1: Brig 4D 12
Beeding Av. BN3: Hove 5F 11
Beeding Cl. BN15: Somp 2B 22
Beeding Ct. BN1: Brig 3A 12
(off Mill Ri.)
Beeding Ct. BN43: Shor S 2D 24
Beehive Cl. BN12: Fer 3B 32
Beehive La. BN12: Fer 3A 32
Bee Rd. BN10: Peace 4G 39
Belbourne Ct. BN1: Brig 3C 44 (4E 29)
(off Tichbourne St.)
Belfast St. BN3: Hove 3H 27
Belgrave Cres. BN25: Sea 2E 43
Belgrave Pl. BN2: Brig 6H 29
Belgrave Rd. BN25: Sea 3C 42
Belgrave St. BN2: Brig 4F 29
Belle Vue Cotts. BN2: Brig 2B 30
Belle Vue Ct. BN2: Brig 5H 29
Bellevue Ct. BN1: Brig 1D 28
Belle Vue Gdns. BN2: Brig 5G 29
Bellingham Cres. BN3: Hove 2D 26
Bell La. BN7: Lewes 5D 16
Bell Mead BN3: Hove 3B 28
Bell Twr. Ind. Est. BN2: Brig 4B 36
Bellview Ct. BN13: W Tar 5A 20
Bellview Rd. BN13: W Tar 5A 20
Belmaine Ct. BN11: Worth 3C 34
Belmer Ct. BN11: Worth 3A 34
Belmont BN1: Brig 1A 44 (3C 28)
Belmont Ct. BN1: Brig 1A 44 (3D 28)
(off Belmont)
Belmont St. BN1: Brig 1D 44 (3E 29)
Belmont Wlk. BN13: Durr 5F 19
Belsize Cl. BN11: Worth 1A 34
Belsize Rd. BN11: Worth 1B 34
Belton Cl. BN2: Brig 2F 29
(off Belton Rd.)
Belton Rd. BN2: Brig 2F 29
Belvedere BN1: Brig 2C 28
Belvedere Av. BN15: Lan 4B 22
Belvedere Gdns. BN25: Sea 2F 43
Belvedere Ter. BN1: Brig 4C 28
(off Norfolk Ter.)
Bembridge St. BN2: Brig 2G 29
Benbow Cl. BN43: Shor B 4B 24
Benedict Cl. BN11: Worth 1H 35
Benedict Dr. BN11: Worth 1G 35
Benenden Cl. BN25: Sea 3F 43
Benett Av. BN3: Hove 6H 11
Benett Dr. BN3: Hove 6H 11
Benfield Cl. BN41: Ports 1C 26
Benfield Ct. BN41: Ports 2C 26
Benfield Cres. BN41: Ports 1C 26
Benfield Hill Local
Nature Reserve 4C 10
Benfield Valley Golf Course 5C 10
Benfield Valley
Recreation Ground 2C 26
Benfield Way BN41: Ports 2C 26
Bengairn Av. BN1: Brig 1E 13
Benham Ct. BN3: Hove 5H 27
(off King's Esplanade)
Bennett Gdns. BN12: Fer 1A 32
Bennett Rd. BN2: Brig 4A 36
Benson Ct. BN3: Hove 3E 27
Bentham Rd. BN2: Brig 3G 29
Berberis Ct. BN43: Shor S 1D 24
Beresford Ct. BN3: Hove 3B 28
Beresford Ho. BN10: Peace 3G 39
Beresford Rd. BN2: Brig 5H 29
Beresford Rd. BN9: Newh 2G 41
Bergamot Cres. BN43: Shor S 1E 25
Berkeley, The BN3: Hove 2D 26
Berkeley Ct. BN12: Fer 2A 32
(off Ferringham La.)
Berkeley Ct. BN3: Hove 3C 28
(off Davigdor Rd.)
Berkeley Row BN7: Lewes 5C 16
Berkeley Sq. BN11: Worth 2A 34
Berkshire Ct. BN12: Gor S 1D 32
Bernard Pl. BN2: Brig 3G 29
Bernard Rd. BN11: Worth 3H 33
Bernard Rd. BN2: Brig 3G 29
Berriedale Av. BN3: Hove 4E 27
Berriedale Cl. BN15: Somp 3A 22
Berriedale Dr. BN15: Somp 3A 22
Berriedale Ho. BN3: Hove 4E 27
Berry Cl. BN10: Tels C 3E 39
Berwick Cl. BN25: Sea 3C 42
Berwick Rd. BN2: Salt 1B 38
Bessborough Ter. BN15: Lan 6B 22
Besson Ho. BN41: Ports 3C 26
(off Gordon Cl.)
BEVENDEAN 1C 30
Bevendean Av. BN2: Salt 3B 38
Bevendean Cres. BN2: Brig 6A 14
Bevendean Down Local
Nature Reserve 6A 14
Bevendean Rd. BN2: Brig 2H 29
Beverley Ct. BN11: Worth 3B 34
Beverley Ct. BN3: Hove 3D 26
Beverley Ho. BN15: S Lan 6C 22
Beves Ho. BN1: Brig 2A 44 (4D 28)
Bexhill Rd. BN2: W'dean 1F 31
Bigwood Av. BN3: Hove 2B 28
Billam Ho. BN2: Brig 4F 29
(off Belgrave St.)
Billam Ter. BN2: Brig 4F 29
(off Belgrave St.)
Billinton Way BN1: Brig 1C 44 (3E 29)
Biology Rd. BN1: Falm 2D 14
Birch Cl. BN15: Lan 6B 22
Birch Ct. BN42: S'wick 1A 26
Birches Cl. BN13: Durr 5E 19
Birch Gro. Cres. BN1: Brig 3E 13
Birch Lodge BN2: Brig 2F 29
(off Bromley Rd.)
Birch Pl. BN12: Fer 1B 32
Birch Tree Ct. BN11: Worth 1E 35
Birch Villa BN1: Brig 6C 12
(off Preston Rd.)
Birdham Pl. BN2: Brig 5A 14
Birdham Rd. BN2: Brig 5A 14
Birkdale Cl. BN13: Durr 4F 19
Birkdale Rd. BN13: Durr 4F 19
Birling Cl. BN2: Brig 1H 29
Birling Cl. BN25: Sea 3C 42
Bishops Cl. BN14: W Tar 6A 20
Bishops Cl. BN15: Lan 4D 22
Bishops Cl. BN25: Sea 3B 42
Bishops Dr. BN7: Lewes 5C 16
Bishops Rd. BN3: Hove 1A 28
BISHOPSTONE 1B 42
Bishopstone Dr. BN2: Salt 2H 37
Bishopstone Station (Rail) 3A 42
Bishops Wlk. BN1: Brig 4A 44 (5D 28)
Blackbird La. BN12: Gor S 5D 18
Blackdown BN2: Brig 3B 30
Blackdown Rd. BN13: Durr 3H 19
Black Lion La. BN1: Brig 5B 44 (5D 28)
Black Lion St. BN1: Brig 6C 44 (6E 29)
Blackman St. BN1: Brig 2C 44 (4E 29)
Blackmore Ct. BN1: Brig 1C 44 (3E 29)
(off New England St.)
Blackpatch Gro. BN43: Shor S 1B 24
BLACK ROCK 5B 36
Black Rock Station Volk's Electric
Railway 5A 36
Blacksmiths Cres. BN15: Somp 4H 21
Blacksmiths M. BN11: Worth 3C 34
(off Montague St.)
Blackthorn Cl. BN1: Brig 5B 12
Blackthorn Cl. BN41: Ports 6B 10
Blake Ct. BN2: Brig 4F 29
(off Richmond Pl.)
Blakeney Av. BN10: Peace 5C 40
Blaker St. BN2: Brig 5F 29
Blanche Ho. BN1: Brig 2A 44 (4D 28)
Blatchington Cl. BN25: Sea 3E 43
Blatchington Hill BN25: Sea 3D 42
Blatchington Hill Flats
BN25: Sea 2E 43
(off Up. Belgrave Rd.)
Blatchington Rd. BN25: Sea 4D 42
Blatchington Rd. BN3: Hove 3G 27
Blatchington Rd. Ind. Est.
BN25: Sea 4D 42
Blenheim Av. BN13: Durr 4G 19
Blenheim Ct. BN13: High S 2F 19
Blenheim Ct. BN3: Hove 4G 27
(off New Church Rd.)
Blenheim Pl. BN1: Brig 3D 44 (4E 29)
Blenheim Rd. BN15: Lan 6B 22
Blessing Lodge BN43: Shor B 4D 24
(off Britannia Av.)
Bletchley Ct. BN1: Brig 2E 29
Blois Rd. BN7: Lewes 2C 16
Bloomsbury Pl. BN2: Brig 6G 29
Bloomsbury St. BN2: Brig 6G 29
Bluebell Way BN12: Gor S 1C 32
Bluebird Cl. BN43: Shor B 4D 24
Bluebird Ct. BN3: Hove 4G 27
Blue Haze Av. BN25: Sea 3G 43
Blunden's Ride BN13: Clap 6A 6
Boardwalk, The BN2: Brig 5B 36
Boatyard, The BN2: Brig 5C 36
Bodiam Av. BN12: Gor S
Amberley Dr. 4D 32
Bodiam Av. BN12: Gor S
Fernhurst Dr. 2D 32
Bodiam Av. BN2: Brig 1D 30
Bodiam Cl. BN2: Brig 6D 14
Bodiam Cl. BN25: Sea 3H 43
Bodiham Ho. BN3: Hove 3B 28
(off Davigdor Rd.)
Bodmin Cl. BN13: Durr 2F 19
Bodmin Rd. BN13: Durr 2F 19
Boiler Ho. Hill BN1: Falm 1D 14
Bolney Av. BN10: Peace 6G 39
(not continuous)
Bolney Rd. BN2: Brig 4B 14
Bolsover Rd. BN13: Worth 1G 33
Bolsover Rd. BN3: Hove 3E 27
Bonaventure BN43: Shor B 4D 24
(off Britannia Av.)
Bonchurch Rd. BN2: Brig 2G 29
Bond St. BN1: Brig 4C 44 (5E 29)
Bond St. Cotts. BN1: Brig 4C 44 (5E 29)
(off Bond St.)
Bond St. Laine BN1: Brig 4C 44 (5E 29)
(off Bond St.)
Bond St. Row BN1: Brig 4C 44 (5E 29)
(off Bond St.)
Booth Mus. of Natural History 2C 28
Borough Ga. BN44: Stey 3C 4
Borough St. BN1: Brig 4C 28
Borrow King Cl. BN2: Brig 1H 29
Bostal, The BN44: Up B 5H 5
Bost Hill BN13: Fin V 6C 6
Bost Hill BN13: High S 6C 6
Boston St. BN1: Brig 1C 44 (3E 29)
BOTOLPHS 6F 5
Botolphs Rd. BN44: Bramb 6E 5
Boughey Pl. BN7: Lewes 2E 17
Boulevard, The BN12: Worth 6G 19
Boulevard, The BN13: Worth 5F 19
Boulevard Ho. BN1: Brig 4C 44 (5E 29)
(off Regent St.)
Boundary, The BN25: Sea 5D 42
Boundary Cl. BN11: Worth 3B 34
Boundary Pas. BN1: Brig 4C 28
(off York Rd.)
Boundary Rd. BN11: Worth 3A 34
Boundary Rd. BN15: S Lan 5F 23
Boundary Rd. BN2: Brig 5A 36
Boundary Rd. BN3: Hove 4C 26
Boundstone Cl. BN15: Lan 3B 22
Boundstone La. BN15: Lan 4A 22
Boundstone La. BN15: Somp 4A 22
Bourne Cl. BN13: Durr 4D 18
Bourne Ct. BN1: Brig 4B 12
Bowden Ri. BN25: Sea 1D 42
Bowen Ct. BN3: Hove 4A 28
Bowline Point BN43: Shor S 3A 24
Bowmans Cl. BN44: Stey 2C 4
Bowness Av. BN15: Somp 5A 22
Bowring Way BN2: Brig 6H 29
Bowser Ct. BN11: Worth 3B 34
Boxgrove BN12: Gor S 6D 18
Boxgrove Cl. BN15: N Lan 2D 22
Boxgrove Pde. BN12: Gor S 6D 18
Boyce's St. BN1: Brig 5B 44 (5D 28)
Boyles La. BN2: Brig 4A 36
Brackenbury Cl. BN41: Ports 6B 10
Bracken Rd. BN25: Sea 5F 43
(not continuous)
Bradfield Wlk. BN11: Worth 1A 34
Bradford Rd. BN7: Lewes 4D 16
Brading Rd. BN2: Brig 3G 29
Bradley Ho. BN11: Worth 2B 34
Braemar Ho. BN1: Brig 4C 28
(off Norfolk Rd.)
Braemore Ct. BN3: Hove 4F 27
Braemore Rd. BN3: Hove 4E 27
Braeside Av. BN1: Brig 1D 12
Braeside Cl. BN14: Fin 2C 6
BRAMBER 4E 5
Bramber Av. BN10: Peace 6G 39
(not continuous)
Bramber Av. BN3: Hove 5F 11
Bramber Av. Nth. BN10: Peace 4G 39
Bramber Castle 4D 4
Bramber Cl. BN10: Peace 4G 39
Bramber Cl. BN15: Somp 2B 22
Bramber Cl. BN25: Sea 5E 43
Bramber Ct. BN3: Hove 3H 27
Bramber Ct. BN43: Shor S 2D 24
Bramber La. BN25: Sea 5E 43
Bramber Rd. BN14: Broadw 3E 21
Bramber Rd. BN25: Sea 5E 43
Bramber Rd. BN44: Stey 4C 4
Bramble Cl. BN13: Durr 3F 19
Bramble Cres. BN13: Durr 2F 19
Brambledean Rd. BN41: Ports 3B 26
Bramble La. BN13: Durr 3F 19
Bramble Ri. BN1: Brig 3A 12
Brambletyne Av. BN2: Salt 3B 38
Bramble Way BN1: Brig 2G 13
Bramley Cl. BN14: Broadw 4D 20
Bramley Rd. BN14: Broadw 4D 20
Brands Cl. BN9: S Heig 1F 41
Brangwyn Av. BN1: Brig 2C 12
Brangwyn Ct. BN1: Brig 3B 12
Brangwyn Cres. BN1: Brig 2B 12
Brangwyn Dr. BN1: Brig 2B 12
Brangwyn Way BN1: Brig 3C 12
Brasslands Dr. BN41: Ports 6H 9
Braybon Av. BN1: Brig 4D 12
Brazen Cl. BN9: Newh 4C 40
Breach Cl. BN44: Stey 2C 4
Bread St. BN1: Brig 3C 44 (4E 29)
Brecon Cl. BN13: Durr 3H 19
Brecon Ct. BN3: Hove 3A 28
Brede Cl. BN2: Brig 5A 30
Brendon Rd. BN13: Durr 2G 19
Brentwood Cl. BN1: Brig 5F 13
Brentwood Cres. BN1: Brig 5F 13
Brentwood Rd. BN1: Brig 5F 13
Bretts Fld. BN10: Peace 2G 39
Brewer St. BN2: Brig 3F 29
Briar Cl. BN2: W'dean 2F 31
Briarcroft Rd. BN2: W'dean 3F 31
Bricky, The BN10: Peace 4G 39
Bridge Cl. BN12: Gor S 6E 19
Bridge Cl. BN15: S Lan 5C 22
Bridge Ct. BN9: Newh 4F 41
(off Bridge St.)
Bridge Rd. BN14: Broadw 1D 34
Bridge St. BN9: Newh 4F 41
Bri. Way BN43: Shor B 4B 24
Bridgewick Cl. BN7: Lewes 2F 17
Bridgnorth Cl. BN13: Durr 5D 18
Bridle Cl. BN44: Up B 4G 5
Bridle Way BN10: Tels C 3E 39
Brierley Gdns. BN15: Lan 4D 22
Brigden St. BN1: Brig 3D 28
Brighthelm BN1: Falm 1D 14
BRIGHTON 5C 44 (5E 29)
Brighton & Hove Albion FC 2D 14
Brighton & Hove Golf Course 1D 10
Brighton & Hove Greyhound
Stadium 1G 27
Brighton & Hove PRU 3A 44 (4D 28)
(off Dyke Rd.)
Brighton & Hove School Sports
Hall & Fitness Suite 4C 28
Brighton Belle BN1: Brig 1C 44 (3E 29)
(off Stroudley Rd.)
Brighton By-Pass BN43: Shor S 6E 9
Brighton Cen., The 5A 44 (5D 28)

A-Z Brighton & Worthing 47

Castle Ter. – CLIFFE

Castle Ter. BN7: Lewes 4E 17 (off New Rd.)
CASTLE TOWN 5H 5
Castle Way BN13: Worth 6H 19
Castle Way BN44: Stey 3D 4
Catherine Va. BN2: W'dean 2G 31
Causeway, The BN12: Gor S 1F 33
Causeway, The BN2: Brig 4H 29
Causeway, The BN25: Sea 5D 42
Cavell Av. BN10: Peace Homecoast Ho. 5F 39
Cavell Av. BN10: Peace Southview Rd. 6F 39
Cavell Av. Nth. BN10: Peace 4G 39
Cavell Ct. BN10: Peace 5F 39 (off Cavell Av.)
Cavell Ho. BN43: Shor S 2D 24
Cavendish Cl. BN10: Tels C 3F 39
Cavendish Cl. BN12: Gor S 1F 33
Cavendish Ho. BN1: Brig 5C 28 (off Kings Rd.)
Cavendish Ho. BN10: Peace 3G 39
Cavendish M. BN11: Worth 3C 34 (off Heene Pl.)
Cavendish M. BN3: Hove 5B 28 (off Ivy Pl.)
Cavendish Pl. BN1: Brig 5C 28
Cavendish St. BN2: Brig 5F 29
Caversham Ct. BN11: Worth 3B 34 (off West Pde.)
Cawthorne Ho. BN1: Brig 2A 44 (4D 28) (off Dyke Rd.)
Caxton Ct. BN14: Broadw 6D 20
Cecil Ct. BN15: S Lan 6C 22
Cecilian Av. BN14: Broadw 6D 20
Cecilian Ct. BN14: Broadw 6D 20
Cecil Norris Ho. BN43: Shor S 3B 24
Cecil Pashley Way BN43: Shor S 2G 23
Cecil Rd. BN15: S Lan 6C 22
Cedar Av. BN13: Durr 4H 19
Cedar Chase BN14: Fin 3C 6
Cedar Cl. BN12: Fer 3A 32
Cedar Cl. BN13: Durr 4H 19
Cedar Cl. BN15: Lan 6B 22
Cedar Ct. BN11: Worth 1A 34
Cedar Ho. BN1: Brig 6C 12
Cedar Ho. BN14: Fin V 6D 6
Cedar Ho. BN43: Shor S 1D 24
Cedars, The BN1: Brig 5B 12
Cedars, The BN10: Peace 3G 39
Cedars, The BN2: Brig 2F 29 (off Bromley Rd.)
Cedars Gdns. BN1: Brig 5B 12
Cedarwell Cl. BN9: Pidd 1D 40
Cedarwood BN1: Brig 5C 12 (off Curwen Pl.)
Cello Ct. BN2: Brig 5G 29 (off Somerset St.)
Centenary Ho. BN1: Brig 6C 12 (off Cumberland Rd.)
Centenary Ho. BN13: Durr 5F 19
Centenary Ind. Est. BN2: Brig 2F 29
Central Av. BN10: Tels C 5E 39
Central Av. BN14: Fin V 5D 6
Central Ct. BN10: Tels C 5E 39
Centrecourt Cl. BN14: Broadw 6C 20
Centrecourt Rd. BN14: Broadw 6C 20
Centurion Rd. BN1: Brig 3B 44 (4D 28) (not continuous)
Chadborn Cl. BN2: Brig 6H 29
Chaffinch Cl. BN13: Durr 5E 19
Chailey Av. BN2: Rott 2G 37
Chailey Ct. BN1: Brig 3A 12 (off Mill Ri.)
Chailey Cres. BN2: Salt 3C 38
Chailey Rd. BN1: Brig 4A 14
Chain Pier Ho. BN2: Brig 6F 29 (off Marine Pde.)
Chalet Cl. BN12: Fer 4A 32
Chalet Gdns. BN12: Fer 4B 32
Chalet Rd. BN12: Fer 4A 32
Chalfont Ct. BN11: Worth 2B 34
Chalfont Dr. BN3: Hove 5A 12
Chalfont Way BN13: Durr 4F 19
Chalkland Ri. BN2: W'dean 2G 31
Chalky Rd. BN41: Ports 5H 9
Challoners Cl. BN2: Rott 2F 37
Challoners M. BN2: Rott 2F 37
Chalvington Cl. BN1: Brig 2A 14
Chalvington Cl. BN25: Sea 1E 43
Champions Row BN3: Hove 2A 28
Chanctonbury Dr. BN43: Shor S 1A 24
Chanctonbury Rd. BN3: Hove 3C 28
Chancton Cl. BN11: Worth 1H 33
Chancton Vw. Rd. BN11: Worth 1H 33
Chandlers Way BN44: Stey 4B 4
Chandos Rd. BN11: Worth 2D 34
Channel Ct. BN15: S Lan 6C 22
Channel Grange BN10: Tels C 5E 39
Channel Vw. BN42: S'wick 3G 25 (off Whiterock Pl.)
Channel Vw. Rd. BN2: W'dean 2D 30
Channings BN3: Hove 4F 27
Chantry Orchard BN44: Stey 3C 4 (off Tanyard La.)
Chantry Rd. BN13: W Tar 4A 20
Chapel Cl. BN25: Sea 3D 42
Chapel Hill BN7: Lewes 4G 17
Chapel Ho. BN2: Brig 5F 29 (off Chapel St.)
Chapel M. BN3: Hove 5B 28
Chapel Pl. BN41: Ports 3B 26
Chapel Rd. BN11: Worth 1D 34
Chapel Rd. BN41: Ports 3A 26
Chapel St. BN2: Brig 5F 29
Chapel St. BN9: Newh 4F 41 (not continuous)
Chapel Ter. BN2: Brig 6H 29
Chapel Ter. M. BN2: Brig 6H 29
Chapman Ct. BN13: W Tar 4A 20
Chappell Cft. BN11: Worth 2B 34
Charis Ct. BN3: Hove 3A 28 (off Eaton Rd.)
Charlecote Rd. BN11: Worth 2E 35
Charles Busby Ho. BN1: Brig 3D 44 (4E 29) (off Marlborough Pl.)
Charles Cl. BN25: Sea 2C 42
Charles Cl. BN3: Hove 5G 11
Charles Ct. BN11: Worth 1C 34
Charles Ho. BN12: Gor S 2F 33
Charles Kingston Gdns. BN1: Brig 3C 12
Charles St. BN2: Brig 6D 44 (6E 29)
Charlotte St. BN2: Brig 6F 29
Charlston Av. BN9: Newh 6C 40
Charltons, The BN1: Brig 2H 13
Charlton St. BN44: Stey 3B 4
CHARMANDEAN 2D 20
Charmandean La. BN14: Char D 3D 20
Charmandean Rd. BN14: Broadw 4C 20
Chartfield BN3: Hove 6G 11
Chartfield Way BN3: Hove 6G 11 (off Woodland Dr.)
Chartness BN1: Brig 2D 12 (off Warmdene Rd.)
Chartwell Cl. BN25: Sea 1D 42
Chartwell Ct. BN1: Brig 5A 44 (5D 28) (off Russell Sq.)
Chartwell Rd. BN15: Lan 6A 22
Chase, The BN14: Fin 3C 6
Chates Farm Ct. BN2: Brig 4F 29
Chatham Pl. BN1: Brig 1A 44 (3D 28)
Chatham Pl. BN25: Sea 5D 42
Chatham Rd. BN11: Worth 1G 35
Chatsmore Cres. BN12: Gor S 1C 32
Chatsmore Ho. BN12: Gor S 2C 32
Chatsworth Av. BN10: Tels C 3E 39
Chatsworth Cl. BN10: Tels C 4E 39
Chatsworth Cl. BN13: High S 2H 19
Chatsworth Ct. BN1: Brig 2C 28 (off Chatsworth Rd.)
Chatsworth Ct. BN43: Shor B 4B 24
Chatsworth Lodge BN11: Worth 1B 34 (off St Botolph's Rd.)
Chatsworth Pk. BN10: Tels C 3F 39
Chatsworth Rd. BN1: Brig 2C 28
Chatsworth Rd. BN11: Worth 2D 34
Chatsworth Sq. BN3: Hove 3B 28
Chaucer Rd. BN11: Worth 1B 34
Chawton Ga. BN14: Char D 3C 20
Cheal Cl. BN43: Shor B 4B 24
Cheapside BN1: Brig 2C 44 (4E 29)
Cheetahs Gym 5G 27
Chelston Av. BN3: Hove 3D 26
Cheltenham Pl. BN1: Brig 3D 44 (4E 29)
Chelwood Av. BN12: Gor S 3E 33
Chelwood Cl. BN1: Brig 2G 13
Chene Rd. BN10: Peace 5B 40
Chepstow Ct. BN1: Brig 3A 14
Cherrycroft BN1: Brig 3D 12 (off Warmdene Rd.)
Cherry Gdns. BN13: High S 1G 19
Cherry Tree Cl. BN13: High S 1F 19
Cherry Tree Lodge BN15: Lan 4B 22
Cherry Wlk. BN13: High S 1F 19
Cherrywood BN1: Brig 5C 12 (off Curwen Pl.)
Cherwell Rd. BN13: Durr 2E 19
Chesham Cl. BN12: Gor S 2G 33
Chesham Mans. BN2: Brig 6H 29 (off Eaton Pl.)
Chesham Pl. BN2: Brig 6H 29
Chesham Rd. BN2: Brig 6H 29
Chesham St. BN2: Brig 6H 29
Chesley Cl. BN13: Durr 4E 19
Chesswood Cl. BN11: Worth 6F 21
Chesswood Rd. BN11: Worth 1E 35
Chester Av. BN11: Worth 1G 35
Chester Av. BN15: Lan 6B 22
Chester Bldgs. BN14: Worth 6A 20
Chester Ct. BN11: Worth 2A 34
Chester Ct. BN3: Hove 3C 28 (off Davigdor Rd.)
Chesterfield Ct. BN2: Brig 5F 29 (off Marine Vw.)
Chesterfield Rd. BN12: Gor S 1F 33
Chester Ter. BN1: Brig 6E 13
Chesterton Av. BN25: Sea 4G 43
Chesterton Dr. BN25: Sea 4G 43
Chestnut Ct. BN11: Worth 1C 34 (off Victoria Rd.)
Chestnuts, The BN2: Brig 2F 29 (off Prince's Cres.)
Chestnut Wlk. BN13: Durr 5E 19
Chestnut Way BN9: Newh 4D 40
Cheviot Cl. BN13: Durr 2G 19
Cheviot Rd. BN13: Durr 2G 19
Cheyne Ct. BN43: Shor S 3E 25
Chichester Cl. BN10: Peace 4B 40
Chichester Cl. BN2: Brig 6H 29 (off Chichester Pl.)
Chichester Cl. BN2: Salt 3A 38
Chichester Cl. BN25: Sea 3D 42
Chichester Cl. BN3: Hove 4E 11
Chichester Ct. BN11: Worth 3A 34 (off Pevensey Gdn.)
Chichester Ct. BN14: Fin V 5D 6
Chichester Ct. BN25: Sea 4D 42 (off Pelham Rd.)
Chichester Dr. E. BN2: Salt 3A 38
Chichester Dr. W. BN2: Salt 3H 37
Chichester Ho. BN12: Gor S 4G 33
Chichester Lodge BN25: Sea 4D 42
Chichester Pl. BN2: Brig 6H 29
Chichester Rd. BN25: Sea 4D 42
Chichester Ter. BN2: Brig 6H 29
Chiddingly Cl. BN2: Brig 5B 30
Chiddingly Ho. BN3: Hove 3B 28 (off Chatsworth Sq.)
Chilgrove BN1: Brig 2D 12 (off Warmdene Rd.)
Chilgrove Cl. BN12: Gor S 1D 32
Chiltern Cl. BN43: Shor S 2E 25
Chiltern Cres. BN13: Durr 2G 19
Chiltington Cl. BN2: Salt 2A 38
Chiltington Way BN2: Salt 2A 38
Chippers Cl. BN13: Worth 6H 19
Chippers Rd. BN13: Worth 6H 19
Chippers Wlk. BN13: Worth 6H 19
Chorley Av. BN2: Salt 2H 37
Chrisdory Rd. BN41: Ports 5H 9
Christchurch Ct. BN9: Newh 4F 41
Christchurch Ho. BN1: Brig 5C 28 (off Montpelier Rd.)
Christchurch Rd. BN11: Worth 1D 34
Christie Rd. BN7: Lewes 4C 16
Chrome Works, The BN3: Hove 2H 27
Church Cl. BN1: Brig 3D 12
Church Cl. BN10: Tels C 5D 38
Church Cl. BN13: Clap 1B 18
Church Cl. BN15: N Lan 2C 22
Church Cl. BN44: Up B 3F 5
Church Ct. BN3: Hove 1F 27
Church Farm Wlk. BN44: Up B 3F 5
Church Grn. BN43: Shor S 3E 25
Church Hill BN1: Brig 2C 12
Church Hill BN9: Newh 5D 40
Church Ho. Cl. BN42: S'wick 1H 25
Church Ho. Gdns. 6A 20
Churchill Ho. BN25: Sea 3H 43
Churchill Ho. BN3: Hove 6D 10
Churchill Ind. Est. BN15: Lan 6B 22
Churchill Rd. BN25: Sea 2C 42
Churchill Rd. BN7: Lewes 2C 16
Churchill Sq. Shop. Cen. 4A 44 (5D 28)
Church La. BN7: Lewes Riverdale 3E 17
Church La. BN7: Lewes Rotten Row 5D 16
Church La. BN12: Fer 2A 32
Church La. BN15: Somp 3G 21
Church La. BN25: Sea 5D 42
Church La. BN42: S'wick 3F 25
Church La. BN44: Stey 3C 4
Church La. BN44: Up B 3F 5
Church Mead BN44: Stey 3C 4
Church Pl. BN2: Brig 4A 36
Church Rd. BN13: W Tar 5A 20
Church Rd. BN3: Hove 4G 27
Church Rd. BN41: Ports 3B 26
Church Row BN7: Lewes 4F 17
Church St. BN1: Brig 3A 44 (4D 28)
Church St. BN25: Sea 4D 42
Church St. BN41: Ports 3B 26
Church St. BN43: Shor S 3B 24
Church St. BN44: Stey 3C 4
Church Twitten BN7: Lewes 4F 17
Church Wlk. BN11: Worth 2F 35
Church Way BN13: W Tar 5A 20
Church Way BN2: Brig 4F 29 (off Albion St.)
Church Way Cl. BN13: W Tar 5A 20
Chute Av. BN13: High S 2G 19
Chute Way BN13: High S 2G 19
Chyngton Av. BN25: Sea 3G 43
Chyngton Gdns. BN25: Sea 3G 43
Chyngton Ho. BN25: Sea 5H 43
Chyngton La. BN25: Sea 4H 43
Chyngton La. Nth. BN25: Sea 3H 43
Chyngton Pl. BN25: Sea 5G 43
Chyngton Rd. BN25: Sea 5F 43
Chyngton Way BN25: Sea 5G 43
Cineworld Cinema Brighton 5B 36
Cinque Foil BN10: Peace 4G 39
Cinque Ports Way BN25: Sea 3H 43
Circus Pde. BN1: Brig 3E 29 (off New England Rd.)
Circus St. BN2: Brig 4D 44 (5E 29)
Cissbury Av. BN10: Peace 5A 40
Cissbury Av. BN14: Fin V 6D 6
Cissbury Cres. BN2: Salt 3C 38
Cissbury Dr. BN14: Fin V 5D 6
Cissbury Gdns. BN14: Fin V 5E 7
Cissbury Ring 3F 7
Cissbury Rd. BN12: Fer 1A 32
Cissbury Rd. BN14: Broadw 4C 20
Cissbury Rd. BN3: Hove 3C 28
Cissbury Way BN43: Shor S 1A 24
City Pk. BN3: Hove 1H 27
CLAPHAM 1A 18
Clapham Cl. BN13: Clap 1B 18
Clapham Comn. BN13: Clap 2A 18
Claremont Ct. BN25: Sea 4C 42 (off Claremont Rd.)
Claremont Quays BN25: Sea 4D 42 (off Claremont Rd.)
Claremont Rd. BN25: Sea 4B 42
Claremont Rd. BN9: Newh 2H 41
Clarence Ct. BN11: Worth 2F 35 (off Brighton Rd.)
Clarence Gdns. BN1: Brig 4A 44 (5D 28) (off Clarence Sq.)
Clarence M. BN25: Sea 4D 42 (off Richmond Rd.)
Clarence Sq. BN1: Brig 4A 44 (5D 28)
Clarence Yd. BN1: Brig 5C 44 (5E 29)
Clarendon Ho. BN3: Hove 3H 27
Clarendon M. BN11: Worth 3C 34
Clarendon Pl. BN2: Brig 6G 29
Clarendon Pl. BN41: Ports 4C 26
Clarendon Rd. BN14: Broadw 4E 21
Clarendon Rd. BN3: Hove 3H 27
Clarendon Rd. BN43: Shor S 2E 25
Clarendon Ter. BN2: Brig 6H 29
Clarendon Vs. BN3: Hove 3H 27
Clare Rd. BN7: Lewes 3C 16
Clare Wlk. BN2: Brig 5H 29
Clarke Av. BN3: Hove 6E 11
Clarke Ct. BN3: Hove 4F 27
Clarks Ind. Est. BN3: Hove 2H 27
Clayfields BN10: Peace 4F 39
Clays Hill BN44: Bramb 4C 4
Clayton Rd. BN2: Brig 3H 29
Clayton Wlk. BN13: Durr 5F 19 (off Chalfont Way)
Clayton Way BN3: Hove 5F 11
Clementine Av. BN25: Sea 2B 42
Clements Ct. BN43: Shor S 3B 24 (off Raven's Rd.)
Clermont Ct. BN1: Brig 6C 12
Clermont Rd. BN1: Brig 6C 12
Clermont Ter. BN1: Brig 6C 12
Clevedown BN7: Lewes 5C 16
Cleveland Cl. BN13: Durr 2H 19
Cleveland Copse BN13: Durr 2H 19 (off Cleveland Cl.)
Cleveland Rd. BN1: Brig 6E 13
Cleveland Rd. BN13: Durr 2H 19
Cleve Ter. BN7: Lewes 5E 17
Cliff, The BN2: Brig 4B 36
Cliff App. BN2: Brig 4B 36
Cliff Av. BN10: Peace 6A 40
Cliff Cl. BN25: Sea 6E 43
Cliff Ct. BN2: Rott 3F 37 (off Park Rd.)
CLIFFE 4G 17

A-Z Brighton & Worthing 49

Cliffe Bus. Cen. – Curlews, The

Cliffe Bus. Cen. BN7: Lewes 4G 17
............(off Cliffe High St.)
Cliffe High St. BN7: Lewes 4F 17
Cliffe Ind. Est. BN8: Lewes 5H 17
Cliffe Leas BN7: Lewes 4G 17
............(off Foundry La.)
Cliff Gdns. BN10: Tels C 4D 38
Cliff Gdns. BN25: Sea 6E 43
Cliff Pk. Cl. BN10: Peace 4B 40
Cliff Rd. BN2: Brig 4B 36
Cliff Rd. BN25: Sea 6E 43
Clifton Ct. BN1: Brig 1B 44 (3D 28)
............(off Clifton St.)
Clifton Ct. BN11: Worth 1C 34
Clifton Gdns. BN11: Worth 1C 34
Clifton Hill BN1: Brig 2A 44 (4C 28)
Clifton M. BN1: Brig 2A 44 (4D 28)
............(off Clifton Rd.)
Clifton Pl. BN1: Brig 3A 44 (4C 28)
Clifton Rd. BN1: Brig 2A 44 (4D 28)
Clifton Rd. BN11: Worth 1C 34
Clifton Rd. BN9: Newh 4F 41
Clifton St. BN1: Brig 2B 44 (4D 28)
Clifton St. Pas.
BN1: Brig 2B 44 (4D 28)
............(off Clifton St.)
Clifton Ter. BN1: Brig 3A 44 (4D 28)
Cliftonville Ct. BN3: Hove 3H 27
Clifton Way BN10: Tels C 4E 39
Clinton La. BN25: Sea 4D 42
Clinton Pl. BN25: Sea 4D 42
Clive Av. BN12: Gor S 2F 33
Clivedale BN44: Stey 3C 4
Clivedale Gdns. BN44: Stey 3D 4
Cliveden Cl. BN1: Brig 5C 12
Cliveden Ct. BN1: Brig 6C 12
Clock Tower Brighton 4B 44 (5D 28)
Cloisters BN9: Newh 4E 41
Cloisters, The BN14: Broadw 5D 20
Close, The BN1: Brig 3B 12
Close, The BN15: S Lan 6D 22
Close, The BN25: Sea 5E 43
Close, The BN43: Shor S 2B 24
Close, The BN9: Newh 1H 41
Clover La. BN12: Fer 3A 32
Clovers End BN1: Brig 1F 13
Clover Way BN41: Ports 6B 10
Cluny St. BN7: Lewes 5E 17
Clyde Cl. BN13: Durr 2E 19
Clyde Rd. BN1: Brig 2E 29
Clyde Rd. BN13: Durr 3E 19
Clyde Ter. BN44: Stey 3D 4
............(off Station Rd.)
Coach Ho. M. BN11: Worth 2C 34
Coach Ho. M. BN41: Ports 1A 26
Coastal Counties Ho. BN2: Brig 4F 29
............(off Sussex St.)
Coastal Pl. BN3: Hove 4F 27
Coates Ct. BN42: S'wick 3G 25
Cobden Rd. BN11: Worth 2C 34
Cobden Rd. BN2: Brig 3G 29
Cobton Dr. BN3: Hove 5G 11
Cockshut Rd. BN7: Lewes 5E 17
Cokeham Ct. BN15: Somp 3H 21
Cokeham Gdns. BN15: Somp 4A 22
Cokeham La. BN15: Somp 4A 22
Cokeham Rd. BN15: Somp 3A 22
Colbourne Av. BN2: Brig 6H 13
Colbourne Rd. BN3: Hove 3C 28
COLDEAN 2H 13
Coldean La. BN1: Brig 1H 13
Coldharbour La. BN13: Pat 1A 18
Coldstream Ho. BN25: Sea 5E 43
............(off Bramber La.)
Colebrook Cl. BN11: Worth 1F 35
Colebrook Ct. BN11: Worth 1F 35
Colebrook Rd. BN1: Brig 4B 12
Colebrook Rd. BN42: S'wick 3H 25
Coleman Av. BN3: Hove 3E 27
Coleman St. BN2: Brig 4F 29
Coleridge Cl. BN12: Gor S 1D 32
Coleridge Cres. BN12: Gor S 1D 32
Coleridge M. BN12: Gor S 1D 32
Coleridge Rd. BN12: Gor S 1D 32
Coleridge St. BN3: Hove 2G 27
Colgate Cl. BN2: Brig 4B 30
Colindale Rd. BN12: Fer 2A 32
Colindale Rd. Nth. BN12: Fer 2A 32
College Cl. BN41: Ports 5H 9
College Ct. BN2: Brig 5G 29
............(off Eastern Rd.)
College Gdns. BN11: Worth 2A 34
College Gdns. BN2: Brig 6G 29
College Hill BN44: Stey 4C 4
College Pl. BN2: Brig 6G 29
College Rd. BN2: Brig 6G 29
College Rd. BN25: Sea 5D 42
College Rd. BN44: Up B 4H 5
College St. BN2: Brig 6G 29
College Ter. BN2: Brig 5G 29
Collington BN1: Brig 2D 12
............(off Warmdene Rd.)
Collingwood Cl. BN10: Peace 3G 39
Collingwood Ct. BN2: Brig 5C 36
Collingwood Ct. BN43: Shor B 4B 24
Collingwood Rd. BN12: Gor S 6E 19
Colne Cl. BN13: Durr 2E 19
Colonnades, The
BN1: Brig 5C 44 (5E 29)
............(off New Rd.)
Columbia Dr. BN13: Durr 4E 19
Columbia Wlk. BN13: Durr 4E 19
............(off Columbia Dr.)
Colvill Av. BN43: Shor S 2H 23
Combined Court Lewes 4E 17
Commerce Way BN15: Lan 5A 22
Commercial Sq. BN7: Lewes 4E 17
............(off Mt. Pleasant)
Compass Ct. BN41: Ports 5G 9
Compton Av. BN1: Brig 2A 44 (4D 28)
Compton Av. BN12: Gor S 2D 32
Compton Rd. BN1: Brig 1B 28
Compts, The BN10: Peace 3F 39
Coney Furlong BN10: Peace 3H 39
Congreve Rd. BN14: Broadw 6D 20
Conifer Dr. BN13: Durr 6D 18
Coniston Cl. BN15: Somp 4A 22
Coniston Ct. BN3: Hove 3B 28
Coniston Ho. BN3: Hove 3B 28
Coniston Rd. BN12: Gor S 6E 19
Connaught Av. BN43: Shor S 2H 23
Connaught Rd. BN25: Sea 4B 42
Connaught Rd. BN3: Hove 4G 27
Connaught Ter. BN3: Hove 3H 27
Connaught Theatre 2D 34
Connected Hub, The 1F 29
Connell Dr. BN2: W'dean 3G 31
Convent Gdns. BN14: Fin 2C 6
Conway Ct. BN3: Hove 3H 27
............(off Clarendon Rd.)
Conway Pl. BN3: Hove 2H 27
Conway St. BN3: Hove 2H 27
Conwy Ct. BN2: Rott 3F 37
Cooksbridge Rd. BN2: Brig 4A 30
Coolham Dr. BN2: Brig 4A 30
Coolwater Pk. BN1: Brig 4B 12
Coombe Drove BN44: Bramb 4C 4
Coombe Lea BN3: Hove 4A 28
Coombe Lodge BN25: Sea 4B 42
Coombe Mdw. BN2: Salt 1C 38
Coombe Ri. BN14: Fin V 6E 7
Coombe Ri. BN2: Salt 1B 38
Coombe Rd. BN2: Brig 1G 29
Coombe Rd. BN44: Stey 4B 4
Coombe Rd. BN7: Lewes 3F 17
Coombe Ter. BN2: Brig 1G 29
Coombe Va. BN2: Salt 1B 38
Copenhagen Ct. BN2: Brig 6C 36
Copper Beeches BN1: Brig 1C 28
Copse Dr. BN12: Gor S 5D 18
Copse Hill BN1: Brig 3B 12
Copse La. BN12: Gor S 5D 18
Copthorne Cl. BN13: Salv 2A 20
Copthorne Ct. BN3: Hove 4A 28
Copthorne Hill BN13: Salv 3H 19
Coral Cl. BN43: Shor S 2D 24
Coral Health & Fitness Club 1G 27
............(within Brighton & Hove Stadium)
Corbyn Cres. BN43: Shor S 3C 24
Corfe Cl. BN13: Durr 5D 18
Cornelius Av. BN9: Newh 6C 40
Corner Gth. BN12: Fer 3B 32
Cornfield Cl. BN25: Sea 4E 43
Cornfield Rd. BN25: Sea 4E 43
Cornford Cl. BN41: Ports 6B 10
Cornwall Av. BN10: Peace 6A 40
............(not continuous)
Cornwall Ct. BN3: Hove 3A 28
Cornwall Gdns. BN1: Brig 5C 12
Cornwall Ho. BN1: Brig 6D 12
Coronation Bldgs. BN11: Worth 1G 35
............(off Brougham Rd.)
Coronation Homelets
BN11: Worth 1H 35
Coronation St. BN2: Brig 3G 29
Corsica Cl. BN25: Sea 6E 43
Corsica Rd. BN25: Sea 6E 43
Cortis Av. BN14: Broadw 5C 20
Corvill Ct. BN11: Worth 3B 34
COTE 2E 19
Cote St. BN13: High S 2E 19
Cotswold Cl. BN13: Durr 2G 19
Cotswold Pl. BN2: Brig 5B 30
............(off Findon Rd.)
Cotswold Rd. BN13: Durr 2G 19
Cotswolds, The BN42: S'wick 3G 25
Cottage Cl. BN9: Newh 2F 41
Cottenham Rd. BN11: Worth 1F 35
Countryside Farm Pk. Homes
BN44: Up B 3F 5
County Court
Brighton 4D 44 (5E 29)
County Court Worthing 2D 34
County Oak Av. BN1: Brig 2F 13
Courcels BN2: Brig 5A 36
............(off Arundel St.)
Course, The BN7: Lewes 5E 17
Court Cl. BN1: Brig 1C 12
Courtenay Ga. BN3: Hove 5H 27
Courtenay Ter. BN3: Hove 5H 27
Court Farm Cl. BN9: Pidd 1C 40
Court Farm Rd. BN2: Rott 1E 37
Court Farm Rd. BN3: Hove 6F 11
Court Farm Rd. BN9: Newh 6E 41
Courtfields BN15: Lan 5B 22
Court Flats, The BN11: Worth 1H 35
Courtlands BN2: Brig 4F 29
............(off Ashton Ri.)
Courtlands BN9: Newh 4E 41
Courtlands Cl. BN12: Gor S 3G 33
Courtlands Way BN11: Worth 3H 33
Courtlands Way BN12: Gor S 3G 33
Court Leet BN25: Sea 5D 42
............(off Steyne Rd.)
Courtney King Ho. BN2: Brig 6H 29
Court Ord Cotts. BN2: Rott 1F 37
Court Ord Rd. BN2: Rott 1E 37
Court Rd. BN7: Lewes 4F 17
Courtyard, The BN1: Falm 2E 15
Courtyard, The BN11: Worth 1B 34
............(off St Botolph's Rd.)
Courtyard, The BN12: Gor S 5D 18
Courtyard, The BN14: Salv 4A 20
Courtyard, The BN3: Hove 2H 27
Courtyard, The BN44: Stey 3C 4
Courtyard La. BN3: Hove 4F 27
Coventina Cl. BN43: Shor S 1E 25
Coventry Ct. BN11: Worth 2A 34
............(off Pevensey Gdns.)
Coventry St. BN1: Brig 2C 28
Covers, The BN25: Sea 5E 43
Cowden Rd. BN2: Salt 4B 38
Cowdens Cl. BN3: Hove 4D 10
Cowdray Cl. BN12: Gor S 3F 33
Cowdray Ct. BN12: Gor S 4D 32
............(off Marine Dr.)
Cowdray Ct. BN3: Hove 3A 28
Cowdray Dr. BN12: Gor S 3F 33
Cowfold Rd. BN2: Brig 5A 30
Cowley Dr. BN15: S Lan 5D 22
Cowley Dr. BN2: W'dean 2H 31
Cowper Rd. BN11: Worth 2B 34
Cowper St. BN3: Hove 3G 27
Coxham La. BN44: Stey 2B 4
Coxwell Cl. BN25: Sea 2G 43
Crabtree Arc. BN15: Lan 4C 22
............(off Grand Av.)
Crabtree Av. BN1: Brig 3E 13
Crabtree La. BN15: Lan 4B 22
Crabtree Lodge BN15: Lan 3B 22
Cradle Hill Ind. Est. BN25: Sea 1G 43
Cradle Hill Rd. BN25: Sea 2G 43
Cradock Pl. BN13: Durr 2G 19
Craignair Av. BN1: Brig 1D 12
Cranbourne St.
BN1: Brig 4B 44 (5D 28)
Cranbrook BN2: Brig 4F 29
............(off John St.)
Cranedown BN7: Lewes 6C 16
Cranleigh Av. BN2: Rott 3H 37
Cranleigh Ct. BN11: Worth 2C 34
Cranleigh Rd. BN14: Worth 5B 20
Cranley Ct. BN3: Hove 3D 26
Cranmer Av. BN3: Hove 1F 27
Cranmer Cl. BN7: Lewes 3F 17
Cranmer Rd. BN13: Worth 1A 34
Cranworth Rd. BN11: Worth 1F 35
Craven Ct. BN15: Lan 3C 22
Craven Path BN2: Brig 4H 29
Craven Pl. BN2: Brig 5H 29
Craven Rd. BN2: Brig 4H 29
Crawley Rd. BN1: Brig 2H 13
Crayford Rd. BN2: Brig 1H 29
Crescent, The BN15: Lan 6B 22
Crescent, The BN2: Brig 6A 14
Crescent, The BN42: S'wick 2H 25
Crescent, The BN44: Stey 4C 4
Crescent, The BN9: Newh 2H 41
Crescent Cl. BN2: W'dean 2G 31
Crescent Ct. BN11: Worth 1H 35
............(off Seamill Pk. Cres.)
Crescent Ct. BN2: Brig 3F 29
............(off Park Cres. Ter.)
Crescent Dr. Nth. BN2: W'dean 2F 31
Crescent Dr. Sth. BN2: W'dean 4F 31
Crescent Mans. BN2: Brig 2F 29
............(off Prince's Cres.)
Crescent Pl. BN2: Brig 6G 29
Crescent Rd. BN11: Worth 2C 34
Crescent Rd. BN2: Brig 2F 29
Crespin Way BN1: Brig 6G 13
Cresta Ct. BN10: Peace 5G 39
............(off Sth. Coast Rd.)
Cresta Rd. BN9: Newh 5C 40
Crest Rd. BN9: Newh 2H 41
Crest Way BN41: Ports 5B 10
Crestway, The BN1: Brig 6G 13
Crestway Pde. BN1: Brig 6G 13
............(off The Crestway)
Cricketers Pde. BN14: Broadw 4D 20
Cricketfield Ct. BN25: Sea 5E 43
Cricketfield Rd. BN25: Sea 5E 43
Cripps Av. BN10: Peace 3H 39
Cripps La. BN44: Stey 3D 4
Crisp Rd. BN7: Lewes 2C 16
Crockhurst Hill BN13: Salv 2H 19
Crocks Dean BN10: Peace 2H 39
Crocodile Wlk. BN3: Hove 2C 28
Croft, The BN42: S'wick 2G 25
Croft Av. BN42: S'wick 3G 25
Croft Ct. BN25: Sea 4D 42
Croft Dr. BN41: Ports 5A 10
Crofters Wood BN44: Bramb 4E 5
Cft. La. BN25: Sea 4D 42
Cft. Mdw. BN44: Stey 3C 4
Croft Rd. BN1: Brig 4B 12
Cromleigh Way BN42: S'wick 6G 9
Cromwell Ct. BN3: Hove 3A 28
Cromwell Pl. BN7: Lewes 4D 16
Cromwell Rd. BN3: Hove 3A 28
Cromwell St. BN2: Brig 3G 29
Crooked La. BN25: Sea 5E 43
Crosby Cl. BN13: Durr 4F 19
Croshaw Cl. BN15: Lan 5B 22
Crossbush Rd. BN2: Brig 4A 30
Crosshaven Pl. BN7: Lewes 2G 17
Cross La. BN14: Fin 2C 6
Cross Rd. BN42: S'wick 1F 25
Cross Rd. Cl. BN42: S'wick 2F 25
Cross St. BN1: Brig 1C 44 (3E 29)
Cross St. BN11: Worth 1C 34
Cross St. BN3: Hove 5B 28
Cross Way BN7: Lewes 4C 16
Crossway, The BN1: Brig 6F 13
Crossway, The BN41: Ports 6A 10
Crossways Av. BN12: Gor S 6C 18
Crouch, The BN25: Sea 5D 42
............(off Crouch La.)
Crouchfield Cl. BN25: Sea 5E 43
Crouch La. BN25: Sea 5D 42
Crowborough Dr. BN12: Gor S 2D 32
Crowborough Rd. BN2: Salt 3B 38
Crowhurst Rd. BN1: Brig 1F 13
Crown Bldgs. BN15: Lan 6A 22
Crown Cl. BN3: Hove 4B 28
............(off Palmeira Av.)
Crown Gdns. BN1: Brig 3B 44 (4D 28)
............(off Queen's Rd.)
Crown Hill BN2: Brig 4G 29
............(off Finsbury Rd.)
Crown Hill BN25: Sea 1D 42
Crown Rd. BN41: Ports 2A 26
Crown Rd. BN43: Shor S 2D 24
Crown St. BN1: Brig 4A 44 (5D 28)
Crypt Gallery, The 5D 42
Cubitt Ter. BN2: Brig 6H 29
............(off Chichester Pl.)
Cuckfield Cres. BN13: Salv 4H 19
Cuckmere Ct. BN25: Sea 4D 42
............(off Sutton Pk. Rd.)
Cuckmere Rd. BN25: Sea 5G 43
Cuckmere Rd. BN9: Newh 6C 40
Cuckmere Way BN1: Brig 2G 13
Cuckoo Ga. BN12: Gor S 6D 18
CUILFAIL 4G 17
CUILFAIL TUNNEL 4G 17
Culpepper Cl. BN2: Brig 6H 13
Culver Ct. BN15: Lan 4C 22
Culver Rd. BN15: Lan 4C 22
Cumberland Av. BN12: Gor S 5F 19
Cumberland Dr. BN1: Brig 6C 12
Cumberland Lodge BN1: Brig 6C 12
............(off Cumberland Rd.)
Cumberland Rd. BN1: Brig 6C 12
Cumberland Ter. BN3: Hove 1G 27
Cumbrian Cl. BN13: Durr 3G 19
Cunningham Ct. BN25: Sea 5D 42
Curlews, The BN43: Shor S 2C 24

50 A-Z Brighton & Worthing

Curve, The – Eastern Cl.

Curve, The BN2: Brig 5F **29**
(off Carlton Hill)
Curvins Way BN15: Lan 3D **22**
Curwen Pl. BN1: Brig 5C **12**
Curzon Cl. BN13: Durr 4H **19**
Curzon Ct. BN2: Salt 4A **38**
Cuthbert Rd. BN2: Brig 5G **29**
Cygnets, The BN43: Shor S 2B **24**
Cypress Av. BN13: Durr 5E **19**
Cypress Cl. BN43: Shor S 1B **24**
Cypress Villa BN1: Brig 6C **12**
(off Preston Rd.)
Cyril Richings Bus. Cen. BN43: Shor S 3D **24**

D

Dacre Rd. BN9: Newh 4F **41**
Dagmar St. BN11: Worth 1D **34**
Dairy Farm Flats BN12: Gor S 1C **32**
Daisy Ct. BN1: Brig 5B **44** (5D **28**)
(off Middle St.)
Dale Av. BN1: Brig 3D **12**
Dale Cres. BN1: Brig 2D **12**
Dale Dr. BN1: Brig 2D **12**
Dale Rd. BN11: Worth 6H **21**
Dale Rd. BN7: Lewes 5C **16**
Dale Vw. BN3: Hove 6D **10**
Dale Vw. Gdns. BN3: Hove 6D **10**
Dallington Rd. BN3: Hove 2F **27**
Damon Cl. BN10: Peace 5G **39**
Dana Lodge BN10: Tels C 5E **39**
Dane Cl. BN25: Sea 5C **42**
Dane Hgts. BN25: Sea 5D **42**
Danehill Rd. BN2: Brig 5B **30**
Dane Rd. BN25: Sea 5C **42**
Daneswood Ho. BN11: Worth 2A **34**
(off Southview Dr.)
Daniel Cl. BN15: Lan 3D **22**
Dankton Gdns. BN15: Somp 3H **21**
Dankton La. BN15: Somp 1H **21**
Dannfields Ho. BN25: Sea 4C **42**
Danny Sheldon Ho. BN2: Brig 6G **29**
(off Eastern Rd.)
Darcey Dr. BN1: Brig 2E **13**
Dart Cl. BN13: Durr 2F **19**
Dartmouth Cl. BN2: Brig 1B **30**
Dartmouth Cres. BN2: Brig 1A **30**
Darwall Dr. BN25: Sea 4F **43**
D'Aubigny Rd. BN2: Brig 2F **29**
Davenport Ct. BN11: Worth 2H **33**
Davey Dr. BN1: Brig 1F **29**
Davey's La. BN7: Lewes 3G **17**
David Lloyd Leisure Brighton 5A **36**
David Lloyd Leisure Worthing 5D **18**
Davies Ct. BN11: Worth 3A **34**
Davigdor Rd. BN3: Hove 3B **28**
Davison Leisure Cen. 1F **35**
Dawes Av. BN11: Worth 1F **35**
Dawes Cl. BN11: Worth 1F **35**
Dawlish Cl. BN2: Brig 1A **30**
Dawn Cl. BN44: Up B 5G **5**
Dawn Cres. BN44: Up B 5F **5**
Dawson Ct. BN11: Worth 1C **34**
(off Victoria Rd.)
Dawson Ter. BN2: Brig 4G **29**
Deacons Dr. BN41: Ports 6B **10**
Deacons Way BN44: Up B 4F **5**
Deacon Trad. Est. BN14: Broadw 5F **21**
Deacon Way BN14: Broadw 5F **21**
Deal Av. BN25: Sea 2H **43**
Dean Cl. BN2: Rott 2G **37**
Dean Cl. BN41: Ports 6C **10**
Dean Ct. Rd. BN2: Rott 2F **37**
Deanery Cl. BN7: Lewes 2F **17**
Dean Gdns. BN41: Ports 6C **10**
Dean Rd. BN25: Sea 5E **43**
Deans Cl. BN2: W'dean 2G **31**
Deans Leisure Cen. 6G **31**
Dean St. BN1: Brig 4A **44** (5C **28**)
Deanway BN3: Hove 5H **11**
Deborah Ter. BN10: Tels C 5E **39**
De Braose Way BN44: Bramb 4D **4**
Deco Bldg., The BN2: Brig 1G **29**
(off Coombe Rd.)
De Courcel Rd. BN2: Brig 5A **36**
Decoy Rd. BN14: Broadw 5F **21**
Deerswood Cl. BN13: Durr 5D **18**
Deeside, The BN1: Brig 1E **13**
De Grey Cl. BN7: Lewes 3F **17**
Delanair Est. BN7: Lewes 3F **17**
Delaware Rd. BN7: Lewes 5C **16**
De La Warr Grn. BN7: Lewes 2D **16**
Delfryn BN41: Ports 5G **9**
Dell, The 6F **39**
De Montfort Rd. BN2: Brig 3G **29**
De Montfort Rd. BN7: Lewes 4D **16**
Dene, The BN3: Hove 5D **10**
Dene Ct. BN11: Worth 2B **34**
Denecroft BN1: Brig 3B **12**
Deneside BN1: Brig 3B **12**
Denes M. BN2: Rott 3F **37**
Dene Va. BN1: Brig 3B **12**
Deneway, The BN1: Brig 4B **12**
Deneway, The BN15: Somp 4A **22**
Denmark M. BN3: Hove 3H **27**
Denmark Rd. BN41: Ports 3C **26**
Denmark Ter. BN1: Brig 4C **28**
Denmark Vs. BN3: Hove 3H **27**
Dennis Hobden Cl. BN2: Brig 1A **30**
DENTON 2G **41**
Denton Cl. BN12: Gor S 1D **32**
Denton Dr. BN1: Brig 3E **13**
Denton Dr. BN9: Newh 2G **41**
Denton Gdns. 2E **35**
DENTON ISLAND 3E **41**
Denton Island Indoor Bowls Club 3E **41**
Denton Ri. BN9: Newh 1G **41**
Denton Rd. BN9: Newh 2G **41**
Derby Ct. BN3: Hove 3C **28**
(off Davigdor Rd.)
Derby Pl. BN2: Brig 5F **29**
(off Up. Park Pl.)
Derek Av. BN3: Hove 4D **26**
Derek Ho. BN3: Hove 4F **27**
Derek Rd. BN15: N Lan 2B **22**
Dervia Ho. BN3: Hove 3B **28**
(off Palmeira Av.)
Derwent Cl. BN15: Somp 5A **22**
Derwent Ct. BN1: Brig 3A **44** (4D **28**)
(off Buckingham Rd.)
Derwent Dr. BN12: Gor S 5F **19**
Desmond Way BN2: Brig 4B **30**
De Vere Leisure Club Brighton 5A **44** (5D **28**)
(off Kings Rd.)
Devil's Dyke Rd. BN3: Brig 3G **11**
Devonian Cl. BN2: Brig 3F **29**
Devonian Ct. BN2: Brig 3F **29**
(off Park Cres. Pl.)
Devon Lodge BN2: Brig 5F **29**
(off Carlton Hill)
Devonport Pl. BN11: Worth 1G **35**
Devonport Rd. BN11: Worth 1G **35**
Devonshire Ct. BN3: Hove 3A **28**
Devonshire Lodge BN11: Worth 2H **33**
Devonshire Mans. BN2: Brig 5F **29**
(off Devonshire Pl.)
Devonshire Pl. BN2: Brig 5F **29**
De Warrenne Rd. BN7: Lewes 4D **16**
Dewe Rd. BN2: Brig 1G **29**
Dewpond, The BN10: Peace 3F **39**
Diamond Jubilee Cl. BN25: Sea 4E **43**
Diggers, The BN1: Brig 5F **13**
Dinapore Ho. BN2: Brig 4F **29**
(off John St.)
Dingemans BN44: Stey 1C **4**
Ditchling Cl. BN12: Gor S 6D **18**
Ditchling Ct. BN1: Brig 2F **29**
Ditchling Cres. BN1: Brig 3G **13**
Ditchling Gdns. BN1: Brig 1E **29**
Ditchling Pl. BN1: Brig 1E **29**
Ditchling Ri. BN1: Brig 2E **29**
Dog La. BN44: Stey 3C **4**
Dolphin Ct. BN3: Hove 4G **27**
(off Hove St.)
Dolphin Ent. Cen. BN43: Shor S 3D **24**
Dolphin Lodge BN11: Worth 3A **34**
Dolphin M. BN2: Brig 6D **44** (6E **29**)
(off Steine St.)
Dolphin M. BN43: Shor S 3C **24**
Dolphin Rd. BN43: Shor S 3C **24**
Dolphin Way BN43: Shor S 3D **24**
Dome Cinema 3E **35**
(off Marine Pde.)
Dominion Bldgs. BN14: Broadw 6F **21**
Dominion Cl. BN14: Broadw 6E **21**
Dominion Rd. BN14: Broadw 5E **21**
Dominion Rd. Recreation Ground 6E **21**
Dominion Way BN14: Broadw 5F **21**
Dominion Way W. BN14: Broadw 5F **21**
Donald Hall Rd. BN2: Brig 5H **29**
Donkey M. BN3: Hove 5B **28**
Donnington Rd. BN2: W'dean 4G **31**
Doone End BN12: Fer 4B **32**
Dorchester Ct. BN1: Brig 5C **28**
(off Norfolk Sq.)
Dorchester Gdns. BN11: Worth 2A **34**
Dorita Ct. BN10: Peace 5G **39**
(off Sth. Coast Rd.)
Dorothy Av. BN10: Peace 6G **39**
(not continuous)
Dorothy Av. Nth. BN10: Peace 4G **39**
Dorothy Rd. BN3: Hove 2D **26**
Dorothy Stringer Sports Cen. 5D **12**
Dorset Ct. BN3: Hove 4F **27**
Dorset Gdns. BN2: Brig 5F **29**
Dorset M. BN2: Brig 5D **44** (5E **29**)
(off Dorset St.)
Dorset Pl. BN14: W Tar 5A **20**
Dorset Pl. BN2: Brig 5F **29**
Dorset Rd. BN7: Lewes 5F **17**
Dorset St. BN2: Brig 5D **44** (5E **29**)
Douglas Av. BN11: Worth 2H **33**
Douglas Cl. BN11: Worth 2H **33**
Dovecote M. BN15: Somp 2A **22**
Dover Cl. BN25: Sea 2H **43**
Dover Rd. BN1: Brig 6E **13**
Dover Rd. BN11: Worth 3A **34**
Dower Cl. BN2: O'dean 1D **36**
Down, The BN3: Hove 4C **10**
Downash Cl. BN2: Brig 4A **30**
Downes Ct. BN43: Shor S 2E **25**
(off Wilmot Rd.)
Downe Wlk. BN13: Durr 5F **19**
(off East Tyne)
Downford BN2: Brig 5B **30**
(off Whitehawk Rd.)
Downhill Vw. BN2: W'dean 3G **31**
Downland Av. BN10: Peace 4A **40**
Downland Av. BN42: S'wick 1F **25**
Downland Cl. BN14: Fin 2C **6**
Downland Cl. BN2: W'dean 2C **30**
Downland Cl. BN42: S'wick 1F **25**
Downland Cl. BN44: Up B 4G **5**
Downland Ct. BN41: Ports 6A **10**
Downland Cres. BN3: Hove 5F **11**
Downland Dr. BN3: Hove 5F **11**
Downland Pk. BN44: Bramb 5F **5**
Downland Pk. BN9: Newh 6E **41**
Downland Rd. BN2: W'dean 2C **30**
Downland Rd. BN44: Up B 4G **5**
Downlands BN13: High S 6C **6**
Downlands Av. BN14: Broadw 3D **20**
Downlands Bus. Pk. BN14: Char D 2E **21**
Downlands Cl. BN15: Somp 3A **22**
Downlands Gdns. BN14: Broadw 3E **21**
Downlands Pde. BN14: Broadw 3E **21**
(off Up. Brighton Rd.)
Downlands Retail Pk. 3E **21**
Downs, The BN25: Sea 4F **43**
Downsbrook Trad. Est. BN14: Broadw 4E **21**
Downs Cl. BN15: S Lan 4F **23**
Downs Cl. BN7: Lewes 3C **16**
Downs Crematorium 2A **30**
Downscroft BN44: Up B 4G **5**
Downside BN1: Brig 3B **12**
Downside BN3: Hove 5H **11**
Downside BN43: Shor S 1C **24**
Downside BN7: Lewes 5C **16**
Downside Av. BN14: Fin V 5C **6**
Downside Cl. BN14: Fin V 5D **6**
Downside Cl. BN43: Shor S 1B **24**
Downs Leisure Cen. 3F **43**
Downsman Ct. BN3: Hove 5E **11**
Downsmead BN15: Somp 2A **22**
Downs Rd. BN25: Sea 4F **43**
Downs Valley Rd. BN2: W'dean 2G **31**
Downs Vw. BN10: Peace 2H **39**
Downsview BN3: Hove 5D **10**
Downsview Av. BN2: W'dean 2E **31**
Downsview Mnr. BN14: Broadw 4C **20**
Downsview Rd. BN16: King G 4A **32**
Downsview Rd. BN25: Sea 4F **43**
Downsview Rd. BN41: Ports 6A **10**
Downs Vs. BN9: S Heig 1G **41**
Downs Wlk. BN10: Peace 2G **39**
Downsway BN2: W'dean 2F **31**
Downsway BN42: S'wick 6G **9**
Downsway BN43: Shor S 1B **24**
Down Ter. BN2: Brig 4G **29**
Downview Av. BN12: Fer 1A **32**
Downview Ct. BN11: Worth 3A **34**
Downview Rd. BN11: Worth 1A **34**
Downview Rd. BN12: Fer 1A **32**
Downview Rd. BN14: Fin 1C **6**
Drake Av. BN12: Gor S 6F **19**
Drake Ct. BN25: Sea 5D **42**
Drake Ho. BN12: Gor S 3G **33**
Drakes Cl. BN15: S Lan 4F **23**
Draxmont Way BN1: Brig 5D **12**
Draycliff Cl. BN12: Fer 3A **32**
Driftway, The BN44: Up B 3G **5**
Dripping Pan, The 5F **17**
Drive, The BN11: Worth 1H **33**
Drive, The BN15: Lan 6B **22**
Drive, The BN3: Hove 4A **28**
Drive, The BN42: S'wick 1G **25**
Drive, The BN43: Shor S 2B **24**
Drive, The BN9: Newh 6E **41**
Drive Lodge BN3: Hove 3A **28**
Driveway, The BN43: Shor S 2B **24**
Drove, The BN1: Brig 1B **28**
Drove, The BN1: Falm 2E **15**
Drove, The BN7: Off 1C **16**
Drove, The BN9: Newh 3G **41**
Drove Av. BN2: King L 6F **15**
Drove Av. BN7: King L 6G **15**
Drove Cres. BN41: Ports 6A **10**
Drove Retail Pk., The 3G **41**
Drove Rd. BN2: W'dean 2C **30**
Drove Rd. BN41: Ports 1A **26**
Drove Rd. BN9: Newh 3F **41**
Drovers Cl. BN41: Ports 6C **10**
Droveway, The BN3: Hove 6G **11**
(not continuous)
Drummond Ct. BN12: Gor S 3F **33**
(off Marine Cres.)
Drummond Rd. BN12: Gor S 3G **33**
Duchess Dr. BN25: Sea 1D **42**
Dudeney Lodge BN1: Brig 1F **29**
Dudley M. BN3: Hove 5B **28**
(off Brunswick St. W.)
Dudley Rd. BN1: Brig 1F **29**
Dudwell Rd. BN2: W'dean 3G **31**
Duke of York's Picture House 3E **29**
Dukes Cl. BN25: Sea 3C **42**
Duke's Ct. BN1: Brig 4B **44** (5D **28**)
(off Duke St.)
Dukes La. BN1: Brig 5B **44** (5D **28**)
Dukes La. BN44: Stey 3C **4**
Duke's Mound BN2: Brig 6H **29**
Duke's Pas. BN1: Brig 5B **44** (5D **28**)
(off Duke St.)
Duke St. BN1: Brig 5B **44** (5D **28**)
Dukes Yd. BN44: Stey 3C **4**
Dulwich Cl. BN25: Sea 3G **43**
Dumbrell Ct. BN7: Lewes 5D **16**
(off St Pancras Rd.)
Duncan Ct. BN2: Salt 3A **38**
Duncan Ho. BN10: Peace 3G **39**
(off Collingwood Cl.)
Dunster Cl. BN1: Brig 1F **29**
Dunvan Cl. BN7: Lewes 2E **17**
Dunwich BN43: Shor B 4D **24**
(off Sea Spray Av.)
Durham Cl. BN2: Brig 1C **30**
Durham Ct. BN3: Hove 4H **27**
DURRINGTON 3F **19**
Durrington Ct. BN1: Brig 3B **12**
(off Mill Ri.)
Durrington Gdns. BN12: Gor S 1F **33**
Durrington Hill BN13: Durr 3F **19**
Durrington La. BN13: Durr 3F **19**
Durrington-on-Sea Station (Rail) 1G **33**
Dyke Cl. BN3: Hove 4H **11**
Dyke Rd. BN1: Brig 6B **12**
Dyke Rd. BN3: Hove 6B **12**
Dyke Rd. Av. BN1: Brig 4H **11**
Dyke Rd. Av. BN3: Hove 4H **11**
Dyke Rd. Dr. BN1: Brig 2C **28**
Dyke Rd. M. BN1: Brig 1A **44** (3D **28**)
(off Dyke Rd.)
Dyke Rd. Pl. BN1: Brig 5A **12**
Dymchurch Cl. BN25: Sea 2G **43**
Dymock Cl. BN25: Sea 3H **43**

E

Eagle Ct. BN2: Brig 2G **29**
(off Lewes Rd.)
Eardley, The BN11: Worth 2E **35**
(off Marine Pde.)
Earls Cl. BN25: Sea 2B **42**
Earls Gdn. BN7: Lewes 4F **17**
East Albany Rd. BN25: Sea 3E **43**
East Av. BN12: Gor S 3H **33**
Eastbank BN42: S'wick 1H **25**
EAST BLATCHINGTON 1D **42**
Eastbourne Rd. BN2: Brig 1H **29**
Eastbourne Rd. BN25: Sea 4G **43**
Eastbourne Ter. BN25: Sea 4F **43**
(off Eastbourne Rd.)
Eastbridge Rd. BN9: Newh 4G **41**
East Brighton Golf Course 4B **36**
Eastbrook Rd. BN41: Ports 3B **26**
Eastbrook Way BN41: Ports 3A **26**
Eastcourt Rd. BN14: Broadw 6C **20**
East Dean Ri. BN25: Sea 3F **43**
East Dr. BN2: Brig 5G **29**
Eastergate Cl. BN12: Gor S 1B **32**
Eastergate Rd. BN2: Brig 4B **14**
Eastern Av. BN43: Shor S 3C **24**
Eastern Cl. BN43: Shor S 3C **24**

A-Z Brighton & Worthing 51

Firle Cl. – Gosling Croft Bus. Cen.

Firle Cl. BN25: Sea 2D **42**
Firle Cres. BN7: Lewes 3B **16**
Firle Dr. BN25: Sea 2D **42**
Firle Grange BN25: Sea 2D **42**
Firle Rd. BN10: Peace 3F **39**
Firle Rd. BN10: Tels C 3F **39**
Firle Rd. BN15: N Lan 2B **22**
Firle Rd. BN2: Brig 4H **29**
Firle Rd. BN25: Sea 2D **42**
Firle Ter. BN9: S Heig 1F **41**
Firsdown Cl. BN13: High S 6C **6**
Firsdown Rd. BN13: High S 6C **6**
First Av. BN14: Char D 2C **20**
First Av. BN15: Lan 4C **22**
First Av. BN15: N Lan 4C **22**
First Av. BN3: Hove 5A **28**
First Av. BN9: Newh 5E **41**
Fishermans Wlk. BN43: Shor B 5H **23**
FISHERSGATE 3A **26**
Fishersgate Cl. BN41: Ports 3A **26**
Fishersgate Station (Rail) 3A **26**
Fishersgate Ter. BN41: Ports 3A **26**
Fisher St. BN7: Lewes 4F **17**
Fitch Dr. BN2: Brig 1A **30**
Fitness First Brighton 2C **44** (4E **29**)
Fittleworth Cl. BN12: Gor S 6C **18**
Fitzalan Ct. BN10: Peace 5F **39** (off Cavell Av.)
Fitzgerald Av. BN25: Sea 5E **43**
Fitzgerald Ho. BN25: Sea 4D **42**
Fitzgerald Pk. BN25: Sea 5E **43**
Fitzgerald Rd. BN7: Lewes 2F **17**
Fitzherbert Ct. BN2: Brig 2H **29** (off Fitzherbert Dr.)
Fitzherbert Dr. BN2: Brig 2H **29**
Fitzjohn's Rd. BN7: Lewes 3C **16**
Fitzroy Rd. BN7: Lewes 2D **16**
FIVE WAYS 6E **13**
Flag Ct. BN3: Hove 5H **27**
Flag Sq. BN43: Shor B 4B **24**
Fleet St. BN1: Brig 1C **44** (3E **29**)
Fletcher Rd. BN14: Broadw 5E **21**
Fletchers Cft. BN44: Stey 3C **4**
Fletching Cl. BN2: Brig 4B **30**
Flimwell Cl. BN2: Brig 5A **30** (not continuous)
Flint Cl. BN25: Sea 1D **42**
Flint Cl. BN41: Ports 6B **10**
Flint Way BN10: Peace 5H **39**
Floral Clock Brighton 4A **28** (off Western Rd.)
Floraldene Ct. BN14: Fin V 1A **20**
Florence Av. BN3: Hove 2D **26**
Florence Ct. BN1: Brig 6D **12** (off Gordon Rd.)
Florence Pl. BN1: Brig 1F **29**
Florence Rd. BN1: Brig 2E **29**
Florets, The BN44: Up B 5G **5**
Florida Cl. BN12: Fer 4B **32**
Florida Gdns. BN12: Fer 4B **32**
Florida Rd. BN12: Fer 4B **32**
Florlandia Cl. BN15: Somp 4H **21**
Foamcourt Waye BN12: Fer 3A **32**
Folkestone Cl. BN25: Sea 2H **43**
Folly Fld. BN9: Newh 4E **41**
Fonthill Rd. BN3: Hove 2H **27**
Fontwell Cl. BN14: Fin V 2A **20**
Fontwell Dr. BN14: Fin V 2A **20**
Foredown Cl. BN41: Ports 6B **10**
Foredown Dr. BN41: Ports 1B **26**
Foredown Rd. BN41: Ports 4A **10** (not continuous)
Foredown Tower Learning & Vis. Cen. 5B **10**
Forest La. BN13: Clap 2D **18**
Forest Rd. BN1: Brig 3A **14**
Forest Rd. BN14: Broadw 4D **20**
Forge Cl. BN41: Ports 6B **10**
Fort Ga. BN9: Newh 6G **41**
Fort Haven BN43: Shor B 4E **25**
Fort Ri. BN9: Newh 6F **41**
Fort Rd. BN9: Newh 4F **41**
Fort Rd. Recreation Ground 6F **41**
Forward Cl. BN9: S Heig 1G **41**
Fosse, The BN7: Lewes 4F **17** (off Lancaster St.)
Foster Cl. BN25: Sea 3D **42**
Foster Ct. BN3: Hove 4C **28** (off York Av.)
Foundry La. BN7: Lewes 4G **17**
Foundry Pas. BN7: Lewes 4G **17** (off Cliffe High St.)
Foundry St. BN1: Brig 3C **44** (4E **29**)
Foundry Ter. BN7: Lewes 4G **17** (off Foundry La.)
Fountains Cl. BN1: Brig 6F **13**
Founthill Av. BN2: Salt 3H **37**
Founthill Rd. BN2: Salt 3H **37**
Fourth Av. BN14: Char D 3D **20**
Fourth Av. BN15: Lan 3C **22**
Fourth Av. BN3: Hove 5H **27**
Fowey Cl. BN43: Shor B 4D **24**
Foxdown Rd. BN2: W'dean 3H **31**
Foxglove Ct. BN1: Brig 5F **13**
Foxglove Wlk. BN13: Durr 5E **19**
Foxhill BN10: Peace 3F **39**
Foxhunters Rd. BN41: Ports 5H **9**
Fox Lea BN14: Fin 3C **6**
Foxley La. BN13: High S 2G **19**
Fox Way BN41: Ports 5A **10**
Framfield BN2: Brig 5B **30** (off Whitehawk Rd.)
Framfield Cl. BN1: Brig 2A **14**
Framnaes BN3: Hove 3D **26**
Frampton Ct. BN12: Gor S 2E **33**
Frampton Pl. BN43: Shor S 2H **23**
Framroze Ct. BN1: Brig 5F **13**
Francis St. BN1: Brig 1D **44** (3E **29**)
Francome Ho. BN15: Lan 6A **22**
Franklands Cl. BN14: Fin V 1H **19**
Franklin Rd. BN13: Durr 3G **19**
Franklin Rd. BN2: Brig 2G **29**
Franklin Rd. BN41: Ports 3C **26**
Franklin Rd. BN43: Shor S 1E **25**
Franklin St. BN2: Brig 2G **29**
Frant Rd. BN3: Hove 6G **11**
Fraser Ct. BN43: Shor S 2E **25**
Fred Emery Ct. BN1: Brig 5C **28** (off Sillwood St.)
Frederick Gdns. BN1: Brig 3C **44** (4E **29**) (off Frederick St.)
Frederick Pl. BN1: Brig 2C **44** (4E **29**)
Frederick St. BN1: Brig 3B **44** (4E **29**)
Frederick Ter. BN1: Brig 2C **44** (4E **29**) (off Frederick Pl.)
Freehold St. BN43: Shor S 3A **24**
Freehold Ter. BN2: Brig 2F **29**
Freeland Cl. BN25: Sea 1A **42**
Freemans Rd. BN41: Ports 2A **26**
Frenchs Ct. BN25: Sea 5D **42** (off Steyne Rd.)
Freshbrook Cl. BN15: S Lan 5C **22**
Freshbrook Ct. BN15: Lan 5C **22** (off Freshbrook Rd.)
Freshbrook Rd. BN15: Lan 5C **22**
Freshbrook Rd. BN15: S Lan 5C **22**
Freshfield Ind. Est. BN2: Brig 5G **29**
Freshfield Pl. BN2: Brig 5G **29**
Freshfield Rd. BN2: Brig 5G **29**
Freshfields Cl. BN15: Lan 4B **22**
Freshfields Dr. BN15: Lan 4B **22**
Freshfield St. BN2: Brig 4G **29**
Freshfield Way BN2: Brig 5G **29**
Friar Cl. BN1: Brig 4E **13**
Friar Cres. BN1: Brig 4E **13**
Friar Rd. BN1: Brig 4D **12**
Friars Av. BN10: Peace 6A **40** (not continuous)
Friars M. BN7: Lewes 5F **17** (off Pinwell Rd.)
Friar's Wlk. BN7: Lewes 4F **17**
Friar Wlk. BN1: Brig 4D **12**
Friar Wlk. BN13: Worth 1H **33**
Friese Greene Ho. BN3: Hove 3F **27**
Frimley Cl. BN2: W'dean 3H **31**
Friston Cl. BN2: Brig 4B **14**
Friston Cl. BN25: Sea 3B **42**
Frith Rd. BN3: Hove 2G **27**
Frobisher Cl. BN12: Gor S 6F **19**
Frobisher Ho. BN10: Peace 3G **39**
Frobisher Way BN12: Gor S 6F **19**
Fulbeck Av. BN13: Durr 4D **18**
Fulbeck Way BN13: Durr 4D **18**
Fuller Rd. BN7: Lewes 2D **16**
Fullers Pas. BN7: Lewes 4F **17**
Fullwood Av. BN9: Newh 4D **40**
Fulmar Cl. BN3: Hove 1B **28**
Fulmer Ct. BN11: Worth 2B **34**
Furlongs, The BN44: Stey 4C **4**
Furze Cl. BN13: High S 6B **6**
Furze Cft. BN3: Hove 4B **28**
Furzedene BN3: Hove 4B **28**
Furze Hill BN3: Hove 4B **28**
Furze Hill Ct. BN3: Hove 4B **28**
Furze Hill Ho. BN3: Hove 4C **28**
Furzeholme BN13: High S 6C **6**
Furze Rd. BN13: High S 6B **6**

G

G3 Bus. Pk. BN43: Shor S 3E **25**
Gableson Av. BN1: Brig 4H **11**
Gainsborough Av. BN14: Broadw 3E **21**
Gainsborough Ho. BN3: Hove 3A **28** (off Eaton Gdns.)
Gainsborough Lodge BN14: Broadw 6C **20**
Gaisford Cl. BN14: Worth 6C **20**
Gaisford Rd. BN14: Worth 6B **20**
Gala Bingo Worthing 3C **34**
Galleries, The BN3: Hove 3B **28** (off Palmeira Av.)
Galliers Cl. BN1: Brig 2F **13**
Gallops, The BN7: Lewes 4C **16**
Galsworthy Cl. BN12: Gor S 1D **32**
Galsworthy Rd. BN12: Gor S 1D **32**
Gannet Ho. BN3: Hove 1H **27**
Gannon Rd. BN11: Worth 1F **35**
Garcia Trad. Est. BN13: Worth 1H **33**
Garden Cl. BN15: Somp 4A **22**
Garden Cl. BN41: Ports 2C **26**
Garden Cl. BN43: Shor S 1D **24**
Garden Ct. BN3: Hove 3B **28** (off Somerhill Av.)
Garden Ct. BN43: Shor S 1D **24**
Gardener St. BN41: Ports 2A **26**
Garden Ho., The BN1: Brig 3A **44** (4D **28**) (off Clifton Pl.)
Garden Pk. BN12: Fer 4A **32**
Gardens, The BN41: Ports 2C **26**
Gardens, The BN42: S'wick 3H **25**
Garden St. BN7: Lewes 5E **17**
Gardner Cen. Rd. BN1: Falm 2D **14**
Gardner Rd. BN41: Ports 3A **26**
Gardner St. BN1: Brig 4C **44** (5E **29**)
Garland Point BN43: Shor B 4D **24**
Garnet Ho. BN2: Brig 6G **29** (off St George's Rd.)
Garrick Rd. BN14: Broadw 6D **20**
Gatcombe Cl. BN13: Durr 5C **18**
Gatewycke Ter. BN44: Stey 3C **4** (off Tanyard La.)
Gatton Pk. La. BN1: Brig 3A **12**
Gaywood Wlk. BN13: Durr 5F **19**
Geneva Rd. BN9: Newh 5F **41**
George V Av. BN11: Worth 1H **33**
George V Av. BN15: S Lan 5F **23**
George St. BN41: Ports Chapel Rd. 3A **26**
George St. BN41: Ports Ellen St. 3C **26**
George St. BN2: Brig 5D **44** (5E **29**)
George St. BN3: Hove 4H **27**
George Williams M. BN41: Ports 2B **26**
Georgia Av. BN14: Broadw 6D **20**
Gerald Rd. BN11: Worth 3H **33**
Gerald Rd. BN25: Sea 6E **43**
Gerard St. BN1: Brig 2E **29**
Ghyllside BN2: Brig 1A **30**
Gibbon Rd. BN9: Newh 5D **40**
Gibson Ct. BN7: Lewes 3F **17**
Gildredge Rd. BN25: Sea 4E **43**
Gilmour Ho. BN3: Hove 4H **27**
Girton Ho. BN3: Hove 4F **27**
Gladstone Ct. BN2: Brig 2G **29** (off Hartington Rd.)
Gladstone Pl. BN2: Brig 2G **29**
Gladstone Rd. BN41: Ports 3B **26**
Gladstone Ter. BN2: Brig 3F **29**
Gladys Av. BN10: Peace 6H **39** (not continuous)
Gladys Rd. BN3: Hove 2D **26**
Glass Pav. BN2: Brig 5D **44** (5E **29**) (off Prince's St.)
Glastonbury Rd. BN3: Hove 4D **26**
Glawood Ho. BN14: Broadw 4E **21**
Glebe, The BN42: S'wick 1H **25**
Glebe Cl. BN15: Lan 3C **22**
Glebe Cl. BN42: S'wick 3G **25**
Glebe Cl. BN7: Lewes 5C **16**
Glebe Dr. BN25: Sea 4D **42**
Glebelands Cl. BN43: Shor S 2D **24**
Glebe Rd. BN14: W Tar 5A **20**
Glebeside Av. BN14: Worth 5A **20**
Glebeside Cl. BN14: Worth 5A **20**
Glebe Vs. BN3: Hove 3D **26**
Glebe Way BN15: Lan 3C **22**
Glen, The BN13: Salv 3A **20**
Glenbarrie Way BN12: Fer 1A **32**
Glendale Rd. BN3: Hove 3B **28**
Glendor Rd. BN3: Hove 4E **27**
Gleneagles Cl. BN25: Sea 5H **41**
Glenfalls Av. BN1: Brig 1E **13**
Glen Gdns. BN12: Fer 2B **32**
Glen Ri. BN1: Brig 3H **11**
Glen Ri. Cl. BN1: Brig 3H **11**
Gleton Av. BN3: Hove 6D **10**
Gloucester Ct. BN11: Worth 3H **33** (off George V Av.)
Gloucester M. BN1: Brig 3D **44** (4E **29**) (off Gloucester Rd.)
Gloucester Pas. BN1: Brig 3D **44** (4E **29**) (off Gloucester St.)
Gloucester Pl. BN1: Brig 3D **44** (4E **29**)
Gloucester Rd. BN1: Brig 3C **44** (4E **29**) (not continuous)
Gloucester St. BN1: Brig 3D **44** (4E **29**)
Gloucester Yd. BN1: Brig 3D **44** (4E **29**) (off Gloucester Rd.)
Glover's Yd. BN1: Brig 1D **28**
Glynde Av. BN12: Gor S Amberley Dr. 4C **32**
Glynde Av. BN12: Gor S Thakeham Dr. 2C **32**
Glynde Av. BN2: Salt 2B **38**
Glyndebourne Av. BN2: Salt 2A **38**
Glyndebourne Ct. BN43: Shor S 3B **24** (off Ham Rd.)
Glynde Cl. BN12: Fer 2B **32**
Glynde Cl. BN9: Newh 1F **41**
Glynde Ho. BN3: Hove 4B **28**
Glynde Rd. BN2: Brig 4H **29**
Glynleigh BN2: Brig 4F **29** (off Ashton Ri.)
Glynn Ri. BN10: Peace 3F **39**
Glynn Rd. BN10: Peace 3G **39**
Glynn Rd. W. BN10: Peace 3G **39**
Gochers Ct. BN2: Brig 3G **29** (off Islingword Rd.)
Godfrey Cl. BN7: Lewes 2E **17**
Godstalls La. BN44: Stey 3B **4**
Godwin Rd. BN3: Hove 1D **26**
Golby Ct. BN10: Tels C 5E **39**
Golden La. BN1: Brig 5B **28**
Golden Sands Cvn. Pk. BN15: S Lan 6E **23**
Gold La. BN10: Peace 2G **39**
Goldsmid M. BN3: Hove 4B **28** (off Farm M.)
Goldsmid Rd. BN3: Hove 1A **44** (3C **28**)
Goldsmith Rd. BN14: Broadw 6E **21**
Goldstone Cl. BN3: Hove 6G **11**
Goldstone Ct. BN3: Hove 5G **11**
Goldstone Cres. BN3: Hove 5G **11**
Goldstone Ho. BN3: Hove 3H **27** (off Clarendon Rd.)
Goldstone La. BN3: Hove 2H **27**
Goldstone Retail Pk. 2H **27**
Goldstone Rd. BN3: Hove 3H **27**
Goldstone St. BN3: Hove 3H **27**
Goldstone Vs. BN3: Hove 3H **27**
Goldstone Way BN3: Hove 6G **11**
Golf Dr. BN1: Brig 5F **13**
Goodwood Ct. BN3: Hove 3B **28**
Goodwood Rd. BN13: Salv 3A **20**
Goodwood Way BN2: Brig 5A **14**
Gordon Av. BN43: Shor S 3C **24**
Gordon Cl. BN41: Ports 3C **26**
Gordon M. BN41: Ports 3C **26**
Gordon Rd. BN41: Ports Chapel Rd. 3A **26**
Gordon Rd. BN41: Ports Gordon Cl. 3C **26**
Gordon Rd. BN1: Brig 6D **12**
Gordon Rd. BN11: Worth 1D **34**
Gordon Rd. BN15: Lan 4B **22**
Gordon Rd. BN43: Shor S 3B **24**
Gorham Av. BN2: Rott 2G **37**
Gorham Cl. BN2: Rott 2G **37**
Gorham Ct. BN10: Tels C 4C **38**
Gorham Way BN10: Tels C 4C **38**
Goring Bus. Pk. BN12: Gor S 1E **33**
GORING-BY-SEA 2E **33**
Goring-by-Sea Station (Rail) 1C **32**
Goring Chase BN12: Gor S 6C **18**
Goring Ct. BN1: Brig 3B **14**
Goring Ct. BN44: Stey 4C **4** (off Bramber Rd.)
GORING CROSSWAYS 6C **18**
GORING HALL BMI HOSPITAL 2D **32**
Goring Rd. BN12: Gor S 2E **33**
Goring Rd. BN12: Worth 2E **33**
Goring Rd. BN44: Stey 4C **4**
Goring St. BN12: Gor S 6C **18**
Goring Way BN12: Fer 2B **32**
Goring Way BN12: Gor S 2B **32**
Gorringe Cl. BN43: Shor S 3F **25**
Gorse Av. BN14: Salv 4B **20**
Gorse Cl. BN41: Ports 4H **9**
Gorse Dr. BN25: Sea 1E **43**
Gorse La. BN13: High S 6C **6**
Gosling Croft Bus. Cen. BN13: Clap 2A **18**

A-Z Brighton & Worthing 53

Gosport Ct. BN43: Shor B 4D **24**
(off Harbour Way)
Graffham Cl. BN2: Brig 4A **30**
Grafton Dr. BN15: Somp 4A **22**
Grafton Gdns. BN15: Somp 4A **22**
Grafton Pl. BN11: Worth 2D **34**
Grafton Rd. BN11: Worth 2D **34**
Grafton St. BN2: Brig 6F **29**
Graham Av. BN1: Brig 4C **12**
Graham Av. BN41: Ports 4H **9**
Graham Cl. BN41: Ports 4H **9**
Graham Ct. BN11: Worth 2H **33**
Graham Ct. BN15: Somp 4A **22**
Graham Cres. BN41: Ports 4H **9**
Graham Rd. BN11: Worth 2D **34**
Grand Av. BN11: Worth 1A **34**
Grand Av. BN15: Lan 4C **22**
Grand Av. BN25: Sea 2B **42**
Grand Av. BN3: Hove 5A **28**
Grand Av. Mans. BN3: Hove 4A **28**
(off Grand Av.)
Grand Cres. BN2: Rott 3G **37**
Grand Junc. Rd.
BN1: Brig 6C **44** (6E **29**)
Grand Ocean BN2: Salt 3B **38**
Grand Pde. BN2: Brig 4D **44** (5E **29**)
Grand Pde. M. BN2: Brig 4D **44** (5E **29**)
Grange, The BN2: Salt 4B **38**
Grange Cl. BN1: Brig 1C **28**
Grange Cl. BN12: Fer 3A **32**
Grange Ct. BN12: Fer 2A **32**
(off Ferring Grange Gdns.)
Grange Ct. BN3: Hove 2F **27**
(off Payne Av.)
Grange Ct. BN42: S'wick 3G **25**
Grange Ct. BN7: Lewes 5E **17**
Grange Farm Cotts. BN2: O'dean 6F **31**
(off Greenways)
Grange Ind. Est., The
BN42: S'wick 3G **25**
Grange Mus. & Art Gallery, The 2G **37**
Grange Pk. BN12: Fer 3A **32**
Grange Rd. BN3: Hove 3E **27**
Grange Rd. BN42: S'wick 3G **25**
Grange Rd. BN7: Lewes 5E **17**
Grange Wlk. BN1: Brig 3C **12**
Grangeways BN1: Brig 3C **12**
Grantham Rd. BN1: Brig 1E **29**
Grantsmead BN15: N Lan 2C **22**
Grant St. BN2: Brig 3F **29**
Granville Ct. BN25: Sea 5D **42**
Granville Ct. BN3: Hove 3H **27**
(off Denmark Vs.)
Granville Rd. BN3: Hove 3C **28**
Graperies, The BN2: Brig 5G **29**
Grasmere Av. BN15: Somp 4H **21**
Grassmere Av. BN10: Tels C 4D **38**
Grassmere Ct. BN10: Tels C 4E **39**
Gratwicke Rd. BN11: Worth 2C **34**
Gravelly Cres. BN15: Lan 4D **22**
Gt. College St. BN2: Brig 6G **29**
Greatham Ct. BN1: Brig 2C **12**
(off Old London Rd.)
Greatham Rd. BN14: Fin V 1H **19**
Gt. Wilkins BN1: Falm 3D **14**
Green, The BN2: Rott 2F **37**
Green, The BN3: Hove 6A **12**
Green, The BN42: S'wick 3G **25**
Greena Ct. BN11: Worth 2C **34**
Greenacre BN10: Peace 2H **39**
Greenacres BN1: Brig 1D **28**
Greenacres BN10: Tels C 5E **39**
Greenacres BN43: Shor S 2A **24**
Greenacres BN44: Stey 4C **4**
Greenbank Av. BN2: Salt 3A **38**
Green Cl. BN42: S'wick 3G **25**
Green Ct. BN42: S'wick 3G **25**
(off The Green)
Grn. Diamond BN1: Brig 6C **44** (6E **29**)
(off Bartholomews)
Greene Ct. BN7: Lewes 5D **16**
Green Fld. Cl. BN42: S'wick 2G **25**
Greenfield Cl. BN1: Brig 3E **13**
Greenfield Cres. BN1: Brig 3D **12**
Green Ga. BN10: Peace 3G **39**
Greenhill Way BN10: Peace 2G **39**
Greenland Cl. BN13: Durr 3G **19**
Greenland Rd. BN13: Durr 4F **19**
Greenland Wlk. BN13: Durr 3G **19**
Green La. BN2: W'dean 4G **31**
Green La. BN25: Sea 5D **42**
Green La. BN7: Lewes 5E **17**
Greenleas BN3: Hove 6D **10**
Greenleaves BN44: Bramb 5D **4**
Greenoaks BN15: N Lan 2B **22**
Green Pk. BN12: Fer 1B **32**
Grn. Ridge BN1: Brig 3H **11**

Greentrees BN11: Worth 2B **34**
Greentrees BN15: Somp 5A **22**
Greentrees Cl. BN15: Somp 4A **22**
Greentrees Cres. BN15: Somp 4A **22**
Green Wlk. BN25: Sea 5G **43**
Grn. Wall BN7: Lewes 4F **17**
Green Way, The BN12: Gor S 6D **18**
Greenway Ct. BN2: Rott 3G **37**
Greenways BN2: O'dean 6F **31**
Greenways BN41: Ports 1B **26**
Greenways BN42: S'wick 1H **25**
Greenways Cnr. BN2: O'dean 6E **31**
Greenways Cres. BN12: Fer 3B **32**
Greenways Cres. BN43: Shor S 1C **24**
Greenwell Cl. BN25: Sea 3G **43**
Greenwich Way BN10: Peace 5F **39**
Greet Rd. BN15: Lan 3B **22**
Grenville Av. BN12: Gor S 1F **33**
Grenville Cl. BN12: Gor S 1E **33**
Grenville Ho. BN10: Peace 3H **39**
Grenville St. BN1: Brig 5B **44** (5D **28**)
Greyfriars BN3: Hove 2B **28**
Greyfriars Cl. BN13: Salv 4A **20**
Greyfriars Ct. BN7: Lewes 4F **17**
Grey Point Ho. BN14: Fin 2C **6**
Greystoke M. BN12: Fer 2A **32**
Greystoke Rd. BN12: Fer 2A **32**
Greystone Av. BN13: Worth 5H **19**
Griffiths Av. BN15: N Lan 2B **22**
Grinstead Av. BN15: Lan 4C **22**
Grinstead La. BN15: Lan 5C **22**
Grinstead Mt. BN2: Brig 5B **30**
Grosvenor Ct. BN1: Brig 5C **12**
Grosvenor Ct. BN25: Sea 4C **42**
Grosvenor Mans. BN3: Hove 4H **27**
Grosvenor M. BN25: Sea 3C **42**
Grosvenor Rd. BN11: Worth 2D **34**
Grosvenor Rd. BN25: Sea 4C **42**
Grosvenor St. BN2: Brig 5F **29**
Grove, The BN12: Fer 2A **32**
Grove, The BN9: Newh 1G **41**
Grove Bank BN2: Brig 4F **29**
(off Albion St.)
Grove Ct. BN3: Hove 4A **28**
Grove Hill BN2: Brig 4F **29**
Grovelands, The BN15: S Lan 6C **22**
Grove Lodge BN14: Broadw 4C **20**
GROVE LODGE RDBT. 3C **20**
Grover Av. BN15: Lan 3B **22**
Grove Rd. BN14: Broadw 4C **20**
Grove Rd. BN25: Sea 4E **43**
Grove St. BN2: Brig 4F **29**
Grove Villa BN1: Brig 1A **44** (3D **28**)
(off New England Rd.)
Guardian Ct. BN13: Salv 4A **20**
Guardswell Pl. BN25: Sea 4E **43**
Guernsey Rd. BN12: Fer 4B **32**
Guildbourne Cen., The 2D **34**
Guildford Cl. BN14: Worth 6A **20**
Guildford Rd. BN1: Brig 2B **44** (4D **28**)
Guildford Rd. BN14: Worth 1A **34**
Guildford St. BN1: Brig 2B **44** (4D **28**)
Guinness Ct. BN9: Newh 1G **41**
Guinness Trust Bungs. BN9: S Heig 1G **41**
Gundreda Rd. BN7: Lewes 3C **16**
Gwydyr Mans. BN3: Hove 4B **28**
Gym Wigan, London
Road, The 1D **44** (3E **29**)
(off London Rd.)
Gym Wigan, Madeira
Drive, The 6E **29**

H

Haddington Cl. BN3: Hove 4H **27**
Haddington St. BN3: Hove 3H **27**
Hadley Av. BN14: Broadw 3D **20**
Hadlow Cl. BN2: Brig 4H **29**
Hadlow Way BN15: Lan 4D **22**
Hadrian Av. BN42: S'wick 2A **26**
Haig Av. BN1: Brig 2H **13**
Haigh Cl. BN15: S Lan 4F **23**
Hailsham Av. BN2: Salt 1B **38**
Hailsham Rd. BN11: Worth 3H **33**
Hairpin Cft. BN10: Peace 3G **39**
Halewick Cl. BN15: Somp 2A **22**
Halewick La. BN15: Somp 2A **22**
Half Moon Ct. BN13: Salv 3H **19**
(off Half Moon La.)
Half Moon La. BN13: Salv 2H **19**
Half Moon Pde. BN13: Salv 3H **19**
(off Half Moon La.)
Halfway Station Volk's
Electric Railway 6G **29**
Halifax Dr. BN13: Durr 4E **19**
Halland Rd. BN2: Brig 4B **14**
Hall Av. BN14: Salv 3A **20**

Hall Cl. BN14: Salv 3A **20**
Hallett Rd. BN2: Brig 3H **29**
Hallyburton Rd. BN3: Hove 2D **26**
Halsbury Cl. BN11: Worth 1E **35**
Halsbury Rd. BN11: Worth 1F **35**
Hamble Ct. BN15: Somp 4H **21**
Hamble Gdns. BN13: Durr 3E **19**
Hamble Rd. BN15: Somp 4H **21**
Hamble Way BN13: Durr 3E **19**
Ham Bri. Trad. Est.
BN14: Broadw 6G **21**
Ham Bus. Cen. BN43: Shor S 3C **24**
Ham Cl. BN11: Worth 6G **21**
Hamfield Av. BN43: Shor S 2B **24**
Hamilton Cl. BN14: Broadw 5E **21**
Hamilton Cl. BN41: Ports 5A **10**
Hamilton Ct. BN12: Gor S 6F **19**
(off Drake Av.)
Hamilton Ct. BN2: Brig 5C **36**
Hamilton Ho. BN25: Sea 3D **42**
Hamilton Mans. BN3: Hove 5H **27**
Hamilton M. BN15: Somp 4A **22**
Hamilton Rd. BN1: Brig 2D **28**
Hamilton Rd. BN15: Lan 3B **22**
Ham La. BN7: Lewes 5F **17**
Hammond Cl. BN13: Durr 2G **19**
Hammond Dr. BN13: Durr 2G **19**
Hammy Cl. BN43: Shor S 2D **24**
Hammy La. BN43: Shor S 2D **24**
Hammy Way BN43: Shor S 2D **24**
Hampden Ct. BN11: Worth 6F **21**
Hampden Gdns. BN9: S Heig 1F **41**
Hampden Rd. BN2: Brig 3G **29**
Hampshire Ct. BN2: Brig 6F **29**
Hampstead Rd. BN1: Brig 1B **28**
Hampton Pl. BN1: Brig 5C **28**
Hampton St. BN1: Brig 5C **28**
Hampton Ter. BN1: Brig 3A **44** (4C **28**)
(off Upper Nth. St.)
Ham Rd. BN11: Worth 6G **21**
Ham Rd. BN43: Shor S 3B **24**
Hamsey Cl. BN2: Brig 5B **30**
Hamsey Cres. BN7: Lewes 3B **16**
Hamsey La. BN25: Sea 5H **43**
Hamsey Rd. BN2: Salt 3B **38**
Ham Way BN11: Worth 6G **21**
Hancock Way BN43: Shor B 4D **24**
HANGLETON 6A **18**
HANGLETON 6E **11**
Hangleton Cl. BN3: Hove 6D **10**
Hangleton Gdns. BN3: Hove 1D **26**
Hangleton Grange BN12: Fer 1A **32**
Hangleton La. BN12: Fer 1A **32**
Hangleton La. BN3: Hove 6C **10**
Hangleton La. BN41: Ports 6B **10**
(not continuous)
Hangleton Link Rd. BN41: Ports 5C **10**
Hangleton Mnr. Cl. BN3: Hove 6C **10**
Hangleton Rd. BN3: Hove 2D **26**
Hangleton Valley Dr. BN3: Hove 6C **10**
Hangleton Way BN3: Hove 1D **26**
Hanover Cl. BN25: Sea 1A **42**
Hanover Ct. BN14: Broadw 4C **20**
(off Rectory Gdns.)
Hanover Ct. BN2: Brig 3F **29**
Hanover Cres. BN2: Brig 3F **29**
Hanover Lofts BN2: Brig 4F **29**
(off Finsbury Rd.)
Hanover M. BN2: Brig 3F **29**
Hanover Pl. BN2: Brig 3F **29**
(off Lewes Rd.)
Hanover St. BN2: Brig 3F **29**
Hanover Ter. BN2: Brig 3F **29**
Hanson Rd. BN9: Newh 5D **40**
Happy Days Cvn. Pk.
BN15: S Lan South Lancing 5E **23**
Harbour Ct. BN42: S'wick 3H **25**
(off Whiterock Pl.)
HARBOUR HEIGHTS 6D **40**
Harbour Ho. BN43: Shor B 4D **24**
Harbour M. BN3: Hove 4C **26**
Harbour Vw. Cl. BN25: Sea 1A **42**
Harbour Vw. Cl. BN9: Newh 5D **40**
Harbour Vw. Rd. BN9: Newh 6D **40**
Harbour Way BN43: Shor B 4C **24**
Hardwicke Ho. BN25: Sea 5D **42**
(off Esplanade)
Hardwick Rd. BN3: Hove 5E **11**
Hardwick Way BN3: Hove 5E **11**
(not continuous)
Hardy Cl. BN43: Shor B 4B **24**
Harebell Dr. BN41: Ports 5A **10**
Harefield Av. BN13: Worth 6H **19**
Harewood Ct. BN3: Hove 4A **28**
Harfield Cl. BN9: Newh 1H **41**
Harison Rd. BN25: Sea 3F **43**
Harlech Cl. BN13: Durr 5D **18**

Harley Ct. BN11: Worth 2B **34**
Harmsworth Cres. BN3: Hove 5E **11**
Harpers Rd. BN9: Newh 4E **41**
Harriet Pl. BN43: Shor B 4D **24**
Harrington Ct. BN1: Brig 6C **12**
Harrington Mans. BN1: Brig 6C **12**
Harrington Pl. BN1: Brig 6F **13**
Harrington Rd. BN1: Brig 6C **12**
Harrington Vs. BN1: Brig 6D **12**
Harrison Ct. BN14: Broadw 5E **21**
Harrison Rd. BN14: Broadw 5E **21**
Harrow Cl. BN25: Sea 3F **43**
Harrow Rd. BN11: Worth 1B **34**
Hartfield Av. BN1: Brig 4E **13**
Hartfield Ct. BN3: Hove 4A **28**
Hartfield Rd. BN2: Salt 3B **38**
Hartfield Rd. BN25: Sea 4F **43**
Harting Cl. BN12: Gor S 6D **18**
Hartington Pl. BN2: Brig 2G **29**
Hartington Rd. BN2: Brig 2G **29**
Hartington Ter. BN2: Brig 2G **29**
Hartington Vs. BN3: Hove 2H **27**
Hartland Ho. BN11: Worth 2A **34**
(off Southview Dr.)
Hartley Ct. BN1: Brig 1B **44** (3D **28**)
(off Howard Pl.)
Harvard Cl. BN7: Lewes 2E **17**
Harvest Cl. BN10: Tels C 2F **39**
Harvey Rd. BN12: Gor S 3G **33**
Harvey's Way BN7: Lewes 4G **17**
Harwood Av. BN12: Gor S 6F **19**
Hastings Av. BN25: Sea 2H **43**
Hastings Ct. BN11: Worth 3A **34**
Hastings Rd. BN11: Worth 3A **34**
Hastings Rd. BN2: Brig 2G **29**
Hatfield Wlk. BN13: Durr 5F **19**
Hathaway M. BN11: Worth 1B **34**
Havelock Rd. BN1: Brig 6D **12**
Haven, The BN15: S Lan 6D **22**
Haven Brow BN25: Sea 3F **43**
Havenside BN43: Shor B 4A **24**
Haven Way BN9: Newh 5D **40**
Havercroft Bldgs. BN11: Worth 2D **34**
Hawkenbury Way BN7: Lewes 4C **16**
Hawkhurst Pl. BN1: Brig 2H **13**
Hawkhurst Rd. BN1: Brig 1H **13**
Hawkins Cl. BN43: Shor S 1F **25**
Hawkins Cres. BN43: Shor S 6F **9**
Hawkins Rd. BN43: Shor S 1F **25**
Hawth Cl. BN25: Sea 3B **42**
Hawth Cres. BN25: Sea 3B **42**
Hawth Gro. BN25: Sea 2B **42**
Hawth Hill BN25: Sea 2A **42**
Hawthorn Bank BN2: Brig 4B **14**
Hawthorn Cl. BN2: Salt 2A **38**
Hawthorn Cres. BN14: Broadw 4D **20**
Hawthorn Est. BN9: Newh 3G **41**
Hawthorn Gdns. BN14: Broadw 4D **20**
Hawthorn Ri. BN9: Newh 4D **40**
Hawthorn Rd. BN14: Broadw 4D **20**
Hawthorn Way BN41: Ports 5A **10**
Hawth Pk. Rd. BN25: Sea 3B **42**
Hawth Pl. BN25: Sea 3B **42**
Hawth Ri. BN25: Sea 2B **42**
Hawth Valley Ct. BN25: Sea 3B **42**
Hawth Way BN25: Sea 3C **42**
Haybourne Cl. BN2: Brig 3A **30**
Haybourne Rd. BN2: Brig 3A **30**
Hayes Cl. BN41: Ports 2C **26**
Hayley Rd. BN15: Lan 3D **22**
Hayling Gdns. BN13: High S 1G **19**
Hayling Ri. BN13: High S 1G **19**
Hayloft M. BN1: Brig 1E **29**
Haynes Rd. BN14: Worth 6A **20**
Haynes Way BN14: Worth 6B **20**
Hayton Ct. BN13: Durr 5D **18**
(off Chestnut Wlk.)
Hayward Rd. BN7: Lewes 2C **16**
Haywards Rd. BN1: Brig 2E **13**
Hazel Bank BN2: Brig 3F **29**
(off Bromley Rd.)
Hazel Cl. BN41: Ports 5C **10**
Hazel Cl. BN9: Newh 4D **40**
Hazeldene BN25: Sea 4G **43**
Hazeldene Meads BN1: Brig 5B **12**
Hazel Holt BN41: Ports 5H **9**
Hazelhurst Cres. BN14: Fin V 5D **6**
Hazelwood BN1: Brig 5B **12**
(off Curwen Pl.)
Hazelwood Cl. BN14: Broadw 5F **21**
Hazelwood Lodge BN15: S Lan 5D **22**
Hazelwood Trad. Est.
BN14: Broadw 5F **21**
Headborough BN15: S Lan 6C **22**
(off Alma St.)
Headborough Ct. BN15: S Lan 6C **22**
Headland Av. BN25: Sea 4F **43**

Lavender Ho. – Manor Ct.

Lavender Ho. BN2: Brig ... 6F 29
... (off Lavender St.)
Lavender St. BN2: Brig ... 6F 29
Lavington Rd. BN14: Worth ... 4B 20
Lavinia Ct. BN12: Gor S ... 1E 33
Law Courts Brighton ... 5F 29
Law Courts Worthing ... 2D 34
Lawes Av. BN9: Newh ... 4E 41
Lawns, The BN15: Somp ... 3H 21
Lawrence Rd. BN3: Hove ... 3F 27
Laylands Ct. BN41: Ports ... 3A 26
... (off Chapel Rd.)
Laylands Rd. BN41: Ports ... 3A 26
Leach Ct. BN2: Brig ... 5G 29
Leahurst Ct. BN1: Brig ... 5B 12
Leahurst Ct. Rd. BN1: Brig ... 5B 12
Lea Rd. BN10: Peace ... 4F 39
Leas, The BN10: Peace ... 6B 40
Leconfield Rd. BN15: Lan ... 5A 22
Lee Bank BN2: Brig ... 4F 29
... (off Grove Hill)
Lee Ct. BN9: Newh ... 3E 41
... (off Elphick Rd.)
Leeds Cl. BN13: Durr ... 5D 18
Lee Rd. BN7: Lewes ... 3D 16
Lees, The BN2: Brig ... 4A 36
Leeward Cl. BN13: W Tar ... 5H 19
Leeward Rd. BN13: W Tar ... 5H 19
Lee Way BN9: Newh ... 3E 41
Legacy, The BN3: Hove ... 3A 28
Leicester Rd. BN7: Lewes ... 4D 16
Leicester St. BN2: Brig ... 5F 29
Leicester Vs. BN3: Hove ... 3D 26
Leigh Rd. BN14: Broadw ... 4D 20
Leighside Ho. BN7: Lewes ... 4F 17
... (off Court Rd.)
Leighton Av. BN14: Broadw ... 4E 21
Leighton Rd. BN3: Hove ... 2G 27
Lenham Av. BN2: Salt ... 3H 37
Lenham Rd. E. BN2: Rott ... 3H 37
Lenham Rd. E. BN2: Salt ... 3H 37
Lenham Rd. W. BN2: Rott ... 3G 37
Lenhurst Way BN13: Worth ... 6H 19
Lennox M. BN11: Worth ... 1D 34
... (off Chapel Rd.)
Lennox Rd. BN11: Worth ... 1D 34
Lennox Rd. BN3: Hove ... 2F 27
Lennox Rd. BN43: Shor S ... 2D 24
Lennox St. BN2: Brig ... 5F 29
Leopold Rd. BN1: Brig ... 3A 44 (4D 28)
Lesser Foxholes BN43: Shor S ... 1H 23
Letchworth Cl. BN12: Fer ... 3A 32
Level, The ... 3F 29
LEWES ... 4F 17
Lewes Athletics Track ... 5G 17
Lewes Bus. Cen. &
Waterside Cen. BN7: Lewes ... 3E 17
Lewes Bus Station ... 4F 17
Lewes Castle ... 4E 17
Lewes Cl. BN2: Salt ... 3C 38
Lewes Cres. BN2: Brig ... 4A 36
... (not continuous)
Lewes FC ... 5F 17
Lewes Golf Course ... 5H 17
Lewes Leisure Cen. ... 5G 17
Lewes Little Theatre ... 4F 17
Lewes Martyrs' Memorial ... 4G 17
Lewes M. BN2: Brig ... 4A 36
Lewes Railway Land Local
Nature Reserve ... 5G 17
Lewes Rd. BN1: Brig ... 4A 14
Lewes Rd. BN2: Brig ... 4F 29
Lewes Rd. BN9: Newh ... 2D 40
Lewes Southern By-Pass
BN7: Lewes ... 6B 16
Lewes Station (Rail) ... 5F 17
Lewes St. BN2: Brig ... 4F 29
Lewes Tourist Info. Cen. ... 4F 17
LEWES VICTORIA HOSPITAL ... 4C 16
Lewin Cl. BN15: Lan ... 3D 22
Lewis Cl. BN9: Newh ... 1H 41
Lewis Ct. BN13: Durr ... 5D 18
Lewis Rd. BN15: N Lan ... 2B 22
Lewis's Bldgs. BN1: Brig ... 4B 44 (5D 28)
... (off Ship St.)
Lewry Cl. BN9: Newh ... 4D 40
Lexden Ct. BN25: Sea ... 3F 43
Lexden Dr. BN25: Sea ... 2E 43
Lexden Rd. BN25: Sea ... 1E 43
Leybourne Cl. BN2: Brig ... 1C 30
Leybourne Pde. BN2: Brig ... 1C 30
... (off Leybourne Rd.)
Leybourne Rd. BN2: Brig ... 6C 14
Library Pl. BN11: Worth ... 2E 35
Library Rd. BN1: Falm ... 1D 14
Lichfield Ct. BN11: Worth ... 3A 34
Lichfield Ct. BN2: Brig ... 5B 30
Lido Worthing, The ... 3D 34
Lilac Cl. BN13: Durr ... 5D 18
Lilac Ct. BN1: Brig ... 4B 12
Lilac Way BN43: Shor S ... 1D 24
Lily Gdns. BN13: Durr ... 3H 19
Limbrick Cl. BN12: Gor S ... 1E 33
Limbrick Cnr. BN12: Gor S ... 6E 19
Limbrick La. BN12: Gor S ... 6E 19
... (not continuous)
Limbrick Way BN12: Gor S ... 6D 18
Lime Rd. BN14: Fin ... 2C 6
Limes, The BN14: Fin ... 1C 6
Limes, The BN2: Brig ... 2F 29
... (off Bromley Rd.)
Lime Tree Av. BN14: Fin V ... 5D 6
Limney Rd. BN2: Brig ... 3A 30
Lincett Av. BN13: Worth ... 6H 19
Lincett Ct. BN13: Worth ... 6H 19
Lincett Dr. BN13: Worth ... 1H 33
Linchmere BN2: Brig ... 3B 30
Linchmere Av. BN2: Salt ... 3A 38
Lincoln Av. BN10: Peace ... 5E 39
Lincoln Av. Sth. BN10: Peace ... 5E 39
Lincoln Cotts. BN2: Brig ... 4F 29
Lincoln Ct. BN10: Peace ... 5E 39
Lincoln Ct. BN15: Lan ... 6C 22
Lincoln Ct. BN3: Hove ... 2A 28
Lincoln Rd. BN13: Worth ... 6H 19
Lincoln Rd. BN41: Ports ... 3B 26
Lincoln St. BN2: Brig ... 4F 29
Linden Lodge BN11: Worth ... 2C 34
... (off Tennyson Rd.)
Lindens, The BN2: Brig ... 3F 29
... (off Canterbury Dr.)
Lindfield BN41: Ports ... 1B 26
... (off Windlesham Cl.)
Lindfield Av. BN25: Sea ... 5H 43
Lindfield Cl. BN2: Salt ... 2H 37
Lindfield Ct. BN1: Brig ... 1G 29
... (off The Crestway)
Lindum Rd. BN13: W Tar ... 5H 19
Lindum Way BN13: Worth ... 5H 19
Linemans Vw. BN43: Shor S ... 3A 24
... (off Broad Reach)
Lingfield Cl. BN13: Salv ... 4H 19
Link Pl. BN1: Brig ... 1F 29
Links Av. BN10: Peace ... 4C 40
Links Cl. BN25: Sea ... 4F 43
Links Cl. BN41: Ports ... 2C 26
Links Rd. BN14: Fin V ... 2A 20
Links Rd. BN15: Lan ... 4D 22
Links Rd. BN25: Sea ... 5F 43
Links Rd. BN41: Ports ... 2C 26
Linkway, The BN1: Brig ... 1F 29
Linkway, The BN11: Worth ... 1C 34
Linthouse Cl. BN10: Peace ... 2H 39
Linton Rd. BN3: Hove ... 2F 27
Lion M. BN3: Hove ... 3F 27
Lions Ct. BN2: Brig ... 5A 30
Lions Dene BN1: Brig ... 4B 12
Lions Gdns. BN1: Brig ... 6B 12
Lions Ga. BN3: Hove ... 1E 27
Lions Pl. BN25: Sea ... 5E 43
Liphook Cl. BN1: Brig ... 1G 29
Lisher Rd. BN15: Lan ... 3D 22
Litlington Ct. BN25: Sea ... 3B 42
Little Cres. BN2: Rott ... 3G 37
Little Dr. BN12: Fer ... 3A 32
Lit. Drove BN44: Bramb ... 4C 4
Little E. St. BN1: Brig ... 6C 44 (6E 29)
Little E. St. BN7: Lewes ... 4F 17
Lit. Gables BN13: Durr ... 4H 19
Lit. George St. BN2: Brig ... 5D 44 (5E 29)
Littlehampton Rd. BN12: Fer ... 6D 18
Littlehampton Rd. BN12: Gor S ... 6D 18
Littlehampton Rd. BN13: Gor S ... 6D 18
Littlehampton Rd. BN13: Salv ... 6D 18
Littlehampton Rd. BN13: Worth ... 6D 18
Lit. High St. BN11: Worth ... 1D 34
Lit. High St. BN43: Shor S ... 3A 24
Lit. Mead BN12: Gor S ... 2E 33
... (off Marlborough Rd.)
Lit. Paddocks BN12: Fer ... 3A 32
Lit. Paddocks Ho. BN12: Fer ... 3B 32
... (off Lit. Paddocks Way)
Lit. Paddocks Way BN12: Fer ... 3B 32
Lit. Pembrokes BN11: Worth ... 1A 34
Little Pl. La. BN25: Sea ... 4D 42
... (off Place La.)
Lit. Preston St. BN1: Brig ... 5C 28
Littlestone Rd. BN13: Durr ... 4G 19
Lit. Twitten
Recreation Ground ... 2B 32
Lit. Western St. BN1: Brig ... 5B 28
Lit. Western St.
BN3: Brig ... 4B 44 (5B 28)
Littleworth Cl. BN2: W'dean ... 3H 31
Liverpool Bldgs. BN11: Worth ... 2D 34
... (off Liverpool Rd.)
Liverpool Gdns. BN11: Worth ... 2D 34
Liverpool Rd. BN11: Worth ... 2D 34
Liverpool Ter. BN11: Worth ... 2D 34
Livesay Cres. BN14: Broadw ... 6D 20
Livingstone Ho. BN3: Hove ... 3H 27
Livingstone Rd. BN3: Hove ... 3H 27
Livingstone St. BN2: Brig ... 5H 29
LivingWell Health
Club Brighton ... 5A 44 (5D 28)
... (off Kings Rd.)
Llandaff Ct. BN11: Worth ... 2A 34
Lloyd Cl. BN3: Hove ... 1A 28
Lloyd Rd. BN3: Hove ... 2A 28
Locks Ct. BN42: S'wick ... 3G 25
Locks Cres. BN41: Ports ... 2B 26
Locks Hill BN41: Ports ... 1B 26
Lockwood Cl. BN2: W'dean ... 3G 31
Lockwood Cres. BN2: W'dean ... 2G 31
Loddon Cl. BN13: Durr ... 2E 19
Loder Gdns. BN14: Broadw ... 5C 20
Loder Pl. BN1: Brig ... 6D 12
Loder Rd. BN1: Brig ... 6D 12
Lodge, The BN2: Brig ... 2F 29
Lodge Cl. BN41: Ports ... 6H 9
Lodge Cl. BN7: Lewes ... 5C 16
Lodge Ct. BN43: Shor S ... 1A 24
Lodsworth BN2: Brig ... 2B 30
Lodsworth Cl. BN2: Brig ... 3A 30
Lomond Av. BN1: Brig ... 1F 13
London Rd. BN1: Brig
Coolwater Pk. ... 4B 12
London Rd. BN1: Brig
Mill Rd. Rdbt. ... 1B 12
London Rd. BN1: Brig
Viaduct Rd. ... 3E 29
London Road Station
(Rail) Brighton ... 2E 29
London St. BN11: Worth ... 1C 34
London Ter. BN1: Brig ... 3E 29
Loney Ct. BN43: Shor S ... 2E 25
Longcroft BN43: Shor S ... 3A 24
Longfellow Rd. BN11: Worth ... 1B 34
Long Furlong BN13: Clap ... 2A 18
Long Furlong BN13: Fin ... 2A 18
Long Furlong BN13: Pat ... 2A 18
Long Furlong BN14: Fin ... 3A 6
Longhill Cl. BN2: O'dean ... 6G 31
Longhill Rd. BN2: O'dean ... 6F 31
Longlands BN14: Char D ... 2D 20
Longlands Glade BN14: Char D ... 2D 20
Longlands Gro. BN14: Char D ... 2D 20
Longlands Spinney
BN14: Char D ... 2D 20
Longley Ind. Est. BN1: Brig ... 3E 29
Long Mdw. BN14: Fin V ... 4D 6
Longridge Av. BN2: Salt ... 4A 38
Looes Barn Cl. BN2: Salt ... 1B 38
Lookout, The BN10: Peace ... 1G 39
Loose La. BN15: Somp ... 5G 21
Lords, The BN25: Sea ... 1D 42
Loriners Ct. BN3: Hove ... 2D 26
Lorna Rd. BN3: Hove ... 3A 28
Lorne Rd. BN1: Brig ... 2E 29
Lorne Vs. BN1: Brig ... 6C 12
Lorraine Ct. BN3: Hove
Davigdor Rd. ... 3C 28
... (off Davigdor Rd.)
Lorraine Ct. BN3: Hove Osborne Vs. 4H 27
Lorraine Rd. BN9: Newh ... 4F 41
Lotts La. BN15: Somp ... 4A 22
Louvain Gdns. BN10: Tels C ... 2F 39
Lovegrove Ct. BN3: Hove ... 2E 27
Love La. BN7: Lewes ... 5C 16
Lover's Wlk. BN1: Brig ... 2D 28
Lover's Wlk. Cotts. BN1: Brig ... 2D 28
Lovett Ct. BN12: Gor S ... 6E 19
Lwr. Beach Rd. BN43: Shor B ... 4B 24
LOWER BEVENDEAN ... 1B 30
Lwr. Bevendean Av. BN2: Brig ... 1A 30
Lwr. Chalvington Pl. BN2: Brig ... 5A 30
LOWER COKEHAM ... 5A 22
Lower Dr. BN25: Sea ... 2E 43
Lower Dr. BN42: S'wick ... 1G 25
Lower Mkt. St. BN3: Hove ... 5B 28
Lower Pl. BN9: Newh ... 4E 41
Lwr. Rock Gdns. BN2: Brig ... 6F 29
Lwr. Stoneham BN8: Lewes ... 1G 17
Lowther Rd. BN1: Brig ... 6E 13
Lowther Rd. BN13: Durr ... 3H 19
Loxley Gdns. BN14: Worth ... 6C 20
Loxwood Av. BN14: Worth ... 4B 20
Loyal Pde. BN1: Brig ... 3A 12
Lucerne Cl. BN41: Ports ... 1B 26
Lucerne Rd. BN1: Brig ... 1D 28
Lucinda Way BN25: Sea ... 2E 43
Lucraft Rd. BN2: Brig ... 3B 14
Ludlow Ct. BN11: Worth ... 2F 35
Ludlow Ri. BN2: Brig ... 1C 30
Lulham Cl. BN10: Tels C ... 2F 39
Lullington Av. BN3: Hove ... 2F 27
Lullington Cl. BN25: Sea ... 5G 43
Lureland Ct. BN10: Peace ... 6G 39
Lustrells Cl. BN2: Salt ... 2H 37
Lustrells Cres. BN2: Salt ... 2H 37
Lustrells Rd. BN2: Rott ... 2G 37
Lustrells Va. BN2: Salt ... 2H 37
Luther M. BN2: Brig ... 3G 29
Luther St. BN2: Brig ... 3G 29
Lychpole Wlk. BN12: Gor S ... 6D 18
Lyminster Av. BN1: Brig ... 4E 13
Lynchet Cl. BN1: Brig ... 6G 13
Lynchet Down BN1: Brig ... 6G 13
Lynchets, The BN7: Lewes ... 2G 17
Lynchets Cres. BN3: Hove ... 5D 10
Lynchette, The BN43: Shor S ... 1B 24
Lynchet Wlk. BN1: Brig ... 6G 13
Lynchmere Av. BN15: N Lan ... 2B 22
Lynden Ct. BN1: Brig ... 6C 12
Lyndhurst Cnr. BN3: Hove ... 3B 28
... (off Lyndhurst Rd.)
Lyndhurst Ct. BN3: Hove ... 3B 28
Lyndhurst Rd. BN11: Worth ... 2E 35
Lyndhurst Rd. BN3: Hove ... 3B 28
Lyn Rd. BN13: Durr ... 4E 19
Lynton St. BN2: Brig ... 3G 29
Lynwood Rd. BN2: Salt ... 4A 38
Lyon Cl. BN3: Hove ... 3B 28
Lyons Way BN14: Char D ... 2E 21

M

McKerchar Cl. BN15: Lan ... 3D 22
Mackie Av. BN1: Brig ... 2D 12
McKinlay Way BN9: Newh ... 3G 41
McNair Ct. BN3: Hove ... 3E 27
McWilliam Rd. BN2: W'dean ... 1E 31
Madehurst Cl. BN2: Brig ... 5H 29
Madeira Av. BN11: Worth ... 1E 35
Madeira Colonnade BN2: Brig ... 6F 29
... (off Madeira Dr.)
Madeira Dr. BN2: Brig ... 6D 44 (6F 29)
Madeira Pl. BN2: Brig ... 6F 29
Mafeking Rd. BN2: Brig ... 1G 29
Magistrates' Court Brighton ... 5F 29
Magistrates' Court Worthing ... 2D 34
Magnolia Cl. BN13: Durr ... 5D 18
Magnus Pl. BN43: Shor S ... 3A 24
... (off Broad Reach)
Magpie Way BN41: Ports ... 4H 9
Maines Farm Rd. BN44: Up B ... 5G 5
Mainstone Rd. BN3: Hove ... 3F 27
Major Cl. BN1: Brig ... 1F 29
Malcolm Cl. BN12: Fer ... 3A 32
Maldon Rd. BN1: Brig ... 6B 12
Malines Av. BN10: Peace ... 5E 39
Malines Av. Sth. BN10: Peace ... 5E 39
Mallett Cl. BN25: Sea ... 5D 42
MALLING ... 2D 16
Malling Cl. BN7: Lewes ... 2F 17
Malling Down BN7: Lewes ... 2G 17
Malling Down ... 3H 17
Malling Hill BN7: Lewes ... 2G 17
Malling Ind. Est. BN7: Lewes ... 3F 17
Malling St. BN7: Lewes ... 4G 17
Mallory Rd. BN3: Hove ... 6A 12
Malthouse, The BN7: Lewes ... 5E 17
... (off Cluny St.)
Malthouse Cl. BN15: Somp ... 3H 21
Malthouse Cotts. BN12: Gor S ... 2E 33
Malthouse Ct. BN2: Brig ... 5F 29
Malthouse La. BN2: Brig ... 4F 29
Malthouse Trad. Est.
BN43: Shor S ... 3D 24
Maltings Barn, The BN7: Lewes ... 4G 17
... (off Foundry La.)
Maltings Grn. BN44: Stey ... 4C 4
... (off Castle La.)
Malvern Cl. BN11: Worth ... 1H 35
Malvern St. BN3: Hove ... 3H 27
Manchester St. BN2: Brig ... 6D 44 (6E 29)
Mandalay Ct. BN1: Brig ... 4B 12
Manhattan Ct. BN1: Brig ... 4B 12
... (off Tongdean La.)
Manitoba Way BN13: Durr ... 4E 19
Mannings BN43: Shor S ... 3B 24
Manor, The BN11: Worth ... 2B 34
Manor Cl. BN11: Worth ... 2B 34
Manor Cl. BN15: Lan ... 3D 22
Manor Cl. BN2: Brig ... 5A 30
Manor Cl. BN25: Sea ... 4G 43
Manor Cl. BN42: S'wick ... 2A 26
Manor Ct. BN11: Worth ... 3B 34

A-Z Brighton & Worthing 57

Oakapple Rd. – Pelham Rd.

O

Oakapple Rd. BN42: S'wick 6G 9
Oak Cl. BN1: Brig 5C 12
Oak Cl. BN13: High S 1G 19
Oakdene Av. BN41: Ports 5G 9
Oakdene Cl. BN41: Ports 5H 9
Oakdene Cres. BN41: Ports 5G 9
Oakdene Gdns. BN41: Ports 5G 9
Oakdene Ri. BN41: Ports 4G 9
Oakdene Way BN41: Ports 4G 9
Oakendene BN2: Brig 4B 14
Oak Est. BN9: Newh 2F 41
Oakland Ct. BN11: Worth 2C 34
Oakland Ct. BN12: Gor S 2C 32
Oakland Ct. BN43: Shor S 3B 24
Oaklands BN12: Fer 2B 32
Oaklands BN15: S Lan 5C 22
Oaklands Av. BN2: Salt 3A 38
Oaklands Bus. Cen. BN11: Worth 1H 33
Oakleigh Cl. BN11: Worth 6G 21
Oakleigh Ct. BN11: Worth 6G 21
Oakleigh Rd. BN11: Worth 6G 21
Oakley Ho. BN2: Brig 5F 29
(off Leicester St.)
Ocean Bldg., The
BN1: Brig 3B 44 (4D 28)
(off Queens Rd.)
Ocean Cl. BN12: Fer 4A 32
Ocean Dr. BN12: Fer 4A 32
Ocean Pde. BN12: Fer 4A 32
Ocean Reach BN2: Rott 3G 37
Octagon, The BN2: Brig 5B 36
Odeon Cinema Brighton 5A 44 (5D 28)
Offham Cl. BN25: Sea 2E 43
Offham Ct. BN25: Sea 3B 42
Offham Ter. BN7: Lewes 4E 17
(off White Hill)
OFFINGTON 4A 20
Offington Av. BN14: Salv 3A 20
OFFINGTON CNR. 2A 20
Offington Ct. BN14: Salv 4C 20
Offington Dr. BN14: Salv 3A 20
Offington Gdns. BN14: Salv 4A 20
Offington La. BN14: Salv 4A 20
Old Barn Way BN42: S'wick 3A 26
Old Boat Wlk. BN1: Brig 1F 13
Oldbury Row BN1: Brig 1F 29
Old Church Hall, The BN1: Brig 2E 29
Old Coastguard Cotts. BN9: Newh 5F 41
Old College Ho. BN2: Brig 3F 29
(off Malthouse La.)
Old Cotts. BN14: Fin 1C 6
Old Ct. Cl. BN1: Brig 4D 12
Old Dairy Cl. BN42: S'wick 2G 25
Olde Pl. M. BN2: Rott 3F 37
Old Farm Ct. BN43: Shor S 4G 23
Old Farm Rd. BN1: Brig 3D 12
Oldfield Cres. BN42: S'wick 3F 25
Old Fort Rd. BN43: Shor B 4B 24
Old London Rd. BN1: Brig 2C 12
Old Malling Way BN7: Lewes 2E 17
Old Mkt. Sq. BN44: Stey 3D 4
(off Station Rd.)
Old Mill Cl. BN1: Brig 3C 12
Old Mill Cl. BN41: Ports 3A 26
(off Chapel Rd.)
Old Mill Ct. BN11: Worth 2A 34
Old Mill M. BN1: Brig 2C 28
Old Nursery Cl. BN25: Sea 2G 43
Old Parish La. BN2: W'dean 2E 31
Old Patcham M. BN1: Brig 2C 12
Old Pl. Ct. BN2: Rott 3F 37
(off High St.)
Old Police Cells Mus. 5C 44 (5E 29)
Old Racecourse, The BN7: Off 2A 16
Old Rectory Gdns. BN42: S'wick 2F 25
Old Refectory, The BN43: Shor S 1D 24
Old Salts Farm Rd. BN15: Lan 4D 22
Old Salts Farm Rd. BN15: S Lan 4D 22
Old School Pl. BN3: Hove 1D 26
OLD SHOREHAM 2H 23
Old Shoreham Rd. BN1: Brig 3C 28
Old Shoreham Rd. BN15: N Lan 2D 22
Old Shoreham Rd. BN15: Shor S 2D 22
Old Shoreham Rd. BN3: Hove 2D 26
Old Shoreham Rd. BN41: Ports 2A 26
Old Shoreham Rd. BN42: S'wick 1F 25
Old Shoreham Rd. BN43: Shor S 2H 23
Old Shoreham Toll Bridge 1H 23
Old Stable Block, The BN1: Stan 1B 14
Old Steine BN1: Brig 5D 44 (5E 29)
Old Steine Gdns. 6D 44 (6E 29)
(off Old Steine)
Old Stocks BN14: Fin 2C 6
(off Nepcote La.)
Old Tree Pde. BN25: Sea 4D 42
(off Broad St.)
Old Viaduct Ct. BN2: Brig 2G 29
Oliver Ho. BN3: Hove 5H 27
Olive Rd. BN3: Hove 2D 26
Olivier Cl. BN2: Brig 5G 29
Onslow Cvn. Pk. BN12: Fer 2A 32
Onslow Ct. BN11: Worth 1H 35
Onslow Dr. BN12: Fer 2A 32
Onslow Pde. BN12: Fer 2B 32
Onslow Rd. BN3: Hove 1A 28
Ontario Cl. BN13: Durr 4E 19
Ontario Gdns. BN13: Durr 4E 19
Open Mkt., The
BN1: Brig 1D 44 (3E 29)
Ophir Rd. BN11: Worth 1G 35
Orange Row BN1: Brig 4C 44 (5E 29)
Orchard, The BN43: Shor S 1D 24
Orchard Av. BN14: Worth 5A 20
Orchard Av. BN15: Lan 4C 22
Orchard Av. BN3: Hove 1G 27
Orchard Cl. BN12: Fer 1A 32
Orchard Cl. BN14: Worth 5B 20
Orchard Cl. BN42: S'wick 2H 25
Orchard Cl. BN43: Shor S 2A 24
Orchard Ct. BN11: Worth 1A 34
(off Downview Rd.)
Orchard Gdns. BN3: Hove 1G 27
Orchard Ho. BN15: Lan 4C 22
Orchard Ho. BN3: Hove 1H 27
Orchard M. BN9: Newh 1G 41
Orchard Rd. BN3: Hove 1G 27
Orchard Rd. BN7: Lewes 3G 17
Orchards, The BN2: Brig 5A 14
(off Moulsecoomb Way)
Orchard Valley Ct. BN7: Lewes 3G 17
Orchard Wlk. BN1: Brig 3E 29
Orchard Way BN15: Lan 3C 22
Orchid Vw. BN1: Brig 2G 13
Oriental Pl. BN1: Brig 5C 28
Orient Rd. BN15: S Lan 5F 23
Orion BN2: Brig 6B 36
Orkney Ct. BN13: Durr 5D 18
Orme Cl. BN15: Lan 6B 22
Orme Rd. BN11: Worth 1C 34
Ormonde Way BN43: Shor B 4H 23
Orpen Rd. BN3: Hove 1B 28
Osborne Cl. BN15: Somp 4A 22
Osborne Dr. BN15: Somp 4A 22
Osborne Rd. BN1: Brig 6D 12
Osborne Vs. BN3: Hove 4H 27
Osbourne Ct. BN43: Shor S 2E 25
Osmonde Cl. BN14: Broadw 6C 20
Osmonde Ct. BN14: Broadw 6C 20
Osmond Gdns. BN3: Hove 3C 28
(off Osmond Rd.)
Osmond Rd. BN3: Hove 3C 28
Osprey Ho. BN1: Brig 5C 28
(off Sillwood Pl.)
Osprey Wlk. BN43: Shor B 4D 24
Otium Leisure Club
Brighton 6C 44 (6E 29)
(off Kings Rd.)
Ousedale Cl. BN7: Lewes 4D 16
Ouse Estuary Nature Reserve 4H 41
Outlook Av. BN10: Peace 5B 40
Oval, The BN13: W Tar 5A 20
Oval, The BN14: Fin 1C 6
Oval Cl. BN10: Peace 2G 39
Oval Waye BN12: Fer 4A 32
Overdown Ri. BN41: Ports 4H 9
Overhill BN42: S'wick 6G 9
Overhill Dr. BN1: Brig 3C 12
Overhill Gdns. BN1: Brig 3C 12
Overhill Way BN1: Brig 2C 12
Overmead BN43: Shor S 2A 24
Over St. BN1: Brig 3C 44 (4E 29)
Overton Rd. BN13: Worth 1G 33
OVINGDEAN 6F 31
Ovingdean Cl. BN2: O'dean 5F 31
Ovingdean Rd. BN2: O'dean 6F 31
Oxen Av. BN43: Shor S 2B 24
Oxford Ct. BN1: Brig 1D 44 (3E 29)
Oxford M. BN3: Hove 3A 28
Oxford Pl. BN1: Brig 1D 44 (3E 29)
Oxford Rd. BN11: Worth 1C 34
Oxford St. BN1: Brig 1D 44 (3E 29)
Oxford Ter. BN44: Stey 3C 4
(off Jarvis La.)
Oxon Ct. BN43: Shor S 2B 24

P

Pacific Ct. BN43: Shor B 4B 24
Pacific Hgts. BN2: Salt 3A 38
(off Suez Way)
Paddock, The BN3: Hove 1A 28
Paddock, The BN43: Shor S 1H 23
Paddock Cl. BN14: Worth 6B 20
(off Haynes Rd.)
Paddock Ct. BN41: Ports 5H 9
Paddock Fld. BN1: Falm 3D 14
Paddock La. BN7: Lewes 4E 17
Paddock Rd. BN7: Lewes 4E 17
Paddocks, The BN15: S Lan 5D 22
Paddocks, The BN44: Up B 3G 5
Paddock Ter. BN7: Lewes 4E 17
(off New Rd.)
Paddock Way BN14: Fin 2C 6
Padua Ho. BN2: W'dean 2H 31
Padua Ho. Flats BN2: W'dean 2G 31
Pages La. BN11: Worth 6G 21
Paine's Twitten BN7: Lewes 5E 17
(off Stewards Inn La.)
Palace M. BN1: Brig 1A 44 (3D 28)
(off Bath St.)
Palace of Fun 6D 44 (6E 29)
Palace Pl. BN1: Brig 5D 44 (5E 29)
Palatine Rd. BN12: Gor S 6E 19
Pallant, The BN12: Gor S 6D 18
Palm Ct. BN13: Durr 3G 19
Palm Ct. BN3: Hove 4B 28
Palm Dr. BN2: Brig 5B 36
Palmeira Av. BN3: Hove 4A 28
Palmeira Ct. BN3: Hove 5A 28
(not continuous)
Palmeira Grande BN3: Hove 4B 28
(off Holland Rd.)
Palmeira Ho. BN3: Hove 3B 28
Palmeira Mans. BN3: Hove 4A 28
(off Church Rd.)
Palmeira Pl. BN3: Hove 3B 28
Palmeira Sq. BN3: Hove 5A 28
(not continuous)
Palmerston Av. BN12: Gor S 2E 33
Palmerston Rd. BN9: Newh 2H 41
Palmers Way BN13: High S 1F 19
Pankhurst Av. BN2: Brig 4G 29
Panorama Ho. BN41: Ports 3C 26
Pantiles, The BN12: Fer 3A 32
Parade, The BN1: Brig 4A 12
Parade, The BN3: Hove 6E 11
Paradise Pk. 2F 41
Parham Cl. BN14: Fin V 1H 19
Parham Cl. BN2: Brig 5H 29
Parham Ct. BN11: Worth 2A 34
Parham Ho. BN3: Hove 3B 28
(off Chatsworth Sq.)
Parham Rd. BN14: Fin V 1H 19
Park, The BN2: Rott 3G 37
Park & Ride Withdean 4B 12
Park Av. BN10: Tels C 4E 39
Park Av. BN11: Worth 1B 34
Park Av. BN3: Hove 3E 27
Park Av. BN43: Shor S 2C 24
Park Cl. BN1: Brig Old London Rd. 2C 12
Park Cl. BN1: Brig Park Rd. 3A 14
Park Cl. BN14: Salv 3A 20
Park Cl. BN3: Hove 5E 11
Park Cl. BN41: Ports 1B 26
Park Ct. BN1: Brig Old London Rd. 2C 12
Park Ct. BN1: Brig Preston Pk. Av. 1D 28
Park Ct. BN10: Peace 5F 39
(off Roderick Av.)
Park Ct. BN2: Brig 4G 29
(off Southover St.)
Park Ct. BN3: Hove 3B 28
(off Davigdor Rd.)
Park Cres. BN11: Worth 2C 34
Park Cres. BN2: Brig 3F 29
Park Cres. BN2: Rott 3F 37
(not continuous)
Park Cres. BN41: Ports 2A 26
Park Cres. Pl. BN2: Brig 3F 29
Park Cres. Rd. BN2: Brig 3F 29
Park Cres. Ter. BN2: Brig 3F 29
Park Dr. BN12: Fer 2B 32
Park Dr. BN9: Newh 1H 41
Park Dr. Cl. BN9: Newh 1H 41
Parker Ct. BN41: Ports 6B 10
Parkfield Ct. BN13: W Tar 6A 20
Parkfield Rd. BN13: W Tar 6A 20
Park Ga. BN3: Hove 4B 28
Pk. Hill BN2: Brig 5F 29
Park Ho. BN11: Worth 1H 35
Park Ho. BN3: Hove 1H 27
Parkland Bus. Cen. BN15: Lan 6B 22
Parklands BN43: Shor S 2E 25
Parklands Av. BN12: Gor S 3F 33
Parklands Ct. BN12: Gor S 2F 33
Park La. BN42: S'wick 3F 25
Pk. Lodge BN11: Worth 2E 35
Pk. Lodge BN3: Hove 2B 28
Park Mnr. BN1: Brig 5B 12
Parkmead BN2: Brig 3F 29
Park M., The BN1: Brig 4B 12
(off London Rd.)
Parkmore Ter. BN1: Brig 2D 28
Park Ri. BN3: Hove 5E 11
Park Rd. BN1: Brig 3A 14
Park Rd. BN10: Peace 5B 40
Park Rd. BN11: Worth 1E 35
Park Rd. BN2: Rott 3F 37
Park Rd. BN25: Sea 4C 42
Park Rd. BN43: Shor S 2C 24
Park Rd. BN7: Lewes 4E 17
Park Rd. Ter. BN2: Brig 5F 29
Pk. Royal BN1: Brig 4C 28
Parks, The BN41: Ports 5B 10
Parkside BN11: Worth 1E 35
Parkside BN43: Shor S 1C 24
Parkside Rd. BN25: Sea 3E 43
Park Sq. BN2: Brig 5B 36
Park St. BN1: Falm 1E 15
(not continuous)
Park St. BN2: Brig 5F 29
Parks Vw. BN2: Brig 5F 29
(off Up. Park Pl.)
Park Ter. BN2: Rott 3F 37
(off West St.)
Park Vw. BN1: Brig 2C 28
Park Vw. BN2: Brig 4G 29
Park Vw. Cl. BN10: Tels C 3E 39
Park Vw. Ri. BN10: Tels C 4E 39
Park Vw. Rd. BN3: Hove 1H 27
Park Vw. Ter. BN1: Brig 2C 28
(off Stanford Rd.)
Park Village, The BN1: Falm 1C 14
Park Village Rd. BN1: Falm 1C 14
Park Way BN42: S'wick 2H 25
Park Way Cl. BN42: S'wick 2H 25
Parnell Ct. BN3: Hove 4H 27
Parochial M. BN2: Brig 5D 44 (5E 29)
(off Prince's St.)
Parochial Ter. BN2: Brig 5D 44 (5E 29)
(off Steine Gdns.)
Pashley Ct. BN43: Shor S 3B 24
Paston Pl. BN2: Brig 6H 29
PATCHAM 2C 12
Patcham By-Pass BN1: Brig 2C 12
Patcham Grange BN1: Brig 3C 12
Patchdean BN1: Brig 3D 12
(not continuous)
PATCHING 1A 18
Patching Cl. BN12: Gor S 6D 18
Patching Lodge BN2: Brig 5G 29
Patricia Av. BN12: Gor S 3F 33
Patricia Cl. BN12: Gor S 3F 33
Patterson's Wlk. BN12: Fer 4A 32
Pavilion Bldgs.
BN1: Brig 5C 44 (5E 29)
Pavilion Ct. BN2: Brig 4D 44 (5E 29)
(off Grand Pde. M.)
Pavilion Ct. BN3: Hove 1A 44 (3C 28)
(off Goldsmid Rd.)
Pavilion M. BN1: Brig 4C 44 (5E 29)
Pavilion Pde. BN2: Brig 5D 44 (5E 29)
Pavilion Point BN1: Brig 5D 44 (5E 29)
(off Old Steine)
Pavilion Retail Pk. 1G 29
Pavilion Rd. BN1: Falm 1E 15
Pavilion Rd. BN14: Worth 1B 34
Pavilion St. BN2: Brig 5D 44 (5E 29)
Pavilion Theatre Worthing 3D 34
Paxmead Cres. BN14: Broadw 4F 21
Payne Av. BN3: Hove 2F 27
Payne Ter. BN1: Brig 1F 29
Paythorne Cl. BN42: S'wick 1F 25
Peace Cl. BN1: Brig 1G 29
Peace Gdns. 3C 12
(off London Road)
PEACEHAVEN 5G 39
Peacehaven Golf Course 5C 40
PEACEHAVEN HEIGHTS 6B 40
Peacehaven Leisure Cen. 5G 39
Peacock Ind. Est. BN3: Hove 3B 28
Peacock La. BN1: Brig 4C 12
Pearsons Retreat BN11: Worth 1H 35
Pebble La. BN12: Fer 3A 32
Pebble Way BN43: Shor S 2E 25
Peckham Cl. BN7: Lewes 2E 17
Peel Rd. BN2: Brig 4B 36
Pegasus Ct. BN11: Worth 2C 34
(off Shelley Rd.)
Pelham Cl. BN10: Peace 3H 39
Pelham Ct. BN13: W Tar 5A 20
Pelham Ct. BN25: Sea 5D 42
Pelham Pl. BN25: Sea 4D 42
(off Pelham Rd.)
Pelham Ri. BN10: Peace 3G 39
Pelham Rd. BN13: W Tar 5H 19

60 A-Z Brighton & Worthing

Pelham Rd. – Rectory Cl.

Pelham Rd. BN25: Sea ... 5D 42
Pelham Sq. BN1: Brig ... 2D 44 (4E 29)
Pelham St. BN1: Brig ... 2D 44 (4E 29)
Pelham Ter. BN2: Brig ... 1G 29
Pelham Ter. BN7: Lewes ... 3E 17
Pelham Yd. BN25: Sea ... 5D 42
Pellbrook Rd. BN7: Lewes ... 2C 16
Pells Pool ... 3F 17
Pemberton Cl. BN15: Lan ... 3C 22
Pembroke Av. BN11: Worth ... 2H 33
Pembroke Av. BN3: Hove ... 4G 27
Pembroke Ct. BN3: Hove ... 4G 27
... (off New Church Rd.)
Pembroke Cres. BN3: Hove ... 3G 27
Pembroke Gdns. BN3: Hove ... 4G 27
Pembury Cl. BN14: Broadw ... 6D 20
Pembury Rd. BN14: Broadw ... 6D 20
Pende Cl. BN15: Somp ... 2B 22
Pendine Av. BN11: Worth ... 1G 35
Pendragon Ct. BN3: Hove ... 2G 27
Penfold Rd. BN14: Broadw ... 4E 21
Penfold Way BN44: Stey ... 4C 4
Penhill Ct. BN15: S Lan ... 5D 22
Penhill Rd. BN15: S Lan ... 5C 22
Penhurst Ct. BN13: Durr ... 5D 18
... (off Ashburnham Cl.)
Penhurst Pl. BN2: Brig ... 4B 30
Penlands Cl. BN44: Stey ... 4C 4
Penlands Ct. BN44: Stey ... 4C 4
Penlands Ri. BN44: Stey ... 4B 4
Penlands Va. BN44: Stey ... 4B 4
Penlands Way BN44: Stey ... 4C 4
Penleigh Cl. BN15: S Lan ... 5D 22
Penns Ct. BN44: Stey ... 2B 4
Pennycress Av. BN13: Durr ... 5C 18
Penrith Ct. BN14: Broadw ... 5D 20
Penstone Cl. BN15: Lan ... 4B 22
Penstone Ct. BN43: Shor S ... 2E 25
Penstone Pk. BN15: Lan ... 4B 22
Pentland Rd. BN13: Durr ... 3G 19
Pepperscoombe La. BN44: Up B ... 3F 5
Percival Mans. BN2: Brig ... 6H 29
... (off Percival Ter.)
Percival Ter. BN2: Brig ... 6H 29
Percy & Wagner Almshouses
BN2: Brig ... 3F 29
... (off Hanover M.)
Perrots La. BN44: Stey ... 4B 4
Perry Hill BN2: Salt ... 1A 38
Perth Cl. BN25: Sea ... 4H 43
Peter Rd. BN15: Lan ... 6A 22
Pett Cl. BN2: Brig ... 4B 30
Petworth Av. BN12: Gor S ... 4E 33
Petworth Ho. BN3: Hove ... 3B 28
... (off Davigdor Rd.)
Petworth Rd. BN1: Brig ... 2F 13
Pevensey Cl. BN25: Sea ... 3G 43
Pevensey Gdn. BN11: Worth ... 3A 34
Pevensey Rd. BN11: Worth ... 3H 33
Pevensey Rd. BN2: Brig ... 2G 29
Pevensey Rd. BN9: Newh ... 6C 40
Peverel Rd. BN14: W Tar ... 6A 20
Peverels, The BN25: Sea ... 2F 43
Peveril Cl. BN15: Somp ... 4G 21
Peveril Dr. BN15: Somp ... 4G 21
Philip Ct. BN3: Hove ... 3A 28
Phoenix Brewery Student
Residences BN2: Brig ... 4F 29
... (off Southover St.)
Phoenix C'way. BN7: Lewes ... 4F 17
Phoenix Cres. BN42: S'wick ... 2F 25
Phoenix Ho. BN11: Worth ... 1D 34
... (off Chapel Rd.)
Phoenix Ind. Est. BN7: Lewes ... 3F 17
Phoenix M. BN25: Sea ... 5D 42
... (off South St.)
Phoenix Pl. BN2: Brig ... 4F 29
Phoenix Pl. BN7: Lewes ... 4F 17
Phoenix Ri. BN2: Brig ... 4F 29
Phoenix Way BN42: S'wick ... 2F 25
Phoenix Works BN7: Lewes ... 3F 17
Phrosso Rd. BN11: Worth ... 3H 33
Phyllis Av. BN10: Peace
Heathy Brow ... 3F 39
Phyllis Av. BN10: Peace
Margaret Ct. ... 5E 39
... (not continuous)
Picton St. BN2: Brig ... 3G 29
PIDDINGHOE ... 1D 40
Piddinghoe Av. BN10: Peace ... 6H 39
... (not continuous)
Piddinghoe Cl. BN10: Peace ... 5H 39
Piddinghoe Mead BN9: Newh ... 3D 40
Pierre Cl. BN41: Ports ... 6B 10
Pilgrims Cl. BN14: Worth ... 6A 20
Pilgrims Ter. BN13: Worth ... 1A 34
Pilgrims Wlk. BN13: Worth ... 1A 34
Pilot Ho. BN2: Brig ... 5F 29
Piltdown Rd. BN2: Brig ... 4B 30
Pimms Gdns. BN1: Brig ... 3C 44 (4E 29)
... (off Orange Row)
Pine Cl. BN9: Newh ... 2G 41
Pine Ct. BN25: Sea ... 2E 43
... (off Up. Belgrave Rd.)
Pines, The BN2: Brig ... 2F 29
... (off Canterbury Dr.)
Pines, The BN3: Hove ... 4C 28
Pines Av. BN14: Char D ... 3D 20
Pine Tree Cl. BN9: Newh ... 4E 41
Pinewood BN1: Brig ... 5C 12
Pinewood Cl. BN1: Brig ... 6C 12
Pinewood Cl. BN25: Sea ... 3E 43
Pinfold Cl. BN2: W'dean ... 4G 31
Pinwell Rd. BN7: Lewes ... 5F 17
Pipe Pas. BN7: Lewes ... 4E 17
Pipers Cl. BN3: Hove ... 5C 10
Pitt Dr. BN25: Sea ... 2F 43
Pitt Gdns. BN2: W'dean ... 2F 31
Place La. BN25: Sea ... 4D 42
Plainfields Av. BN1: Brig ... 1E 13
Plaistow Cl. BN2: Brig ... 4B 30
Plantation, The BN13: Salv ... 3H 19
Plantation Cl. BN13: Salv ... 3H 19
Plantation Ri. BN13: Salv ... 3A 20
Plantation Way BN13: Salv ... 3H 19
Playden Cl. BN2: Brig ... 4A 36
Plaza Ho. BN1: Brig ... 3C 44 (4E 29)
... (off Jubilee St.)
Plumpton Rd. BN2: Brig ... 4H 29
Plymouth Av. BN2: Brig ... 1A 30
Poling Cl. BN12: Gor S ... 6D 18
Pollard Ct. BN11: Worth ... 2A 34
Polperro Cl. BN12: Fer ... 3A 32
Pond La. BN13: Durr ... 4F 19
Pond M. BN13: Durr ... 4F 19
Pond Rd. BN43: Shor S ... 3B 24
Pondsyde Ct. BN25: Sea ... 3E 43
Pony Farm BN14: Fin ... 2D 6
Pool Pas. BN1: Brig ... 6C 44 (6E 29)
... (off Pool Valley)
Pool Valley BN1: Brig ... 6C 44 (6E 29)
Pool Valley
Coach Station ... 6D 44 (6E 29)
Popes Folly BN2: Brig ... 1G 29
Poplar Av. BN3: Hove ... 5E 11
Poplar Cl. BN1: Brig ... 6D 12
Poplar Cl. BN3: Hove ... 5E 11
Poplar Rd. BN13: Durr ... 5E 19
Poplars, The BN12: Fer ... 4A 32
Poplars, The BN2: Brig ... 2F 29
... (off Prince's Cres.)
Portfield Av. BN1: Brig ... 2E 13
Port Hall Av. BN1: Brig ... 2C 28
Port Hall M. BN1: Brig ... 2C 28
Port Hall Pl. BN1: Brig ... 2C 28
Port Hall Rd. BN1: Brig ... 2C 28
Port Hall St. BN1: Brig ... 2C 28
Portland Av. BN3: Hove ... 3E 27
Portland Bus. Pk. BN3: Hove ... 2E 27
Portland La. BN3: Hove ... 3D 26
Portland M. BN2: Brig ... 6G 29
Portland Pl. BN2: Brig ... 6G 29
Portland Recreation Ground ... 3F 27
Portland Rd. BN11: Worth ... 2D 34
Portland Rd. BN3: Hove ... 2D 26
Portland Rd. Trad. Est.
BN3: Hove ... 2D 26
Portland Sq. BN11: Worth ... 2D 34
Portland St. BN1: Brig ... 4B 44 (5D 28)
Portland Ter. BN9: S Heig ... 1F 41
Portland Vs. BN3: Hove ... 3D 26
Portside BN2: Brig ... 5B 36
PORTSLADE ... 1A 26
PORTSLADE-BY-SEA ... 3C 26
Portslade M. BN41: Ports ... 3C 26
Portslade Sports Cen. ... 5A 10
Portslade Station (Rail) ... 2D 26
Port Vw. BN9: S Heig ... 1G 41
Portway BN44: Stey ... 4B 4
Pot La. BN12: Fer ... 3A 18
Pot La. BN12: Pat ... 3A 18
Pot La. BN13: Pat ... 3A 18
Potters La. BN7: Lewes ... 5E 17
Poulter's La. BN14: Worth ... 4A 20
Pound La. BN44: Up B ... 4G 5
Powell Gdns. BN9: Newh ... 2F 41
Powis Gro. BN1: Brig ... 3A 44 (4D 28)
Powis Rd. BN1: Brig ... 3A 44 (4C 28)
Powis Sq. BN1: Brig ... 2A 44 (4C 28)
Powis Vs. BN1: Brig ... 3A 44 (4D 28)
Poynings Cl. BN25: Sea ... 5H 43
Poynings Ct. BN14: Fin V ... 5D 6
Poynings Dr. BN3: Hove ... 5F 11
Poynter Rd. BN3: Hove ... 2G 27
Pratton Av. BN15: Lan ... 3B 22
PRESTON ... 1C 28
Preston Cir. BN1: Brig ... 3E 29
Preston Drove BN1: Brig ... 6C 12
Preston Grange BN1: Brig ... 1C 28
Preston Indoor Bowls Club ... 1C 28
Preston Manor ... 1C 28
Preston Mans. BN1: Brig ... 2D 28
Preston Pk. Av. BN1: Brig ... 6D 12
Preston Park Station (Rail) ... 6B 12
Preston Rd. BN1: Brig ... 6C 12
Preston St. BN1: Brig ... 5C 28
Preston Village M. BN1: Brig ... 1C 28
... (off Middle Rd.)
Prestonville Ct. BN1: Brig ... 3D 28
... (off Dyke Rd.)
Prestonville Rd. BN1: Brig ... 3D 28
Prestonville Ter. BN1: Brig ... 3D 28
... (off Old Shoreham Rd.)
Primrose Ct. BN44: Stey ... 4C 4
Prince Albert St.
BN1: Brig ... 5C 44 (5E 29)
Prince Av. BN15: S Lan ... 5F 23
Prince Charles Cl. BN42: S'wick ... 1H 25
Prince Charles Rd. BN7: Lewes ... 2G 17
Prince Edward's Rd.
BN7: Lewes ... 4D 16
Prince of Wales Ct. BN3: Hove ... 4F 27
... (off Kingsway)
Prince Regent's Cl. BN2: Brig ... 4A 36
Prince Regents Ct. BN2: Brig ... 5A 30
Prince Regent Swimming
Complex ... 4C 44 (5E 29)
Princes Av. BN3: Hove ... 4G 27
Princes Cl. BN25: Sea ... 2D 42
Princes Ct. BN3: Hove ... 4G 27
Princes Ct. BN43: Shor B ... 4H 23
Prince's Cres. BN2: Brig ... 2F 29
Princes Cres. BN3: Hove ... 4G 27
Princes Ga. BN11: Worth ... 2H 33
Princes Ho. BN1: Brig ... 5C 44 (5E 29)
... (off North St.)
Prince's Pl. BN1: Brig ... 5C 44 (5E 29)
Prince's Rd. BN2: Brig ... 2F 29
Princess Av. BN13: Worth ... 1H 33
Princess Ct. BN13: Worth ... 1H 33
Princess Dr. BN25: Sea ... 2B 42
Princes Sq. BN3: Hove ... 4G 27
Prince's St. BN2: Brig ... 5D 44 (5E 29)
Princes Ter. BN2: Brig ... 4A 36
Prince William Cl. BN14: Fin V ... 2A 20
Prinsep Rd. BN3: Hove ... 2G 27
Priors Cl. BN44: Up B ... 4F 5
Priory, The BN1: Brig ... 3B 12
Priory, The BN3: Hove ... 5H 27
Priory Cl. BN14: W Tar ... 6A 20
Priory Cl. BN15: Somp ... 3H 21
Priory Ct. BN1: Brig ... 2D 28
... (off Stanford Av.)
Priory Ct. BN7: Lewes ... 5F 17
Priory Cres. BN7: Lewes ... 5E 17
Priory Fld. BN44: Up B ... 4F 5
Priory Flats BN7: Lewes ... 5E 17
Priory Ga. BN15: Lan ... 4C 22
... (off North Rd.)
Priory Ho. BN7: Lewes ... 5F 17
Priory St. BN7: Lewes ... 5E 17
Priory Ter. BN7: Lewes ... 5F 17
... (off Mountfield Rd.)
Promenade BN25: Sea ... 4B 42
Promenade, The BN10: Peace ... 5E 39
... (not continuous)
Promenade, The BN11: Worth ... 3D 34
Prospect Pl. BN11: Worth ... 3D 34
Providence Pl. BN1: Brig ... 1C 44 (3E 29)
... (not continuous)
Providence Ter. BN11: Worth ... 1E 35
Providence Way BN43: Shor B ... 4D 24
Pulborough Cl. BN2: Brig ... 3B 30
Pump Ho., The BN3: Hove ... 2D 26
Purbeck Ho. BN2: Brig ... 5F 29
... (off Dorset Gdns.)
Puregym Brighton ... 1D 44 (3E 29)
... (off London Road)
PureGym (Central)
Brighton ... 3B 44 (4E 29)
Puttick Dr. BN13: Worth ... 1G 33

Q

Quadrangle, The BN14: Fin ... 4C 6
Quadrant, The BN12: Gor S ... 1E 33
Quantock Cl. BN13: Durr ... 2H 19
Quantock Rd. BN13: Durr ... 2H 19
Quarry Bank Rd. BN1: Brig ... 6F 13
Quarry La. BN25: Sea ... 2F 43
Quarry Rd. BN9: Newh ... 6E 41
Quarry Rd. Ind. Est. BN9: Newh ... 5E 41
Quashetts, The BN14: Broadw ... 5D 20
... (not continuous)
Quay, The BN43: Shor B ... 4C 24
Quay Ct. BN43: Shor B ... 4D 24
Quayside, The BN43: Shor B ... 4C 24
Quebec St. BN2: Brig ... 4F 29
Queen Alexandra Av. BN3: Hove ... 5G 11
Queen Anne's Cl. BN7: Lewes ... 4E 17
Queen Caroline Cl. BN3: Hove ... 5G 11
Queen Mary Av. BN3: Hove ... 5G 11
Queensborough Ct. BN11: Worth ... 1A 34
Queensbury M. BN1: Brig ... 5A 44 (5C 28)
Queens Ct. BN11: Worth ... 3H 33
... (off Aglaia Rd.)
Queensdown School Rd.
BN1: Brig ... 5G 13
Queensdown School Rd.
BN2: Brig ... 6H 13
Queen's Gdns. BN1: Brig ... 3C 44 (4E 29)
Queen's Gdns. BN3: Hove ... 5A 28
Queen's Mans. BN11: Worth ... 3C 34
... (off Wordsworth Rd.)
Queen's Pde. BN3: Hove ... 6E 11
Queens Pde. BN15: Lan ... 4C 22
... (off North Rd.)
Queens Pk. Gdns. BN25: Sea ... 3B 42
Queen's Pk. M. BN2: Brig ... 4G 29
Queen's Pk. Ri. BN2: Brig ... 4G 29
Queen's Pk. Rd. BN2: Brig ... 5F 29
Queen's Pk. Ter. BN2: Brig ... 4G 29
Queen's Pl. BN1: Brig ... 1D 44 (3E 29)
Queen's Pl. BN3: Hove ... 4A 28
Queen's Pl. BN43: Shor S ... 3B 24
Queen Sq. BN1: Brig ... 4B 44 (5D 28)
Queen's Rd. BN1: Brig ... 4B 44 (5D 28)
Queen's Rd. BN11: Worth ... 3C 34
Queen's Rd. BN7: Lewes ... 2F 17
Queens Rd. BN15: S Lan ... 5D 22
Queens Rd. BN42: S'wick ... 1G 25
Queen's Rd. Quad.
BN1: Brig ... 3B 44 (4D 28)
Queen St. BN14: Broadw ... 5C 20
Queensway BN15: Lan ... 4C 22
Queensway BN2: Brig ... 4H 29
Queensway BN25: Sea ... 2F 43
Queen Victoria Av. BN3: Hove ... 5G 11
Querneby Cl. BN43: Shor S ... 3F 25
Quicksilver St. BN13: Worth ... 1G 33
Quinta Carmen BN11: Worth ... 3B 34
... (off Seaview Rd.)
Quoin Est., The BN15: Lan ... 6B 22

R

RACE HILL ... 3B 30
Rackham Cl. BN13: Worth ... 5H 19
Rackham Rd. BN13: Worth ... 5G 19
Radbone Cl. BN14: Broadw ... 4E 21
Radinden Dr. BN3: Hove ... 1B 28
Radinden Mnr. Rd. BN3: Hove ... 2A 28
Radnor Cl. BN13: Worth ... 6H 19
Radnor Rd. BN13: Worth ... 6H 19
Raglan Av. BN13: Durr ... 5G 19
Raglan Ct. BN1: Brig ... 4B 44 (5E 29)
... (off Portland St.)
Raglan Ct. BN11: Worth ... 2A 34
Railway App. BN11: Worth ... 1C 34
Railway App. BN9: Newh ... 4F 41
Railway La. BN7: Lewes ... 4F 17
Railway Quay BN9: Newh ... 4F 41
Railway Rd. BN9: Newh ... 4F 41
Railway St. BN1: Brig ... 2B 44 (4D 28)
Rainbow Sq. BN43: Shor S ... 2D 24
Raleigh Cl. BN43: Shor B ... 4A 24
Raleigh Cres. BN12: Gor S ... 1F 33
Raleigh Way BN12: Gor S ... 6E 19
Ranalah Est. BN9: Newh ... 3F 41
Ranelagh Vs. BN3: Hove ... 2H 27
Ranscombe Hill BN8: Glyn ... 6H 17
Raphael Rd. BN3: Hove ... 3F 27
Ravensbourne Av.
BN43: Shor S ... 1B 24
Ravensbourne Cl.
BN43: Shor S ... 1B 24
Raven's Rd. BN43: Shor S ... 3B 24
Ravenswood Ct. BN13: W Tar ... 5H 19
Ravenswood Dr. BN2: W'dean ... 4H 31
Rayford Cl. BN10: Peace ... 5G 39
Rayford Ct. BN25: Sea ... 5D 42
... (off St John's Rd.)
Raymond Cl. BN25: Sea ... 2F 43
Reading Rd. BN2: Brig ... 4B 36
Read's Wlk. BN44: Stey ... 1C 4
Reba Ct. BN2: Salt ... 4B 38
Rectory Cl. BN3: Hove ... 3D 26
Rectory Cl. BN43: Shor S ... 3F 25

A-Z Brighton & Worthing 61

Rectory Cl. – St Ann's Well Gdns.

Rectory Cl. BN9: Newh. ... 5E **41**
Rectory Ct. BN43: Shor S ... 2E **25**
... *(off Pebble Way)*
Rectory Farm Rd. BN15: Somp ... 3H **21**
Rectory Gdns. BN14: Broadw ... 4C **20**
Rectory La. BN13: Clap ... 1A **18**
Rectory Rd. BN14: W Tar ... 6A **20**
Rectory Rd. BN43: Shor S ... 3E **25**
Rectory Rd. BN9: Newh. ... 1G **41**
Rectory Wlk. BN15: Somp ... 3A **22**
Redcotts BN11: Worth ... 1B **34**
Redcross St. BN1: Brig ... 2D **44** (4E **29**)
... *(off Trafalgar St.)*
Redhill Cl. BN1: Brig ... 3A **12**
Redhill Dr. BN1: Brig ... 3A **12**
Red Sq. Retail Pk. ... 3E **21**
Redvers Rd. BN2: Brig ... 1H **29**
Redwood Cl. BN13: Durr ... 5E **19**
Reed Ct. BN7: Lewes ... 2E **17**
Rees Cl. BN13: Durr ... 4D **18**
Reeves Hill BN1: Brig ... 3H **13**
Refectory Rd. BN1: Falm ... 1D **14**
Regency Apts. BN11: Worth ... 3C **34**
... *(off Crescent Rd.)*
Regency Ct. BN1: Brig ... 5B **12**
Regency Ct. BN12: Fer ... 2B **32**
Regency Ct. BN13: Salv ... 4A **20**
Regency M. BN1: Brig ... 5C **28**
Regency Rd. BN1: Brig ... 5A **44** (5D **28**)
... (not continuous)
Regency Sq. BN1: Brig ... 5C **28**
Regency Town House ... 5B **28**
Regent Arc. BN1: Brig ... 5C **44** (5E **29**)
... *(off Market St.)*
Regent Cl. BN15: S Lan ... 4F **23**
Regent Hill BN1: Brig ... 4A **44** (5D **28**)
Regent Row BN1: Brig ... 4A **44** (5D **28**)
Regents Cl. BN25: Sea ... 2D **42**
Regent St. BN1: Brig ... 4C **44** (5E **29**)
Regis Ct. BN11: Worth ... 3A **34**
Reigate Ct. BN11: Worth ... 2H **33**
... *(off Reigate Rd.)*
Reigate Rd. BN1: Brig ... 1B **28**
Reigate Rd. BN11: Worth ... 2H **33**
Rendezvous Casino ... 5B **36**
Reynolds Rd. BN3: Hove ... 3F **27**
Richard Allen Ct. BN1: Brig ... 1G **29**
Richardson Ct. BN3: Hove ... 3F **27**
Richardson Rd. BN3: Hove ... 3F **27**
Richardsons Yd. BN1: Brig ... 3D **28**
... *(off New England Rd.)*
Rich Ind. Est. BN9: Newh ... 2G **41**
Richington Way BN25: Sea ... 3G **43**
Richmond Ct. BN11: Worth ... 2C **34**
Richmond Ct. BN25: Sea ... 4D **42**
... *(off Richmond Rd.)*
Richmond Ct. BN3: Hove ... 3C **28**
... *(off Osmond Rd.)*
Richmond Gdns. BN2: Brig ... 4F **29**
Richmond Hgts. BN2: Brig ... 4F **29**
Richmond M. BN25: Sea ... 4D **42**
... *(off Richmond Rd.)*
Richmond Pde. BN2: Brig ... 4E **29**
Richmond Pl. BN2: Brig ... 2D **44** (4E **29**)
Richmond Rd. BN11: Worth ... 2B **34**
Richmond Rd. BN2: Brig ... 2F **29**
Richmond Rd. BN25: Sea ... 4D **42**
Richmond St. BN2: Brig ... 4F **29**
Richmond Ter. BN2: Brig ... 3F **29**
... *(off Lewes Rd.)*
Richmond Ter. BN25: Sea ... 4D **42**
Ride, The BN1: Brig ... 1D **28**
Ridge Cl. BN41: Ports ... 4A **10**
Ridgeside Av. BN1: Brig ... 3C **12**
Ridge Vw. BN1: Brig ... 3A **14**
Ridgeway BN42: S'wick ... 1H **25**
Ridgeway, The BN25: Sea ... 2E **43**
Ridgeway Cl. BN42: S'wick ... 1H **25**
Ridgeway Gdns. BN2: W'dean ... 3G **31**
Ridgewood Av. BN2: Salt ... 1A **38**
Ridgway, The BN2: W'dean ... 2F **31**
Ridgway Cl. BN2: W'dean ... 2F **31**
Ridings, The BN10: Tels C ... 3F **39**
Ridings, The BN2: O'dean ... 6F **31**
Ridings, The BN25: Sea ... 2E **43**
Ridings, The BN44: Bramb ... 5C **4**
Rifeside Gdns. BN12: Fer ... 1A **32**
Rife Way BN12: Fer ... 2A **32**
Rigden Rd. BN3: Hove ... 2A **28**
Riley Rd. BN2: Brig ... 2G **29**
Ringmer Cl. BN1: Brig ... 4A **14**
Ringmer Dr. BN1: Brig ... 4B **14**
Ringmer Rd. BN1: Brig ... 4A **14**
Ringmer Rd. BN13: Worth ... 5G **19**
Ringmer Rd. BN25: Sea ... 5D **42**
Ringmer Rd. BN8: Lewes ... 2G **17**
Ringmer Rd. BN8: Ring ... 2G **17**
Ringmer Rd. BN9: Newh ... 5C **40**
Ring Rd. BN15: N Lan ... 1C **22**
Ripley Rd. BN11: Worth ... 2H **33**
Ripon Ct. BN11: Worth ... 2A **34**
... *(off Pevensey Gdns.)*
Riptide Health & Fitness ... 1H **27**
Rise, The BN41: Ports ... 6H **9**
Risings, The BN25: Sea ... 3E **43**
Rissom Ct. BN1: Brig ... 6C **12**
Riverbank BN43: Shor B ... 4A **24**
Riverbank Bus. Cen.
BN43: Shor S ... 3A **24**
River Cl. BN43: Shor B ... 4A **24**
Riverdale BN7: Lewes ... 3E **17**
Riverside BN42: S'wick ... 4G **25**
Riverside BN43: Shor B ... 4B **24**
Riverside BN44: Up B ... 4F **5**
Riverside BN9: Newh ... 4F **41**
Riverside Bus. Cen.
BN43: Shor S ... 3B **24**
Riverside Bus. Cen. BN7: Lewes ... 3F **17**
Riverside Cvn. Pk.
BN44: Up B Bramber ... 4F **5**
Riverside Ct. BN9: Newh ... 4E **41**
... *(off North La.)*
Riverside Ho. BN9: Newh ... 5F **41**
Riverside Ind. Est. BN7: Lewes ... 3F **17**
Riverside Nth. BN9: Newh ... 4F **41**
Riverside Rd. BN43: Shor B ... 4B **24**
Robert Lodge BN2: Brig ... 4B **36**
Roberts Marine Mans.
BN11: Worth ... 3H **33**
... *(off West Pde.)*
Robertson Rd. BN1: Brig ... 6B **12**
Roberts Rd. BN15: S Lan ... 6C **22**
Robert St. BN1: Brig ... 3C **44** (4E **29**)
Robin Davis Cl. BN2: Brig ... 2A **30**
Robin Dene BN2: Brig ... 4B **36**
Robinia Lodge BN1: Brig ... 6C **12**
Robin Rd. BN12: Gor S ... 5D **18**
Robinson Cl. BN15: Lan ... 4C **22**
Robinson Rd. BN9: Newh ... 3E **41**
Robins Row BN41: Ports ... 1A **26**
Robson Ct. BN12: Gor S ... 1G **33**
Robson Rd. BN12: Gor S ... 2G **33**
Rochester Cl. BN13: Durr ... 5D **18**
Rochester Cl. BN3: Hove ... 4B **28**
Rochester Ct. BN11: Worth ... 2A **34**
... *(off Pevensey Gdns.)*
Rochester Ct. BN3: Hove ... 4B **28**
... *(off Rochester Gdns.)*
Rochester Gdns. BN3: Hove ... 4B **28**
Rochester St. BN2: Brig ... 5H **29**
Rochford Way BN25: Sea ... 1A **42**
Rock Cl. BN42: S'wick ... 3G **25**
... *(off Whiterock Pl.)*
Rock Gro. BN2: Brig ... 6H **29**
Rockingham Cl. BN13: Durr ... 4G **19**
Rockingham Ct. BN13: Durr ... 4G **19**
Rock Pl. BN2: Brig ... 6F **29**
Rock St. BN2: Brig ... 4A **36**
Roderick Av. BN10: Peace
Cavell Av. ... 6F **39**
... (not continuous)
Roderick Av. BN10: Peace
Southview Rd. ... 4G **39**
... (not continuous)
Roderick Av. Nth. BN10: Peace ... 1G **39**
Roderick Ct. BN10: Peace ... 4G **39**
... *(off Roderick Av.)*
Rodmell Av. BN2: Salt ... 3B **38**
Rodmell Ct. BN25: Sea ... 3B **42**
Rodmell Pl. BN1: Brig ... 2E **13**
Rodmell Rd. BN13: Worth ... 5G **19**
Rodmell Rd. BN25: Sea ... 5G **43**
Roedale Rd. BN1: Brig ... 1F **29**
ROEDEAN ... 5D **36**
Roedean Cl. BN25: Sea ... 3F **43**
Roedean Ct. BN2: Brig ... 4B **36**
Roedean Cres. BN2: Brig ... 4C **36**
Roedean Hgts. BN2: Brig ... 4C **36**
Roedean Path BN2: Brig ... 5D **36**
Roedean Rd. BN13: Durr ... 4G **19**
Roedean Rd. BN2: Brig ... 4B **36**
Roedean Ter. BN2: Brig ... 5D **36**
Roedean Va. BN2: Brig ... 5D **36**
Roedean Way BN2: Brig ... 5C **36**
Rogate Cl. BN13: Salv ... 4A **20**
Rogate Cl. BN15: Somp ... 3H **21**
Rogate Rd. BN13: Salv ... 4H **19**
Roger's La. BN14: Fin ... 3C **6**
Roman Cl. BN25: Sea ... 1A **42**
Roman Cres. BN42: S'wick ... 2G **25**
Roman Rd. BN3: Hove ... 4D **26**
Roman Rd. BN42: S'wick ... 2G **25**
Roman Rd. BN44: Stey ... 4D **4**
Roman Wlk. BN15: Somp ... 3H **21**
Roman Way BN42: S'wick ... 2G **25**
Romany Cl. BN41: Ports ... 2B **26**
Romany Rd. BN13: Durr ... 5D **18**
Romney Cl. BN25: Sea ... 4H **43**
Romney Ct. BN11: Worth ... 3H **33**
Romney Rd. BN11: Worth ... 3H **33**
Romney Rd. BN2: Rott ... 3G **37**
Romsey Cl. BN1: Brig ... 6F **13**
Ronuk Ho. BN41: Ports ... 2C **26**
... *(off Carlton Ter.)*
Rookery Cl. BN1: Brig ... 1C **28**
Rookery Cl. BN9: Newh ... 1G **41**
ROOKERY HILL ... 1A **42**
Rookery Way BN25: Sea ... 2A **42**
Rookery Way BN9: Newh ... 1H **41**
Ropes Pas. BN7: Lewes ... 4E **17**
... *(off High St.)*
Ropetackle BN43: Shor S ... 3A **24**
Rope Wlk. BN43: Shor S ... 3A **24**
Rosebery Av. BN12: Gor S ... 2G **33**
Rosebery Av. BN2: W'dean ... 2E **31**
Rose Ct. BN11: Worth ... 1H **35**
Rose Ct. BN43: Shor S ... 1D **24**
Rosecroft Cl. BN15: Lan ... 5C **22**
Rosedene Cl. BN2: W'dean ... 4G **31**
Rose Hill BN2: Brig ... 3F **29**
Rose Hill Cl. BN1: Brig ... 3E **29**
Rose Hill Ct. BN1: Brig ... 3E **29**
... *(off Rose Hill Cl.)*
Rose Hill Ter. BN1: Brig ... 3E **29**
Rosehill Ter. M. BN1: Brig ... 3E **29**
... *(off Rose Hill Ter.)*
Rosemary Av. BN44: Stey ... 3D **4**
Rosemary Cl. BN10: Peace ... 3G **39**
Rosemary Cl. BN44: Stey ... 3D **4**
Rosemary Dr. BN43: Shor S ... 1D **24**
Rosemount Cl. BN25: Sea ... 1A **42**
Rose Wlk. BN12: Gor S ... 2G **33**
Rose Wlk. BN25: Sea ... 3E **43**
Rose Wlk., The BN9: Newh ... 4E **41**
Rose Wlk. Cl. BN9: Newh ... 4D **40**
Rossiter Rd. BN15: N Lan ... 2C **22**
Rosslyn Av. BN43: Shor S ... 3C **24**
Rosslyn Ct. BN43: Shor S ... 2B **24**
Rosslyn Rd. BN43: Shor S ... 3B **24**
Rotary Ho. BN15: S Lan ... 6C **22**
Rotary Lodge BN1: Brig ... 2A **14**
Rotary Lodge BN11: Worth ... 1B **34**
Rotary Point BN41: Ports ... 1A **26**
Rothbury Rd. BN3: Hove ... 3D **26**
Rotherfield Cl. BN1: Brig ... 2F **13**
Rotherfield Cres. BN1: Brig ... 3F **13**
Rother Rd. BN25: Sea ... 5F **43**
Rothesay Cl. BN13: Worth ... 6G **19**
Rothwell Ct. BN9: Newh ... 4C **40**
Rotten Row BN7: Lewes ... 5D **16**
ROTTINGDEAN ... 3G **37**
Rottingdean Pl. BN2: Rott ... 6H **31**
Rotyngs, The BN2: Rott ... 2F **37**
Rough Brow BN25: Sea ... 3F **43**
Roundhay Av. BN10: Peace ... 5A **40**
ROUND HILL ... 2F **29**
Roundhill Cres. BN2: Brig ... 2F **29**
Round Hill Rd. BN2: Brig ... 2F **29**
Round Hill St. BN2: Brig ... 2F **29**
Roundhouse Cres. BN10: Peace ... 5H **39**
Roundway BN1: Brig ... 3A **14**
Roundwood BN13: High S ... 2H **19**
Rowan Av. BN3: Hove ... 1E **27**
Rowan Cl. BN25: Sea ... 4H **43**
Rowan Cl. BN41: Ports ... 1A **26**
Rowan Ho. BN12: Gor S ... 6C **18**
... *(off Goring Chase)*
Rowan Ho. BN2: Brig ... 3F **29**
... *(off Canterbury Dr.)*
Rowans, The BN11: Worth ... 2A **34**
Rowans, The BN43: Shor S ... 2A **24**
Rowans Ct. BN7: Lewes ... 4E **17**
Rowan Way BN2: Rott ... 6G **31**
Rowe Av. BN10: Peace ... 6F **39**
... (not continuous)
Rowe Av. Nth. BN10: Peace ... 4F **39**
Rowenden Ct. BN2: Salt ... 3A **38**
Rowlands Rd. BN11: Worth ... 3A **34**
Rox BN1: Brig ... 4E **29**
Roxburgh Cl. BN13: Durr ... 3H **19**
ROYAL ALEXANDRA CHILDREN'S HOSPITAL ... 6H **29**
Royal Arc. BN11: Worth ... 3D **34**
... *(off South St.)*
Royal Bldgs. BN15: Lan ... 6A **22**
Royal Cres. BN2: Brig ... 6G **29**
Royal Cres. Mans. BN2: Brig ... 6G **29**
... *(off Marine Pde.)*
Royal Cres. M. BN2: Brig ... 6G **29**
Royal Dr. BN25: Sea ... 1D **42**
Royal George Pde. BN43: Shor S ... 1E **25**
Royal Pavilion ... 5D **44** (5E **29**)
ROYAL SUSSEX COUNTY HOSPITAL ... 6H **29**
Royal Sussex Ct. BN7: Lewes ... 5F **17**
Royal Vw. BN2: Brig ... 4D **44** (5E **29**)
... *(off Grand Pde.)*
Royles Cl. BN2: Rott ... 2G **37**
Rudd Ho. BN13: Durr ... 3G **19**
Rudgwick Av. BN12: Gor S ... 2C **32**
Rudyard Cl. BN2: W'dean ... 2G **31**
Rudyard Rd. BN2: W'dean ... 2G **31**
Rufus Cl. BN7: Lewes ... 4E **17**
Rugby Cl. BN25: Sea ... 3G **43**
Rugby Ct. BN11: Worth ... 1A **34**
... *(off Rugby Rd.)*
Rugby Ct. BN2: Brig ... 4A **36**
Rugby Pl. BN2: Brig ... 4A **36**
Rugby Rd. BN1: Brig ... 1E **29**
Rugby Rd. BN11: Worth ... 1H **33**
Rusbridge La. BN7: Lewes ... 4G **17**
Rushey Hill Cvn. Pk.
BN10: Peace ... 5B **40**
Rushlake Cl. BN1: Brig ... 3A **14**
Rushlake Rd. BN1: Brig ... 2A **14**
Ruskin Pl. BN3: Hove ... 2F **27**
Ruskin Rd. BN14: Broadw ... 6F **21**
Ruskin Rd. BN3: Hove ... 2F **27**
Rusper Rd. BN1: Brig ... 2H **13**
Rusper Rd. BN13: Worth ... 5G **19**
Rusper Rd. Sth. BN13: Worth ... 5H **19**
Russell Cl. BN14: Broadw ... 5E **21**
Russell Ct. BN15: S Lan ... 5C **22**
Russell Cres. BN1: Brig ... 1A **44** (3C **28**)
Russell Ho. BN3: Hove ... 3B **28**
Russell M. BN1: Brig ... 4A **44** (5C **28**)
... *(off Castle St.)*
Russell Pl. BN1: Brig ... 5A **44** (5D **28**)
Russell Rd. BN1: Brig ... 5A **44** (5D **28**)
Russell Row BN7: Lewes ... 2E **17**
Russells Dr. BN15: S Lan ... 5C **22**
Russell Sq. BN1: Brig ... 4A **44** (5D **28**)
Rustic Cl. BN10: Peace ... 3F **39**
Rustic Pk. BN10: Tels C ... 2F **39**
... *(off Rustic Rd.)*
Rustic Rd. BN10: Peace ... 2F **39**
Rustington Rd. BN1: Brig ... 3E **13**
Rutland Ct. BN3: Hove ... 3F **27**
Rutland Gdns. BN3: Hove ... 4F **27**
Rutland Rd. BN3: Hove ... 3G **27**
Ryde Ct. BN3: Hove ... 1D **26**
... *(off Hangleton Gdns.)*
Ryde Rd. BN2: Brig ... 3H **29**
Rye Cl. BN11: Worth ... 3A **34**
Rye Cl. BN2: Salt ... 2C **38**
Rye Cl. BN25: Sea ... 3H **43**
Ryecroft BN2: Brig ... 5B **30**
Ryecroft Cl. BN12: Gor S ... 3E **33**
Ryecroft Gdns. BN12: Gor S ... 2E **33**
Ryelands Dr. BN2: Brig ... 5H **13**

S

Sackville Cl. BN7: Lewes ... 4E **17**
Sackville Cres. BN14: Broadw ... 6E **21**
Sackville Gdns. BN3: Hove ... 4F **27**
Sackville Rd. BN14: Broadw ... 6E **21**
Sackville Rd. BN3: Hove ... 4G **27**
Sackville Trad. Est. BN3: Hove ... 2G **27**
Sackville Way BN14: Broadw ... 6E **21**
Sadler Way BN2: Brig ... 4B **30**
Saffron Cl. BN43: Shor S ... 1E **25**
Saffron Ga. BN3: Hove ... 3A **28**
Saffrons Ct. BN11: Worth ... 1A **34**
St Andrews Cl. BN12: Fer ... 2A **32**
St Andrew's Ct. BN9: Newh ... 4D **40**
St Andrew's Dr. BN25: Sea ... 1A **42**
St Andrew's Gdns. BN13: W Tar ... 6A **20**
St Andrew's La. BN7: Lewes ... 4F **17**
St Andrews Pl. BN7: Lewes ... 5F **17**
... *(off St Andrew's La.)*
St Andrew's Rd. BN1: Brig ... 1E **29**
St Andrew's Rd. BN13: W Tar ... 5H **19**
St Andrew's Rd. BN41: Ports ... 3B **26**
St Anne's Ct. BN1: Brig ... 1B **44** (3D **28**)
... *(off Howard Pl.)*
St Anne's Ct. BN2: Brig ... 6G **29**
... *(off Burlington St.)*
St Anne's Cres. BN7: Lewes ... 5D **16**
St Anne's Ho. BN1: Brig ... 1B **44** (3D **28**)
... *(off Buckingham Pl.)*
St Annes Ter. BN7: Lewes ... 4D **16**
... *(off Western Rd.)*
St Annes Well Ho. BN3: Hove ... 4B **28**
St Ann's Ct. BN3: Hove ... 3B **28**
St Anns Mans. BN3: Hove ... 3C **28**
... *(off Davigdor Rd.)*
St Ann's Well Gdns. ... 3B **28**

St Anselm's Rd. – Shakespeare Rd.

St Anselm's Rd. BN14: Worth 6B **20**
St Aubins Ct. BN12: Fer 4B **32**
St Aubins Rd. BN12: Fer 4B **32**
St Aubyns BN3: Hove 4G **27**
St Aubyn's Cres. BN41: Ports 3B **26**
St Aubyn's Gdns. BN3: Hove 4G **27**
St Aubyn's Mans. BN3: Hove 5G **27**
(off King's Esplanade)
St Aubyn's Mead BN2: Rott 3G **37**
St Aubyn's Rd. BN41: Ports
Gordon Rd. 3A **26**
St Aubyn's Rd. BN41: Ports
Norway St. 3C **26**
St Aubyn's Sth. BN3: Hove 5G **27**
ST BARNABAS HOUSE HOSPICE 5C **18**
St Bernard's Ct. BN15: Lan 5C **22**
St Botolph's Ct. BN11: Worth 1B **34**
St Botolph's Rd. BN11: Worth 1B **34**
St Catherine's Ter. BN3: Hove 5G **27**
St Crispians BN25: Sea 4C **42**
St Crispians Ct. BN25: Sea 4C **42**
St Cuthman's Cl. BN2: Brig 4A **30**
St Cuthmans Rd. BN44: Stey 2C **4**
St David's Ct. BN10: Peace 4F **39**
St David's Ga. BN15: Lan 4B **22**
St Dunstan's Rd. BN13: Worth 1A **34**
St Elizabeth's BN25: Sea 3E **43**
St Elmo Rd. BN14: Worth 6B **20**
St George's Gdns. BN11: Worth 2F **35**
St George's M. BN1: Brig 3D **44** (4E **29**)
St George's Pl. BN1: Brig 2D **44** (4E **29**)
St George's Rd. BN11: Worth 1F **35**
St George's Rd. BN2: Brig 6G **29**
St George's Ter. BN2: Brig 6G **29**
St Giles Cl. BN43: Shor S 2D **24**
St Helen's Cres. BN3: Hove 5D **10**
St Helen's Dr. BN3: Hove 5D **10**
St Helen's Rd. BN2: Brig 3H **29**
St Helier Ct. BN12: Fer 4B **32**
St Helier Rd. BN12: Fer 4B **32**
St Heliers Av. BN3: Hove 3E **27**
St James Av. BN15: N Lan 2C **22**
St James' Ho. BN2: Brig 5F **29**
(off High St.)
St James's Av. BN2: Brig 5F **29**
St James's Gdns. BN2: Brig 5F **29**
(off Dorset Gdns.)
St James's Pl. BN2: Brig 5D **44** (5E **29**)
St James's St. BN2: Brig 5D **44** (5E **29**)
St James's St. M. BN2: Brig 5F **29**
St James St. BN7: Lewes 5E **17**
ST JOHN AMBULANCE
HEADQUARTERS 3G **25**
(off The Twitten)
St John's Av. BN12: Gor S 3F **33**
St John's Cl. BN12: Gor S 3F **33**
St John's Ct. BN15: Lan 4B **22**
St John's Hill BN7: Lewes 4E **17**
St John's M. BN2: Brig 6G **29**
St John's Mt. BN2: Brig 5F **29**
(off Mt. Pleasant)
St John's Pde. BN12: Gor S 3E **33**
St John's Pl. BN2: Brig 5F **29**
St John's Pl. BN3: Hove 4A **28**
St John's Rd. BN25: Sea 5D **42**
St John's Rd. BN3: Hove 5A **28**
St John's Ter. BN7: Lewes 4E **17**
St John St. BN7: Lewes 4F **17**
St Joseph's Bus. Pk. BN3: Hove 2G **27**
St Joseph's Cl. BN3: Hove 2G **27**
St Joseph's Trad. Est.
BN3: Hove 2G **27**
St Julians Cl. BN43: Shor S 3E **25**
St Julian's La. BN43: Shor S 3E **25**
St Keyna Av. BN3: Hove 4D **26**
St Laurence Cl. BN10: Tels C 3E **39**
St Lawrence Av. BN14: Worth 6A **20**
St Lawrence Ct. BN14: Worth 6B **20**
St Lawrence La. BN14: Worth 5C **20**
St Lawrence M. BN14: Worth 6A **20**
St Leonard's Av. BN3: Hove 4C **26**
St Leonard's Cl. BN9: Newh 1H **41**
St Leonard's Ct. BN14: Fin V 5D **6**
St Leonard's Gdns. BN3: Hove 4D **26**
St Leonard's Rd. BN2: Brig 2G **29**
St Leonard's Rd. BN3: Hove 4C **26**
St Leonard's Rd. BN9: Newh 1H **41**
St Louie Cl. BN42: S'wick 2A **26**
St Lukes Cl. BN15: Lan 6H **21**
St Lukes Ct. BN9: Newh 5E **41**
St Lukes La. BN9: Newh 4F **41**
St Luke's Rd. BN2: Brig 4G **29**
St Luke's Swimming Pool 4G **29**
St Luke's Ter. BN2: Brig 4G **29**
St Malo Cl. BN12: Fer 4B **32**
St Malo Ct. BN12: Fer 4B **32**
St Margaret's BN2: Rott 3G **37**
St Margaret's Pl.
BN1: Brig 5A **44** (5D **28**)
St Margaret's Ri. BN25: Sea 5H **41**
St Marks Cres. BN15: Lan 6H **21**
St Mark's M. BN2: Brig 4A **36**
(off St Mark's St.)
St Mark's St. BN2: Brig 4A **36**
St Martin's Ct. BN2: Brig 2F **29**
(off St Martin's St.)
St Martins Cres. BN9: Newh 2F **41**
St Martin's Flats BN2: Brig 3G **29**
(off Picton St.)
St Martin's La. BN7: Lewes 5E **17**
St Martin's Pl. BN2: Brig 3F **29**
St Martin's St. BN2: Brig 3F **29**
St Mary Magdalene St. BN2: Brig 2F **29**
St Mary's Cl. BN15: Somp 3H **21**
St Mary's Cl. BN25: Sea 3D **42**
St Mary's Cl. BN43: Shor S 3B **24**
St Marys Ct. BN13: Durr 4F **19**
St Marys Gdns. BN12: Fer 1A **32**
St Mary's House & Gdns. 4E **5**
St Mary's Pl. BN2: Brig 5F **29**
St Marys Pl. BN43: Shor B 4C **24**
St Mary's Rd. BN43: Shor S 3B **24**
St Mary's Sq. BN2: Brig 6H **29**
St Matthews Ct. BN2: Brig 5G **29**
(off College Ter.)
St Matthew's Rd. BN11: Worth 1C **34**
St Maur's Rd. BN12: Fer 2A **32**
St Michaels Cotts. BN44: Stey 3B **4**
(off Tanyard La.)
St Michael's Ct. BN11: Worth 2B **34**
St Michael's Pl. BN1: Brig 4C **28**
St Michael's Rd. BN11: Worth 2B **34**
St Michael's Rd. BN41: Ports 3B **26**
St Michael's Ter. BN7: Lewes 3F **17**
St Michael's Way BN1: Brig 1C **12**
St Nicholas Ct. BN1: Brig 3B **44** (4D **28**)
(off Buckingham Rd.)
St Nicholas Ct. BN15: Lan 4B **22**
(off Penstone Pk.)
St Nicholas Ct. BN43: Shor S 2H **23**
St Nicholas La. BN7: Lewes 4F **17**
St Nicholas Lodge
BN1: Brig 4B **44** (5D **28**)
(off Church St.)
St Nicholas Pl. BN43: Shor B 4C **24**
St Nicholas Rd.
BN1: Brig 3A **44** (4D **28**)
St Nicholas Rd. BN41: Ports 3B **26**
St Nicolas La. BN43: Shor S 2H **23**
St Osmund Rd. BN12: Fer 2A **32**
St Pancras Gdns. BN7: Lewes 5D **16**
St Pancras Rd. BN7: Lewes 5D **16**
St Patrick's Rd. BN3: Hove 3G **27**
St Paul's Av. BN15: Lan 6H **21**
St Paul's St. BN2: Brig 2F **29**
St Peter's Av. BN10: Tels C 4E **39**
St Peter's Cl. BN25: Sea 2D **42**
St Peter's Cl. BN3: Hove 6F **11**
St Peter's Grn. BN44: Up B 4F **5**
St Peter's Ho. BN1: Brig 2D **44** (4E **29**)
(off York Pl.)
St Peter's Pl. BN1: Brig 2D **44** (4E **29**)
St Peter's Pl. BN15: Lan 5A **22**
St Peters Pl. BN7: Lewes 4E **17**
St Peter's Rd. BN25: Sea 2D **42**
St Peter's Rd. BN41: Ports 3B **26**
St Peter's St. BN1: Brig 1D **44** (3E **29**)
St Philips M. BN3: Hove 3F **27**
St Raphael Rd. BN11: Worth 2H **33**
St Richards Cl. BN12: Gor S 1E **33**
St Richard's Ct. BN3: Hove 1D **26**
St Richard's Flat BN41: Ports 3B **26**
St Richard's Rd. BN41: Ports 3B **26**
St Robert's Lodge BN15: Lan 5C **22**
(off Sompting Rd.)
St Saviours Ct. BN1: Brig 2E **29**
(off Ditchling Rd.)
St Swithuns La. BN7: Lewes 5E **17**
St Swithuns Ter. BN7: Lewes 5E **17**
(off Stewards Inn La.)
St Thomas's Rd. BN14: Worth 6B **20**
St Valerie Rd. BN11: Worth 3A **34**
St Wilfred's Rd. BN14: Broadw 6D **20**
St Wilfrid's Flat BN2: Brig 3G **29**
(off Whippingham Rd.)
St Wilfrids Pl. BN25: Sea 4G **43**
Salehurst Cl. BN1: Brig 6G **13**
Salisbury Ho. BN12: Gor S 1C **32**
(off Goring St.)
Salisbury Rd. BN11: Worth 2D **34**
Salisbury Rd. BN25: Sea 4D **42**
Salisbury Rd. BN3: Hove 4A **28**
SALTDEAN 2A **38**
Saltdean Dr. BN2: Salt 3H **37**
Saltdean Lido 3A **38**
Saltdean Pk. Rd. BN2: Salt 3A **38**
Saltdean Va. BN2: Salt 3A **38**
Saltings, The BN15: S Lan 5D **22**
Saltings, The BN43: Shor B 4H **23**
Saltings Way BN44: Up B 4F **5**
Salts Farm Rd. BN15: S Lan 4E **23**
Saltwood Rd. BN25: Sea 3G **43**
Salvington Cl. BN13: Durr 3F **19**
Salvington Ct. BN14: Fin V 6D **6**
Salvington Gdns. BN13: Durr 4H **19**
Salvington Hill BN13: High S 2G **19**
SALVINGTON LODGE 2F **19**
Salvington Rd. BN13: Durr 3F **19**
Salvington Rd. BN13: Salv 3F **19**
Samphire Dr. BN13: Durr 5C **18**
Sanders Ho. BN3: Hove 2E **27**
Sanderstead BN2: Brig 5B **30**
Sandgate Cl. BN25: Sea 2H **43**
Sandgate Rd. BN1: Brig 6E **13**
Sandhurst Av. BN2: W'dean 1F **31**
Sanditon Ct. BN11: Worth 1F **35**
Sanditon Way BN14: Char D 3C **20**
Sandore Cl. BN25: Sea 3F **43**
Sandore Rd. BN25: Sea 3F **43**
Sandown Av. BN12: Gor S 3E **33**
Sandown Cl. BN12: Gor S 3E **33**
Sandown Ct. BN11: Worth 3C **34**
Sandown Ct. BN3: Hove 1D **26**
(off Hangleton Rd.)
Sandown Rd. BN2: Brig 3H **29**
Sandown Rd. BN42: S'wick 2F **25**
Sandringham Cl. BN25: Sea 1F **43**
Sandringham Cl. BN3: Hove 5G **11**
Sandringham Ct. BN15: S Lan 5D **22**
Sandringham Dr. BN3: Hove 5G **11**
Sandringham Lodge BN3: Hove 4A **28**
(off Palmeira Av.)
Sandringham M. BN13: Durr 3F **19**
Sandringham M. BN14: Broadw 4D **20**
(off Shandon Rd.)
Sandwich Rd. BN11: Worth 3H **33**
Sanyhils Av. BN1: Brig 1D **12**
Sapphire Bus. Pk. BN25: Sea 4D **42**
Sark Gdns. BN12: Fer 4B **32**
Sarnia Cl. BN10: Peace 4A **40**
Saunders Hill BN1: Brig 1H **13**
Saunders Pk. Ho. BN2: Brig 2G **29**
(off Hollingdean Rd.)
Saunders Pk. Ri. BN2: Brig 1G **29**
Saunders Pk. Vw. BN2: Brig 1G **29**
(not continuous)
Saxifrage Way BN13: Durr 5C **18**
Saxonbury BN2: Brig 4F **29**
(off Ashton Ri.)
Saxon Cl. BN2: Salt 2A **38**
Saxon Ct. BN3: Hove 4D **26**
Saxon La. BN25: Sea 5D **42**
Saxon Rd. BN3: Hove 4D **26**
Saxon Rd. BN44: Stey 3E **5**
Saxon Rd. BN9: Newh 4E **41**
Saxons BN43: Shor S 1B **24**
Saxons Plain BN13: Clap 3D **18**
Saxon Way BN1: Brig 1C **12**
Saxony Rd. BN14: Broadw 6C **20**
Scarborough Rd. BN1: Brig 1B **28**
Sceptre BN1: Brig 6C **12**
School Cl. BN42: S'wick 3G **25**
School Hill BN14: Fin 2C **6**
School Hill BN7: Lewes 4F **17**
(off High St.)
School La. BN2: Salt 2A **38**
School La. BN44: Stey 3C **4**
School Ri. BN2: Brig 5A **30**
School Rd. BN3: Hove 3F **27**
School Rd. BN44: Up B 4F **5**
School Yd. BN11: Worth 2D **34**
(off Grafton Pl.)
Science Pk. Rd. BN1: Falm 1D **14**
Science Pk. Sq. BN1: Falm 1D **14**
Scotland St. BN2: Brig 4F **29**
Scotney Cl. BN13: Durr 5D **18**
Scott Rd. BN3: Hove 3F **27**
Sculptures Gym 4D **42**
Seabright BN11: Worth 3B **34**
Seabrook Ct. BN15: S Lan 6C **22**
Seacliffe BN10: Tels C 5D **38**
Sea Cl. BN12: Gor S 2G **33**
Sea Cotts. BN25: Sea 5E **43**
Sea Ct. BN12: Gor S 3E **33**
Seadown Pde. BN15: Somp 5H **21**
Sea Dr. BN12: Fer 4B **32**
Seafield Av. BN12: Gor S 3F **33**
Seafield Cl. BN25: Sea 2G **43**
Seafield Rd. BN3: Hove 4H **27**
Seafields BN43: Shor S 2B **24**
SEAFORD 5D **42**
Seaford Ct. BN25: Sea 4D **42**
Seaford Golf Course 1E **43**
Seaford Head Golf Course 6F **43**
Seaford Head Swimming Pool 5F **43**
Seaford Ho. BN25: Sea 5D **42**
(off Crouch La.)
Seaford Mus. Martello
Tower no. 74 6D **42**
Seaford Rd. BN25: Sea 5H **41**
Seaford Rd. BN3: Hove 4C **26**
Seaford Rd. BN9: Newh 3H **41**
Seaford Station (Rail) 4D **42**
Seaford Tourist Info. Cen. 5D **42**
Seaford Way BN43: Shor B 4D **24**
Seagrave Cl. BN25: Sea 1A **42**
Seagrove Way BN25: Sea 1E **43**
Seahaven Gdns. BN43: Shor B 5H **23**
Seahaven Swim & Fitness Cen. 4F **41**
Sea Ho. BN42: S'wick 3G **25**
Sea La. BN12: Fer 2B **32**
Sea La. BN12: Gor S 2E **33**
Sea La. Cl. BN12: Fer 2B **32**
Sea La. Gdns. BN12: Fer 3B **32**
Sea Life Brighton 6D **44** (6E **29**)
Seamill Ct. BN11: Worth 1H **35**
Seamill Pk. Av. BN11: Worth 1H **35**
Seamill Pk. Cres. BN11: Worth 1H **35**
Seamill Way BN11: Worth 1H **35**
Sea Pl. BN12: Gor S 2G **33**
Searle Av. BN10: Peace 5A **40**
Sea-Saw Way BN2: Brig 3B **30**
Seaside Av. BN15: S Lan 5D **22**
Seaside Cl. BN15: S Lan 5D **22**
Seaside Rd. BN15: S Lan 5D **22**
Sea Spray Av. BN43: Shor B 4D **24**
Seaview Av. BN10: Peace 5A **40**
(not continuous)
Seaview Ct. BN11: Worth 3B **34**
Seaview Ct. BN15: Lan 6B **22**
Seaview Est. BN42: S'wick 3H **25**
Seaview Ho. BN9: Newh 5F **41**
Seaview Rd. BN10: Peace 6A **40**
Seaview Rd. BN11: Worth 3B **34**
Seaview Rd. BN2: W'dean 2D **30**
Seaview Rd. BN9: Newh 2H **41**
Sea Vw. Way BN2: W'dean 1F **31**
Second Av. BN14: Char D 3D **20**
Second Av. BN15: Lan 3C **22**
Second Av. BN3: Hove 5A **28**
Second Av. BN9: Newh 4E **41**
Second Rd. BN10: Peace 5E **39**
Sedbury Rd. BN15: Somp 2A **22**
Sefton Cl. BN13: Durr 4F **19**
Sefton Rd. BN41: Ports 5H **9**
Segrave Cl. BN7: Lewes 3D **16**
Selba Dr. BN2: Brig 6A **14**
Selborne Pl. BN3: Hove 3A **28**
Selborne Rd. BN11: Worth 1F **35**
Selborne Rd. BN3: Hove 4A **28**
Selden La. BN11: Worth 2F **35**
Selden Pde. BN13: Salv 3H **19**
(off Salvington Rd.)
Selden Rd. BN11: Worth 1F **35**
Seldens M. BN13: Salv 4H **19**
Selden's Way BN13: Salv 4H **19**
Sele Gdns. BN44: Up B 4G **5**
Selham Cl. BN1: Brig 2A **14**
Selham Dr. BN1: Brig 2H **13**
Selham Pl. BN1: Brig 2H **13**
(off Beatty Av.)
Selhurst Rd. BN2: W'dean 4G **31**
Selkirk Cl. BN13: Worth 6G **19**
Selmeston Ct. BN25: Sea 3B **42**
Selmeston Pl. BN2: Brig 4B **30**
Selsey Cl. BN1: Brig 2A **14**
Selsey Cl. BN13: Worth 5H **19**
Selsfield Dr. BN2: Brig 5H **13**
Semley Rd. BN1: Brig 1E **29**
Senlac Rd. BN9: Newh 4F **41**
Sett, The BN41: Ports 6B **10**
Sevelands Cl. BN2: Brig 3B **30**
SEVEN DIALS 1A **44** (3D **28**)
Seventh Av. BN15: N Lan 2C **22**
Severn Lodge BN2: Brig 5F **29**
(off Mt. Pleasant)
Seville St. BN2: Brig 3G **29**
Seymour Ho. BN2: Brig 6H **29**
(off Seymour Sq.)
Seymour Sq. BN2: Brig 6H **29**
Seymour St. BN2: Brig 6H **29**
Shadwells Cl. BN15: Lan 3D **22**
Shadwells Ct. BN15: Lan 3D **22**
Shadwells Rd. BN15: Lan 3D **22**
Shaftesbury Av. BN12: Gor S 1G **33**
Shaftesbury Pl. BN1: Brig 2E **29**
Shaftesbury Rd. BN1: Brig 2E **29**
Shakespeare Rd. BN11: Worth 1B **34**

A-Z Brighton & Worthing 63

Shakespeare St. – Station Rd.

Shakespeare St. BN3: Hove 2G 27
Shandon Gdns. BN14: Broadw 4D 20
Shandon Rd. BN14: Broadw 3D 20
Shandon Way BN14: Broadw 4D 20
Shanklin Ct. BN2: Brig 2G 29
Shanklin Ct. BN3: Hove 1D 26
(off Hangleton Rd.)
Shanklin Rd. BN2: Brig 2G 29
Shannon Cl. BN10: Tels C 3E 39
Sharpthorne Ct.
BN1: Brig 1C 44 (3E 29)
(off Cheapside)
Sharpthorne Cres. BN41: Ports 6C 10
Shawcross Ho. BN1: Brig 6C 12
Sheepbell Cl. BN41: Ports 5B 10
Sheepcote Valley
Cvn. Club Site BN2: Brig 5C 30
Sheepfair BN7: Lewes 3C 16
Sheepfold, The BN10: Peace 3G 39
Sheep Pen La. BN25: Sea 4F 43
Sheep Pen La. BN44: Stey 3C 4
Sheep Wlk. BN2: Rott 1E 37
Sheffield Ct. BN1: Brig 1C 44 (3E 29)
(off New England St.)
Shelby Rd. BN13: Durr 4E 19
Sheldon Ct. BN11: Worth 3B 34
Shelldale Av. BN41: Ports 3B 26
Shelldale Cres. BN41: Ports 3B 26
Shelldale Rd. BN41: Ports 2B 26
Shelley Cl. BN7: Lewes 4D 16
Shelley Ct. BN11: Worth 2C 34
Shelley Rd. BN11: Worth 2B 34
Shelley Rd. BN3: Hove 3F 27
Shenfield Way BN1: Brig 5F 13
Shepham Av. BN2: Salt 3A 38
Shepherd Ind. Est. BN7: Lewes 3F 17
Shepherds Cl. BN9: Pidd 1D 40
Shepherds Cot BN10: Peace 2H 39
Shepherds Cft. BN1: Brig 4A 12
Shepherds Cft. BN14: Fin 2C 6
(off Southview Rd.)
Shepherd's Mead BN14: Fin V 5E 7
Sheppard Way BN41: Ports 5A 10
Shepway, The BN25: Sea 3G 43
Shepway Pde. BN25: Sea 4D 42
(off Broad St.)
Sherbourne Cl. BN3: Hove 5D 10
Sherbourne Lodge BN11: Worth 1A 34
Sherbourne Rd. BN3: Hove 6D 10
Sherbourne Way BN3: Hove 5D 10
Sherbrooke Cl. BN13: Durr 4F 19
Sheridan Mans. BN3: Hove 2G 27
Sheridan Rd. BN14: Broadw 5E 21
Sheridan Ter. BN3: Hove 2G 27
Shermanbury Ct. BN15: Somp 5A 22
Shermanbury Rd. BN14: Worth 6B 20
Sherrington Rd. BN2: W'dean 2H 31
Sherwood Ri. BN25: Sea 3E 43
Sherwood Rd. BN25: Sea 3E 43
Shetland Ct. BN13: Durr 5D 18
Shield Ter. BN9: Newh 5F 41
Shingle Rd. BN43: Shor B 4C 24
Shipley Rd. BN2: W'dean 3G 31
Ship St. BN1: Brig 6B 44 (6D 28)
Ship St. BN43: Shor S 3A 24
Ship St. BN9: Newh 3E 41
Ship St. Ct. BN1: Brig 5C 44 (5E 29)
(off Ship St.)
Ship St. Gdns. BN1: Brig 5B 44 (5D 28)
Shirley Av. BN3: Hove 6H 11
Shirley Cl. BN14: Salv 3B 20
Shirley Cl. BN43: Shor S 2E 25
Shirley Dr. BN14: Salv 3B 20
Shirley Dr. BN3: Hove 5H 11
Shirley M. BN3: Hove 3H 27
Shirley Rd. BN3: Hove 2A 28
Shirley St. BN3: Hove 3H 27
Shooting Fld. BN44: Stey 2C 4
Shopsdam Rd. BN15: S Lan 6D 22
Shoreham Airport 3G 23
Shoreham Airport Vis. Cen. 3G 23
SHOREHAM BEACH 4B 24
Shoreham Beach Local
Nature Reserve 5B 24
Shoreham By-Pass BN15: Shor S 1G 23
SHOREHAM-BY-SEA 3B 24
Shoreham-by-Sea Station (Rail) 3B 24
Shoreham Ct. BN43: Shor S 2B 24
Shoreham Fort 4E 25
SHOREHAM HEALTH CEN. 3B 24
(off Western Rd.)
Shoreham Lighthouse 4E 25
Shoreham Rd. BN44: Up B 5G 5
Short Brow BN25: Sea 3F 43
Shortgate Rd. BN2: Brig 4B 14
Shrewsbury Ct. BN11: Worth 3B 34
Sidehill Dr. BN41: Ports 6H 9
Sidney Tidy Ho. BN2: Brig 4G 29
(off Queen's Pk. Rd.)
Sillwood Ct. BN1: Brig 5C 28
(off Montpelier Rd.)
Sillwood Hall BN1: Brig 5C 28
(off Montpelier Rd.)
Sillwood M. BN1: Brig 5C 28
(off Sillwood St.)
Sillwood Pl. BN1: Brig 5C 28
Sillwood Rd. BN1: Brig 5C 28
Sillwood St. BN1: Brig 5C 28
Sillwood Ter. BN1: Brig 5C 28
Silver Birch Cl. BN3: Hove 1E 27
Silver Birch Dr. BN13: Durr 5D 18
Silver Birches BN1: Brig 1C 28
Silverdale BN11: Worth 1H 35
Silverdale Av. BN3: Hove 3B 28
Silverdale Ct. BN3: Hove 3B 28
Silverdale Dr. BN15: Somp 5A 22
Silverdale Rd. BN3: Hove 3B 28
Silver La. BN25: Bishop 1B 42
Sinclair Wlk. BN1: Brig 1C 44 (3E 29)
(off Fleet St.)
Singleton Cl. BN12: Fer 1B 32
Singleton Cres. BN12: Fer 1B 32
Singleton Cres. BN12: Gor S 1B 32
Singleton Rd. BN1: Brig 2E 13
Sir George's Pl. BN44: Stey 2B 4
Sirius BN2: Brig 5B 36
Skylark Ri. BN12: Gor S 5D 18
Skyline Vw. BN10: Peace 3H 39
Slindon Av. BN10: Peace 6H 39
(not continuous)
Slindon Cl. BN14: Broadw 4D 20
Slindon Rd. BN14: Broadw 4D 20
Slinfold Cl. BN2: Brig 5H 29
Sloane Ct. BN2: Brig 5G 29
(off Park St.)
SLONK HILL 1D 24
Slonk Hill Rd. BN43: Shor S 6B 8
(not continuous)
Smugglers La. BN44: Up B 4G 5
Smugglers Wlk. BN12: Gor S 3G 33
Soldiers Fld. La. BN14: Fin 2D 6
Solway Av. BN1: Brig 1D 12
Somerhill Av. BN3: Hove 3B 28
Somerhill Ct. BN3: Hove 3B 28
(off Somerhill Av.)
Somerhill Lodge BN3: Hove 4B 28
(off Somerhill Rd.)
Somerhill Rd. BN3: Hove 4B 28
Somerly Gdns. BN42: S'wick 2G 25
Somerset Cl. BN13: W Tar 5A 20
Somerset Cotts. BN13: Clap 1B 18
(off The Street)
Somerset Ct. BN3: Hove 3A 28
(off Wilbury Vs.)
Somerset Point BN2: Brig 6G 29
(off Somerset St.)
Somerset Rd. BN12: Fer 4B 32
Somerset St. BN2: Brig 5G 29
SOMPTING 4H 21
Sompting Av. BN14: Broadw 5D 20
Sompting By-Pass BN14: Char D 3E 21
Sompting Cl. BN2: Brig 3B 30
Sompting Ct. BN43: Shor S 2D 24
Sompting Rd. BN14: Broadw 3E 21
Sompting Rd. BN15: Lan 4B 22
Sonnet Ct. BN11: Worth 2C 34
(off Shelley Rd.)
Sopers La. BN44: Bramb 6A 4
Sorlings Reach BN43: Shor B 4D 24
Southall Av. BN2: Brig 6H 13
Southampton St. BN2: Brig 4F 29
Sth. Ash BN44: Stey 2C 4
South Av. BN12: Gor S 3G 33
South Av. BN2: Brig 5G 29
Sth. Bank Ct. BN15: S Lan 6E 23
Sth. Beach BN43: Shor B 4B 24
Southcliffe BN7: Lewes 4G 17
Sth. Coast Rd. BN10: Peace 4B 38
Sth. Coast Rd. BN10: Salt 4B 38
Sth. Coast Rd. BN10: Tels C 4B 38
Sth. Coast Rd. BN2: Salt 4B 38
South Ct. BN1: Brig 2C 28
South Ct. BN7: Lewes 4G 17
(off Cliffe High St.)
Southcourt Rd. BN14: Broadw 1C 34
Southdown Av. BN1: Brig 1E 29
Southdown Av. BN10: Peace 6H 39
(not continuous)
Southdown Av. BN41: Ports 2C 26
Southdown Av. BN7: Lewes 5C 16
Southdown Cvn. Pk. BN5: Small D 4H 5
Southdown Cl. BN9: Newh 5D 40
Southdown Cnr. BN25: Sea 5F 43
(off Chyngton Rd.)
Southdown Ho. BN12: Gor S 2F 33
(off Goring Rd.)
Southdown Ho. BN3: Hove 3B 28
(off Somerhill Av.)
Southdown M. BN2: Brig 5G 29
Southdown Pl. BN1: Brig 1E 29
Southdown Pl. BN7: Lewes 3G 17
Southdown Rd. BN1: Brig 6E 13
Southdown Rd. BN25: Sea 4E 43
Southdown Rd. BN41: Ports 6A 10
Southdown Rd. BN42: S'wick 3G 25
Southdown Rd. BN43: Shor S 2A 24
Southdown Rd. BN9: Newh 5D 40
Sth. Downs Bus. Pk. BN7: Lewes 3G 17
Southdown Sports Club 6E 17
Sth. Downs Rd. BN7: Lewes 3F 17
Southdown Ter. BN44: Stey 3D 4
(off Station Rd.)
Southdownview Cl.
BN14: Broadw 5E 21
Southdownview Rd.
BN14: Broadw 4E 21
Southdownview Way
BN14: Broadw 4E 21
South Dr. BN12: Fer 4A 32
Southease BN2: Brig 5B 30
(off Whitehawk Rd.)
SOUTHERHAM 6H 17
Southerham La. BN8: Glyn 5H 17
Southerham La. BN8: Lewes 5H 17
Southerham Nature Reserve 5H 17
SOUTHERHAM RDBT. 6H 17
SOUTHERN CROSS 1A 26
Southern Ring Rd. BN1: Falm 2D 14
Southey Rd. BN11: Worth 3C 34
Sth. Farm Industries
BN14: Worth 5C 20
Sth. Farm Rd. BN14: Broadw 4C 20
Sth. Farm Rd. BN14: Worth 4C 20
Southfield Rd. BN14: Broadw 5D 20
SOUTH HEIGHTON 1G 41
SOUTH LANCING 5E 23
Southlands Ct. BN43: Shor S 2C 24
SOUTHLANDS HOSPITAL 2D 24
Southlands Way BN43: Shor S 2D 24
South La. BN9: Newh 4F 41
(off High St.)
Sth. Lodge BN15: Somp 3A 22
(off Cokeham Rd.)
Sth. Lodge BN2: Brig 5B 30
SOUTH MALLING 2F 17
Southmount BN1: Brig 1F 29
Southon Cl. BN41: Ports 5H 9
Southon Vw. BN15: Lan 6A 22
(off Western Rd.)
SOUTHOVER 5E 17
Southover Grange Gdns. 5E 17
Southover High St. BN7: Lewes 5D 16
Southover Mnr. Ho. BN7: Lewes 5E 17
(off Southover High St.)
Southover Pl. BN2: Brig 3F 29
Southover Rd. BN7: Lewes 5E 17
Southover St. BN2: Brig 3F 29
South Pl. BN7: Lewes 4F 17
(off St John St.)
Sth. Point BN43: Shor B 4C 24
South Rd. BN1: Brig 1C 28
South Rd. BN9: Newh 4F 41
South Rd. M. BN1: Brig 1C 28
Southsea Av. BN12: Gor S 2G 33
South St. BN1: Brig 5B 44 (5D 28)
South St. BN1: Falm 2E 15
South St. BN11: Worth 2D 34
South St. BN14: W Tar 6A 20
South St. BN14: Worth 6A 20
South St. BN15: Lan 6C 22
South St. BN25: Sea 5D 42
South St. BN41: Ports 1A 26
South St. BN7: Lewes 4G 17
(not continuous)
South St. BN8: Lewes 5H 17
Southview Cl. BN42: S'wick 1G 25
Southview Cl. BN43: Shor S 3E 25
Southview Dr. BN11: Worth 2A 34
Southview Gdns. BN11: Worth 2A 34
Southview Rd. BN10: Peace 4G 39
Southview Rd. BN14: Fin 2C 6
Southview Rd. BN42: S'wick 2G 25
South Vw. Ter. BN9: S Heig 1F 41
Southwater Cl. BN12: Gor S 1D 32
Southwater Cl. BN2: Brig 4H 29
Sth. Way BN25: Sea 5G 43
Sth. Way BN7: Lewes 4C 16
Sth. Way BN9: Newh 4E 41
Southways Av. BN14: Broadw 4E 21
SOUTHWICK 3G 25
Southwick Sq. BN42: S'wick 3G 25
Southwick Station (Rail) 3G 25
Southwick St. BN42: S'wick 3G 25
SOUTHWICK TUNNEL 5F 9
Southwold Cl. BN13: High S 1G 19
Sth. Woodlands BN1: Brig 3C 12
Sovereign Cl. BN25: Sea 2F 43
Sovereign Ct. BN2: Brig 5C 36
Spa Ct. BN3: Hove 5H 27
(off King's Esplanade)
Sparrows, The BN10: Peace 3H 39
Spears Wlk. BN2: W'dean 2F 31
Speedwell Cl. BN13: Durr 5C 18
Spencer Av. BN3: Hove 5D 10
Spencer Rd. BN15: Lan 5B 22
Spences Ct. BN7: Lewes 3G 17
Spences Fld. BN7: Lewes 2G 17
Spences La. BN7: Lewes 3F 17
Spey Cl. BN13: Durr 2E 19
Spinnals Gro. BN42: S'wick 3F 25
Spinney, The BN3: Hove 5A 12
Spinneys, The BN7: Lewes 3G 17
Spital Rd. BN7: Lewes 4C 16
Splashpoint 2F 35
Springate Rd. BN42: S'wick 2H 25
Springfield Av. BN10: Tels C 4D 38
Springfield Gdns. BN13: Salv 3A 20
Springfield Rd. BN1: Brig 2D 28
Spring Gdns. BN1: Brig 4B 44 (5E 29)
Spring Gdns. BN42: S'wick 3G 25
Spring Gdns. BN7: Lewes 4F 17
Spring St. BN1: Brig 4A 44 (5C 28)
Squadron Dr. BN13: Durr 4D 18
Square, The BN1: Brig 2C 12
Square, The BN14: Fin 2C 6
Stable La. BN14: Fin 2C 6
Stafford Ct. BN2: Brig 5F 29
(off Up. Rock Gdns.)
Stafford Ct. BN25: Sea 4D 42
(off Stafford Rd.)
Stafford Rd. BN1: Brig 2C 28
Stafford Rd. BN25: Sea 4D 42
Stag Ho. BN2: Brig 6G 29
(off Somerset St.)
Stamford Lodge BN1: Brig 6C 12
(off Cumberland Rd.)
Standean Cl. BN1: Brig 2H 13
Standen Ct. BN44: Up B 5G 5
(off Downscroft)
Stanford Av. BN1: Brig 2D 28
Stanford Cl. BN3: Hove 1A 28
Stanford Ct. BN1: Brig 2D 28
(off Stanford Av.)
Stanford Rd. BN1: Brig 2C 28
Stanford Sq. BN11: Worth 2E 35
Stanhope Rd. BN11: Worth 1D 34
Stanley Av. BN41: Ports 4H 9
Stanley Av. Sth. BN41: Ports 5H 9
Stanley Deason Leisure Cen. 5B 30
Stanley Rd. BN1: Brig 3E 29
Stanley Rd. BN10: Peace 3F 39
Stanley Rd. BN11: Worth 1D 34
Stanley Rd. BN41: Ports 2A 26
Stanley St. BN2: Brig 5F 29
STANMER 1B 14
Stanmer Av. BN2: Salt 1B 38
Stanmer Ct. BN1: Brig 6E 13
(off Stanmer Pk. Rd.)
Stanmer Ct. BN1: Falm 2C 14
STANMER HEIGHTS 2F 13
Stanmer Ho. BN1: Brig 6E 13
(off Stanmer Pk. Rd.)
Stanmer House 1B 14
Stanmer Pk. 1B 14
Stanmer Pk. Rd. BN1: Brig 6E 13
Stanmer Rural Mus. 1B 14
Stanmer St. BN1: Brig 6F 13
Stanmer Vs. BN1: Brig 5F 13
Stansfield Rd. BN7: Lewes 3D 16
Stanstead Cres. BN2: W'dean 4H 31
Staplefield Dr. BN2: Brig 5B 14
Stapley Ct. BN3: Hove 2D 26
Stapley Rd. BN3: Hove 2D 26
Starboard Ct. BN2: Brig 5B 36
Station App. BN1: Falm 2D 14
Station App. BN25: Sea 4D 42
Station App. BN3: Hove 2H 27
Station App. BN43: Shor S 3B 24
(off Brunswick Rd.)
Station Pde. BN11: Worth 1A 34
Station Pde. BN15: Lan 5C 22
Station Rd. BN1: Brig 5B 12
Station Rd. BN11: Worth 1D 34
Station Rd. BN25: Sea 3A 42
Station Rd. BN41: Ports 4C 26
Station Rd. BN42: S'wick 3G 25
Station Rd. BN44: Stey 3D 4
Station Rd. BN7: Lewes 5F 17

64 A-Z Brighton & Worthing

Station Rd. – Toronto Cl.

Station Rd. BN9: Newh 2H 41
Station St. BN1: Brig 2C 44 (4E 29)
Station St. BN7: Lewes 4F 17
Steep Cl. BN14: Fin 3C 6
Steepdown Rd. BN15: Somp 2A 22
Steep La. BN14: Fin 3C 6
Steeple Vw. BN13: W Tar 5A 20
Steine Gdns. BN2: Brig 5D 44 (5E 29)
Steine Ho. BN1: Brig 5C 44 (5E 29)
(off Old Steine)
Steine La. BN1: Brig 5C 44 (5E 29)
(off East St.)
Steine St. BN2: Brig 6D 44 (6E 29)
Stephens Rd. BN1: Brig 6F 13
Stepney Ct. BN1: Brig 1C 44 (3E 29)
(off Fleet St.)
Stevens Ct. BN3: Hove 3E 27
Stevenson Rd. BN2: Brig 5G 29
Stewards Inn La. BN7: Lewes 5E 17
Steyne, The BN11: Worth 2E 35
Steyne, The BN25: Sea 5D 42
Steyne Cl. BN25: Sea 5E 43
Steyne Ct. BN25: Sea 5D 42
Steyne Gdns. BN11: Worth 2E 35
Steyne Rd. BN25: Sea 5D 42
STEYNING 3C 4
Steyning Av. BN10: Peace 6G 39
(not continuous)
Steyning Av. BN3: Hove 5F 11
Steyning By-Pass BN44: Stey 1B 4
Steyning Cl. BN12: Gor S 1E 33
Steyning Cl. BN15: Somp 2B 22
Steyning Cl. BN25: Sea 5H 43
Steyning Ct. BN3: Hove 3H 27
Steyning Ho. BN14: Broadw 5D 20
Steyning Leisure Cen. 2B 4
Steyning Mus. 3C 4
Steyning Rd. BN2: Rott 3F 37
Steyning Rd. BN25: Sea 5H 43
Stirling Av. BN25: Sea 3H 43
Stirling Cl. BN25: Sea 4H 43
Stirling Ct. BN3: Hove 3A 28
Stirling Pl. BN3: Hove 3G 27
Stockwell Lodge BN3: Hove 2G 27
Stoke Abbott Ct. BN11: Worth 2D 34
(off Stoke Abbott Rd.)
Stoke Abbott Rd. BN11: Worth 2D 34
Stoke Cl. BN25: Sea 4G 43
Stoke Mnr. Cl. BN25: Sea 3G 43
Stone Cl. BN13: Durr 4H 19
Stonecroft BN44: Stey 3C 4
Stonecroft Cl. BN3: Hove 4E 11
Stonecross Rd. BN2: Brig 4B 14
STONEHAM 1G 17
Stoneham Cl. BN7: Lewes 2E 17
Stoneham Rd. BN3: Hove 3F 27
Stonehurst Ct. BN2: Brig 4G 29
Stonehurst Rd. BN13: W Tar 5H 19
Stone La. BN13: Salv 4H 19
Stoneleigh Av. BN1: Brig 2D 12
Stoneleigh Cl. BN1: Brig 2D 12
Stonery Cl. BN41: Ports 6A 10
(not continuous)
Stonery Rd. BN41: Ports 6A 10
Stone St. BN1: Brig 5C 28
Stonewood Cl. BN25: Sea 3H 43
Stoney La. BN43: Shor S 3E 25
Stony Mere Way BN1: Brig 3C 14
Stony Mere Way BN1: Stan 3C 14
Stopham Cl. BN14: Worth 5B 20
Storrington Cl. BN3: Hove 6E 11
Storrington Ri. BN14: Fin V 4D 6
Stour Cl. BN13: Durr 2E 19
Stour Rd. BN13: Durr 2E 19
Strand, The BN12: Fer 4A 32
Strand, The BN12: Gor S 1D 32
Strand, The BN2: Brig 5B 36
Strand Pde. BN12: Gor S 6F 19
STRAND PARADE RDBT. 1G 33
(off The Boulevard)
Stratheden Ct. BN25: Sea 5D 42
Strathmore Cl. BN13: Worth 6G 19
Strathmore Rd. BN13: Worth 6G 19
Street, The BN13: Clap 1A 18
Street, The BN13: Pat 1A 18
Street, The BN15: N Lan 2C 22
Street, The BN43: Shor S 2H 23
Street, The BN44: Bramb 4E 5
St. Barn BN15: Somp 3G 21
St. Gabriels BN2: Brig 3G 29
Stretton Ct. BN3: Hove 3F 27
(off Rutland Gdns.)
Stringer Way BN1: Brig 5D 12
Strone Ct. BN11: Worth 3H 33
Stroudley Rd. BN1: Brig 3D 28
Stuart Cl. BN11: Worth 6F 21
Studio Theatre Brighton 4C 44 (5E 29)
Styles Fld. BN7: Lewes 4F 17
(off Friar's Wlk.)
Sudeley Pl. BN2: Brig 6H 29
Sudeley St. BN2: Brig 6H 29
Sudeley Ter. BN2: Brig 6H 29
Suez Way BN2: Salt 3A 38
Suffolk Ho. BN11: Worth 1D 34
Suffolk St. BN3: Hove 2F 27
Sugden Rd. BN11: Worth 1F 35
Sullington Cl. BN2: Brig 4B 14
Sullington Gdns. BN14: Fin V 4D 6
Sullington Way BN43: Shor S 2C 24
Summer Cl. BN41: Ports 3A 26
Summerdale Rd. BN3: Hove 6D 10
Summerdown Cl. BN13: Durr 5D 18
Summerdown Ct. BN13: Durr 5D 18
(off Summerdown Cl.)
Summerfields BN14: Fin 2C 6
Summersdeane BN42: S'wick 1H 25
Suncourt BN11: Worth 3A 34
Sunningdale Cl. BN25: Sea 5F 43
Sunningdale Ct. BN12: Gor S 1E 33
Sunningdale Rd. BN13: Durr 4F 19
Sunninghill Av. BN3: Hove 6E 11
Sunninghill Cl. BN3: Hove 6E 11
Sunny Cl. BN12: Gor S 3G 33
Sunnydale Av. BN1: Brig 2E 13
Sunnydale Cl. BN1: Brig 2E 13
Sunnyside Pk. BN25: Sea 3A 42
Sunset Cl. BN10: Tels C 2F 39
Sun St. BN7: Lewes 4E 17
Sunview Av. BN10: Peace 6H 39
(not continuous)
Surrenden Cl. BN1: Brig 4D 12
Surrenden Ct. BN1: Brig 5D 12
(off Varndean Gdns.)
Surrenden Cres. BN1: Brig 5C 12
Surrenden Holt BN1: Brig 5D 12
Surrenden Lodge BN1: Brig 6D 12
Surrenden Pk. BN1: Brig 4E 13
Surrenden Rd. BN1: Brig 5D 12
Surrey Cl. BN25: Sea 3B 42
Surrey Ho. BN2: Brig 6H 29
Surrey Rd. BN25: Sea 3B 42
Surrey St. BN1: Brig 2B 44 (4D 28)
Surrey St. BN11: Worth 3C 34
Surry Ct. BN43: Shor S 3B 24
(off Surry St.)
Surry St. BN43: Shor S 3B 24
SUSSEX BEACON (HOSPICE) 1A 30
Sussex County Cricket Ground 3A 28
Sussex County Lawn Tennis & Croquet Club 3F 25
Sussex Ct. BN3: Hove 4A 28
Sussex Ct. BN43: Shor B 4C 24
Sussex Emmaus 1B 26
SUSSEX EYE HOSPITAL 6H 29
Sussex Hgts. BN1: Brig 5A 44 (5C 28)
(off St Margaret's Pl.)
Sussex Ho. BN10: Tels C 5D 38
Sussex Ho. Bus. Pk. BN3: Hove 2F 27
Sussex M. BN11: Worth 2A 34
Sussex M. BN2: Brig 4A 36
Sussex Pl. BN2: Brig 3D 44 (4F 29)
Sussex Rd. BN11: Worth 1D 34
Sussex Rd. BN15: S Lan 5G 23
Sussex Rd. BN3: Hove 5H 27
Sussex Sq. BN2: Brig 4A 36
Sussex Sq. M. BN2: Brig 4A 36
(off Bristol Pl.)
Sussex St. BN2: Brig 4F 29
Sussex Ter. BN2: Brig 4F 29
Sussex Way BN10: Tels C 5D 38
Sussex Wharf BN43: Shor B 4D 24
Sussex Yacht Club 4H 25
Sutherland Rd. BN2: Brig 5G 29
SUTTON 3G 43
Sutton Av. BN10: Peace 5F 39
Sutton Av. BN25: Sea 5F 43
Sutton Av. Nth. BN10: Peace 4F 39
Sutton Cl. BN2: W'dean 1G 31
Sutton Ct. BN14: Fin V 5D 6
Sutton Cft. La. BN25: Sea 4D 42
Sutton Drove BN25: Sea 3E 43
Sutton M. BN25: Sea 3F 43
Sutton Pk. Rd. BN25: Sea 4D 42
Sutton Pl. BN25: Sea 3G 43
Sutton Rd. BN25: Sea 4D 42
Swallow Ct. BN2: Brig 3B 30
(off Albourne Cl.)
Swallowmead BN44: Stey 4C 4
Swallow Ri. BN41: Ports 4H 9
Swallows, The BN10: Tels C 3F 39
Swallows Cl. BN15: S Lan 5G 23
Swallows Grn. Dr. BN13: Durr 5E 19
Swanborough Ct. BN43: Shor S 3B 24
(off New Rd.)
Swanborough Dr. BN2: Brig 3B 30
Swanborough Pl. BN2: Brig 3B 30
Swanbourne Cl. BN15: N Lan 2D 22
Swandean Cl. BN13: High S 2G 19
Swannee Cl. BN10: Peace 3H 39
Sweda Ct. BN2: Brig 6H 29
Swing Bri. 3F 41
Swiss Gdns. BN43: Shor S 3A 24
Sycamore Cl. BN13: Durr 4E 19
Sycamore Cl. BN2: W'dean 2G 31
Sycamore Cl. BN25: Sea 4H 43
Sycamore Cl. BN41: Ports 5C 10
(not continuous)
Sycamore Ct. BN14: Fin 3C 6
Sycamore Ct. BN2: Brig 2H 29
(off Fitzherbert Dr.)
Sycamores, The BN10: Peace 3G 39
Sydney St. BN1: Brig 3C 44 (4E 29)
Sylvan Rd. BN15: Somp 4H 21
Sylvester Way BN3: Hove 5C 10
Symbister Rd. BN41: Ports 3C 26

T

Taaffe Ho. BN1: Brig 2A 44 (4D 28)
(off Dyke Rd.)
TA Cen. 1D 34
(off Lit. High St.)
Tagalie Sq. BN13: Worth 1G 33
Talbot Cres. BN1: Brig 2H 13
Talbot Ter. BN7: Lewes 4E 17
Talland Pde. BN25: Sea 5D 42
Tamar Av. BN13: Durr 2E 19
Tamar Cl. BN13: Durr 3E 19
Tamarisk Way BN12: Fer 3B 32
Tamplin Ter. BN2: Brig 4F 29
Tamworth Rd. BN3: Hove 3F 27
Tandridge Rd. BN3: Hove 4E 27
Tangmere Pl. BN1: Brig 2E 13
Tangmere Rd. BN1: Brig 2E 13
Tanners Brook BN7: Lewes 5F 17
Tanyard Cotts. BN44: Stey 3B 4
Tanyard La. BN44: Stey 3B 4
Tarmount La. BN43: Shor S 3B 24
Tarner Ho. BN2: Brig 5F 29
(off Tilbury Pl.)
Tarner Rd. BN2: Brig 4F 29
Tarragon Way BN43: Shor S 1E 25
Tarring Cl. BN9: S Heig 1F 41
Tarring Ga. BN14: W Tar 6A 20
Tarring Rd. BN11: Worth 1H 33
Tasman Way BN13: Durr 3E 19
Taunton Gro. BN2: Brig 1C 30
Taunton Pl. BN2: Brig 1C 30
(off Taunton Rd.)
Taunton Rd. BN2: Brig 1B 30
Taunton Way BN2: Brig 1C 30
Tavistock Down BN1: Brig 6G 13
Tavy Cl. BN13: Durr 4E 19
Tavy Rd. BN13: Durr 4E 19
Taw Cl. BN13: Durr 3F 19
Teg Cl. BN41: Ports 6B 10
Teign Wlk. BN13: Durr 2E 19
(off Adur Av.)
Telegraph St. BN2: Brig 6G 29
Telgarth Rd. BN12: Fer 4A 32
TELSCOMBE 1F 39
TELSCOMBE CLIFFS 5E 39
Telscombe Cliffs Way BN10: Tels C 5D 38
Telscombe Cl. BN10: Peace 2H 39
Telscombe Grange BN10: Tels C 5D 38
Telscombe Pk. BN10: Peace 2G 39
Telscombe Rd. BN10: Peace 2E 39
Telscombe Rd. BN10: Tels C 2E 39
Templars, The BN14: Broadw 3E 21
Temple Gdns. BN1: Brig 4C 28
Temple Hgts. BN1: Brig 4C 28
(off Windlesham Rd.)
Temple Ho. BN1: Brig 1C 44 (3E 29)
Temple St. BN1: Brig 4C 28
Ten Acres BN11: Worth 1G 35
Tenantry Down Rd. BN2: Brig 3A 30
Tenantry Rd. BN2: Brig 2H 29
Tennis Rd. BN3: Hove 4E 27
Tennyson Ct. BN3: Hove 3G 27
Tennyson Rd. BN11: Worth 2C 34
Terminus Bldgs. BN25: Sea 4D 42
(off Blatchington Rd.)
Terminus Pl. BN1: Brig 1B 44 (3D 28)
Terminus Rd. BN1: Brig 1B 44 (3D 28)
Terminus St. BN1: Brig 2B 44 (4D 28)
Terrace, The BN12: Gor S 2E 33
Terrace, The BN15: S Lan 6C 22
Terrace Row BN2: Brig 6F 29
(off Broad St.)
Terraces, The BN2: Brig 6D 44 (6F 29)
(off Madeira Dr.)
Terringes Av. BN13: W Tar 6G 19
Terringes Av. BN13: Worth 6G 19
Test Rd. BN15: Somp 4H 21
Teville Ga. BN11: Worth 1D 34
Teville Industrials BN14: Broadw 5F 21
Teville Pl. BN11: Worth 1C 34
Teville Rd. BN11: Worth 1C 34
Teynham Ho. BN2: Salt 4A 38
Thackeray Rd. BN14: Broadw 6F 21
Thakeham Cl. BN12: Gor S 2C 32
Thakeham Dr. BN12: Gor S 2C 32
Thalassa Rd. BN11: Worth 1H 35
Thames Cl. BN2: Brig 5F 29
Thames Ho. BN2: Brig 5F 29
(off Thames Cl.)
Thames Way BN13: Durr 3F 19
Thatch Ct. BN15: N Lan 2C 22
Theatre Royal Brighton 4C 44 (5E 29)
Theobald Ho. BN1: Brig 2C 44 (4E 29)
(off Blackman St.)
Thesiger Cl. BN11: Worth 6G 21
Thesiger Rd. BN11: Worth 6G 21
Third Av. BN14: Char D 3D 20
Third Av. BN15: Lan 3C 22
Third Av. BN3: Hove 5H 27
Third Av. BN9: Newh 5E 41
Third Rd. BN10: Peace 5E 39
Thirlmere Cres. BN15: Somp 5H 21
Thomas Ho. BN1: Brig 2A 44 (4D 28)
(off Dyke Rd.)
Thomas St. BN7: Lewes 3G 17
Thompson Rd. BN1: Brig 1G 29
Thompson Rd. BN9: Newh 1H 41
Thomson Cl. BN13: Durr 4D 18
Thornbush Cres. BN41: Ports 5B 10
Thorndean Rd. BN2: Brig 5H 13
Thornhill Av. BN1: Brig 1E 13
Thornhill Cl. BN3: Hove 5E 11
Thornhill Ri. BN41: Ports 4H 9
Thornhill Way BN41: Ports 5A 10
Thorn Rd. BN11: Worth 3C 34
Thornscroft BN44: Stey 2C 4
Thornsdale BN2: Brig 4F 29
(off Albion Hill)
Thurlow Rd. BN11: Worth 1E 35
Thyme Cl. BN43: Shor S 1E 25
Ticehurst Rd. BN2: Brig 5B 30
Tichborne St. BN1: Brig 4C 44 (5E 29)
TIDE MILLS 6H 41
Tide Mills Way BN25: Sea 3A 42
Tidy St. BN1: Brig 3C 44 (4E 29)
Tilbury Pl. BN2: Brig 5F 29
Tilbury Way BN2: Brig 4F 29
Tilgate Cl. BN2: Brig 4H 29
Tillington BN2: Brig 3A 30
Tillstone Cl. BN2: Brig 6H 13
Tillstone St. BN2: Brig 5F 29
Tilsmore BN2: Brig 5B 30
Timber Cl. BN13: Durr 4E 19
Timberlane Trad. Est. BN14: Broadw 5F 21
Timber Yd. Cotts. BN7: Lewes 4G 17
Timberyard La. BN7: Lewes 4G 17
Tintagel Ct. BN3: Hove 2G 27
Tintagel Ct. BN43: Shor S 3B 24
Tintern Cl. BN1: Brig 1F 29
Tisbury Rd. BN3: Hove 4H 27
Tithe Barn BN15: N Lan 2C 22
Titian Rd. BN3: Hove 3F 27
Titnore La. BN12: Gor S 3C 18
Titnore La. BN13: Clap 3A 18
Titnore La. BN13: Gor S 3A 18
Titnore La. BN13: Pat 3A 18
Titnore Way BN13: Durr 4C 18
Tivoli BN1: Brig 6C 12
Tivoli Cres. BN1: Brig 1B 28
Tivoli Cres. Nth. BN1: Brig 6B 12
Tivoli Pl. BN1: Brig 6B 12
Tivoli Rd. BN1: Brig 6B 12
Tollbridge Ho. BN43: Shor S 2H 23
Tollgate BN10: Peace 3F 39
TONGDEAN 5A 12
Tongdean Av. BN3: Hove 5A 12
Tongdean Ct. BN1: Brig 4B 12
Tongdean La. BN1: Brig Gableson Av. 4H 11
Tongdean La. BN1: Brig Windsor Ct. 4B 12
Tongdean Pl. BN3: Hove 5A 12
Tongdean Ri. BN1: Brig 4A 12
Tongdean Rd. BN3: Hove 5H 11
Toomey Rd. BN44: Stey 1C 4
Tophill Cl. BN41: Ports 6H 9
Torcross Cl. BN2: Brig 1A 30
Toronto Cl. BN13: Durr 4F 19

A-Z Brighton & Worthing 65

Warnham Ri. – Windmill Dr.

Warnham Ri. BN1: Brig 3E 13
Warnham Rd. BN12: Gor S 2F 33
Warren, The BN12: Fer 4B 32
Warren Av. BN2: W'dean 1E 31
Warren Cl. BN14: Salv 3B 20
Warren Cl. BN2: W'dean 2D 30
Warren Cl. BN7: Lewes 5D 16
Warren Ct. BN14: Salv 3B 20
Warren Ct. BN15: Lan 5B 22
Warren Ct. BN42: S'wick 1G 25
Warren Dr. BN7: Lewes 5C 16
Warren Farm Pl. BN14: Fin V 2A 20
Warren Gdns. BN14: Salv 3B 20
Warren Lodge BN10: Tels C 3E 39
Warren Ri. BN2: W'dean 2D 30
Warren Rd. BN14: Salv 2A 20
Warren Rd. BN2: Brig 3A 30
Warren Rd. BN2: W'dean 3A 30
Warren Way BN10: Tels C 3E 39
Warren Way BN2: W'dean 2F 31
Warrior Cl. BN41: Ports 6B 10
Warwick Ct. BN3: Hove 3C 28
(off Davigdor Rd.)
Warwick Gdns. BN11: Worth 2E 35
Warwick La. BN11: Worth 2E 35
(off Warwick St.)
Warwick Mt. BN2: Brig 6G 29
(off Montague St.)
Warwick Pl. BN11: Worth 2E 35
Warwick Rd. BN11: Worth 2E 35
Warwick Rd. BN25: Sea 4D 42
Warwick St. BN11: Worth 2D 34
Warwick Wlk. BN43: Shor S 1B 24
Washington St. BN2: Brig 4F 29
Waterdyke Av. BN42: S'wick 3G 25
Waterford Cl. BN10: Peace 2G 39
Waterfront, The BN12: Gor S 3G 33
Waterfront, The BN2: Brig 5B 36
Watergate La. BN7: Lewes 5E 17
WATERHALL 2H 11
Waterhall Golf Course 2G 11
Waterhall Rd. BN1: Brig 2H 11
Waterloo Pl. BN2: Brig 2D 44 (4F 29)
Waterloo Pl. BN7: Lewes 4F 17
Waterloo St. BN3: Hove 5B 28
Watersfield Rd. BN14: Worth 5B 20
Waterside Rd. BN41: Ports 4B 26
Watling Cl. BN42: S'wick 3G 25
Watling Ct. BN42: S'wick 3G 25
(off Watling Rd.)
Watling Rd. BN42: S'wick 3G 25
Waverley Ct. BN11: Worth 3B 34
Waverley Ct. BN25: Sea 5E 43
Waverley Cres. BN1: Brig 1G 29
Wavertree Rd. BN12: Gor S 1F 33
Wayfield Av. BN3: Hove 1E 27
Wayfield Cl. BN3: Hove 1F 27
Wayland Av. BN1: Brig 4A 12
Wayland Hgts. BN1: Brig 4A 12
Wayside BN1: Brig 2B 12
Wayside BN15: Lan 5A 22
Wayside Av. BN13: Durr 3F 19
Weald Av. BN3: Hove 1F 27
Weald Cl. BN7: Lewes 3E 17
Weald Dyke BN43: Shor B 4B 24
Wear Cl. BN13: Durr 3E 19
Wear Rd. BN13: Durr 3E 19
Weavers Ct. BN43: Shor S 3A 24
(off Ropetackle)
Welbeck Av. BN3: Hove 4E 27
Welbeck Ct. BN25: Sea 4D 42
Welbeck Ct. BN3: Hove 4E 27
Welbeck Mans. BN3: Hove 4E 27
(off Welbeck Av.)
Welesmere Rd. BN2: Rott 1G 37
Welland Cl. BN13: Durr 2F 19
Welland Rd. BN13: Durr 2F 19
Wellend Vs. BN1: Brig 2D 28
Wellesbourne Ri. BN1: Brig 4B 12
Wellesley Av. BN12: Gor S 2F 33
Wellesley Ct. BN11: Worth 3H 33
Wellhouse Pl. BN7: Lewes 4E 17
Wellingham La. BN13: High S 1G 19
Wellington Ct. BN2: Brig
The Strand 5C 36
Wellington Ct. BN11: Worth 2A 34
Wellington Ct. BN2: Brig 3F 29
(off Wellington Rd.)
Wellingtonia Ct. BN1: Brig 5C 12
(off Laine Cl.)
Wellington Pk. BN25: Sea 4F 43
Wellington Rd. BN10: Peace 5A 40
Wellington Rd. BN2: Brig 3F 29
Wellington Rd. BN41: Ports 4B 26
Wellington Rd. BN9: Newh 1G 41
Wellington St. BN2: Brig 3G 29
Wellington St. BN7: Lewes 4F 17
Wellsbourne BN2: Brig 5B 30
(off Findon Rd.)
Wells Ct. BN11: Worth 3A 34
(off Pevensey Gdn.)
Wembley Av. BN15: Lan 4B 22
Wembley Gdns. BN15: Lan 4B 22
Wenban Pas. BN11: Worth 1D 34
(off Wenban Rd.)
Wenban Rd. BN11: Worth 1D 34
Wenceling Cotts. BN15: S Lan 5G 23
Wendale Dr. BN10: Peace 2H 39
Wendover Grange BN3: Hove 4G 27
Went Hill Pk. BN25: Sea 4F 43
Wentworth Cl. BN13: Durr 2H 19
Wentworth Ct. BN11: Worth 2B 34
Wentworth St. BN2: Brig 6F 29
Weppons BN43: Shor S 3B 24
Wessex Ct. BN11: Worth 2C 34
Wessex Wlk. BN43: Shor S 1B 24
West Av. BN11: Worth 2A 34
West Av. BN15: S Lan 5E 23
West Beach BN43: Shor B 5H 23
West Beach Ct. BN25: Sea 3A 42
WEST BLATCHINGTON 6F 11
West Blatchington Windmill 6F 11
Westbourne Av. BN14: Broadw 6D 20
Westbourne Gdns. BN3: Hove 4G 27
Westbourne Gro. BN3: Hove 3G 27
Westbourne Pl. BN3: Hove 4G 27
Westbourne St. BN3: Hove 3G 27
Westbourne Vs. BN3: Hove 4F 27
Westbrook BN2: Salt 2A 38
Westbrooke BN11: Worth 2D 34
Westbrooke Ct. BN11: Worth 2C 34
(off Crescent Rd.)
Westbrook Way BN42: S'wick 3H 25
West Bldgs. BN11: Worth 3C 34
Westbury Ct. BN11: Worth 2B 34
West Cl. BN15: Lan 3C 22
Westcombe BN1: Brig 3C 28
(off Dyke Rd.)
West Ct. BN43: Shor S 3A 24
(off West St.)
Westcourt Pl. BN14: Broadw 6C 20
Westcourt Rd. BN14: Broadw 1C 34
Westdean Av. BN9: Newh 6C 40
West Dean Ri. BN25: Sea 3F 43
Westdean Rd. BN14: Worth 5B 20
WESTDENE 3A 12
Westdene Dr. BN1: Brig 3A 12
Westdene Woods Local
Nature Reserve 3B 12
Westdown Ct. BN11: Worth 1A 34
Westdown Rd. BN25: Sea 3C 42
West Dr. BN12: Fer 4A 32
West Dr. BN2: Brig 5F 29
West End Way BN15: Lan 6B 22
Westergate Cl. BN12: Fer 2B 32
Westergate Rd. BN2: Brig 4A 14
Westerman Complex BN3: Hove 2F 27
Western Cl. BN15: Lan 6A 22
Western Concourse BN2: Brig 6B 36
Western Ct. BN9: Newh 5E 41
Western Esplanade BN3: Hove 4D 26
Western Esplanade BN41: Ports 4D 26
Western Lodge BN15: Somp 3A 22
(off Cokeham Rd.)
Western Pl. BN11: Worth 3C 34
Western Rd. BN1: Brig 4B 28
Western Rd. BN15: Lan 5H 21
Western Rd. BN15: Somp 5H 21
Western Rd. BN3: Hove 4A 28
Western Rd. BN43: Shor S 3B 24
Western Rd. BN7: Lewes 4D 16
Western Rd. BN9: Newh 5D 40
Western Rd. Nth. BN15: Somp 4A 22
Western Row BN11: Worth 3C 34
Western St. BN1: Brig 5B 28
Western Ter. BN1: Brig 5C 28
Western Ter. BN15: Somp 3F 21
Westfield Av. BN2: Salt 1B 38
Westfield Av. Nth. BN2: Salt 1B 38
Westfield Av. Sth. BN2: Salt 1B 38
Westfield Cl. BN1: Brig 4E 13
Westfield Cres. BN1: Brig 3E 13
Westfield Ri. BN2: Salt 1B 38
Westgate St. BN7: Lewes 4E 17
Westham BN2: Brig 5B 30
West Hill BN13: High S 6C 6
West Hill Cl. BN13: High S 6C 6
West Hill Pl. BN1: Brig 2B 44 (4D 28)
West Hill Rd. BN1: Brig 2A 44 (4D 28)
West Hill St. BN1: Brig 2A 44 (4D 28)
West Hove Golf Course 3C 10
West Jetty BN2: Brig 6B 36
Westlake Cl. BN13: Worth 5H 19
Westlake Gdns. BN13: Worth 5H 19
Westland Av. BN14: Worth 6A 20
Westland Ct. BN41: Ports 3A 26
(off West Rd.)
Westlands BN12: Fer 3A 32
West La. BN15: Lan 3C 22
West Mans. BN11: Worth 3B 34
Westmead Gdns. BN11: Worth 2H 33
Westmeston Av. BN2: Salt 2H 37
Westminster Ct. BN11: Worth 2F 35
Westmoreland Wlk.
BN43: Shor S 1A 24
Westmorland Ct.
BN3: Hove 1A 44 (3C 28)
(off Goldsmid Rd.)
Westmount BN2: Brig 4G 29
Westmount Cl. BN42: S'wick 2F 25
West Onslow Cl. BN12: Fer 1A 32
West Pde. BN11: Worth 4H 33
West Pk. La. BN12: Gor S 2G 33
West Point BN43: Shor B 4C 24
West Quay BN2: Brig 6B 36
West Quay BN9: Newh 5F 41
West Rd. BN41: Ports 3A 26
West St. BN1: Brig 5B 44 (5D 28)
West St. BN11: Worth 3C 34
West St. BN15: Somp 3F 21
West St. BN2: Rott 3F 37
West St. BN25: Sea 5D 42
West St. BN41: Ports 3C 26
West St. BN43: Shor S 3A 24
West St. BN7: Lewes 4F 17
WEST TARRING 5A 20
West Tyne BN13: Durr 4F 19
West Vw. BN25: Sea 5D 42
West Vw. BN3: Hove 3A 28
West Vw. Cl. BN2: W'dean 2F 31
Westview Cl. BN10: Peace 4A 40
West Vw. Ct. BN25: Sea 5D 42
Westview Ter. BN14: Fin 2C 6
(off North Vw. Ter.)
Westview Ter. BN9: Newh 1F 41
West Way BN13: High S 1F 19
West Way BN15: S Lan 5E 23
West Way BN3: Hove 6D 10
Westway Cl. BN41: Ports 4G 9
Westway Gdns. BN41: Ports 4G 9
WEST WORTHING 2H 33
West Worthing Station (Rail) 1A 34
West Worthing Tennis
& Squash Club 4C 18
Wharf Rd. BN41: Ports 4D 26
Wheatfield Way BN2: Brig 5B 14
Wheatlands Cl. BN10: Tels C 2F 39
Wheatsheaf Gdns. BN7: Lewes 3G 17
Wheelwright Lodge BN15: Somp 3A 22
(off West St.)
Whichelo Pl. BN2: Brig 4G 29
Whippingham Rd. BN2: Brig 2G 29
Whippingham St. BN2: Brig 2G 29
Whipping Post La. BN2: Rott 3F 37
Whistler Ct. BN1: Brig 1D 28
Whitebeam Rd. BN13: Durr 5E 19
Whitecross St. BN1: Brig 2C 44 (4E 29)
WHITEHAWK 4B 30
Whitehawk Cl. BN2: Brig 5A 30
Whitehawk Cres. BN2: Brig 5A 30
Whitehawk FC 5C 30
Whitehawk Hill Rd. BN2: Brig 5H 29
Whitehawk Race Hill Local
Nature Reserve 3A 30
Whitehawk Rd. BN2: Brig 4A 30
Whitehawk Way BN2: Brig 4B 30
White Hill BN7: Lewes 4E 17
White Horse Sq. BN44: Stey 3C 4
White Ho. Pl. BN13: Durr 2G 19
Whiteley Cl. BN25: Sea 4G 43
White Lion Ct. BN43: Shor S 3A 24
(off Ship St.)
White Lodge BN3: Hove 2A 28
Whitelot Cl. BN42: S'wick 6G 9
Whitelot Way BN42: S'wick 6G 9
Whiterock Pl. BN42: S'wick 3G 25
White St. BN2: Brig 5F 29
White Styles Rd. BN15: Somp 3H 21
White Styles Ter. BN15: Somp 3H 21
Whitethorn Dr. BN1: Brig 4H 11
Whiteway Cl. BN25: Sea 1D 42
Whiteway La. BN2: Rott 2G 37
Whittingehame Gdns. BN1: Brig 5D 12
Whitworth Ho. BN11: Worth 1B 34
(off St Botolph's Rd.)
Whylands Av. BN13: Durr 2F 19
Whylands Cl. BN13: Durr 2F 19
Whylands Cres. BN13: Durr 2F 19
Wick Hall BN3: Hove 4B 28
Wickhurst Cl. BN41: Ports 6H 9
Wickhurst Ri. BN41: Ports 5H 9
Wickhurst Rd. BN41: Ports 6H 9
Wicklands Av. BN2: Salt 3A 38
Widdicombe Way BN2: Brig 6A 14
Widewater Cl. BN15: S Lan 5G 23
Widewater Ct. BN43: Shor B 5G 23
Widewater Lagoon 5G 23
Wigmore Cl. BN1: Brig 1F 29
Wigmore Rd. BN14: Broadw 4D 20
Wigmore Trad. Est.
BN14: Broadw 5F 21
Wilbury Av. BN3: Hove 2H 27
Wilbury Cres. BN3: Hove 3A 28
Wilbury Gdns. BN3: Hove 2A 28
Wilbury Grange BN3: Hove 4A 28
Wilbury Gro. BN3: Hove 4A 28
Wilbury Lodge BN3: Hove 3A 28
Wilbury Mans. BN3: Hove 2B 28
(off Wilbury Vs.)
Wilbury Rd. BN3: Hove 4A 28
Wilbury Vs. BN3: Hove 3A 28
Wilby Av. BN42: S'wick 1G 25
Wild Pk. 4H 13
Wild Pk. Cl. BN2: Brig 5A 14
Wilfrid Rd. BN3: Hove 2D 26
Wilkinson Cl. BN2: Rott 1F 37
Wilkinson Way BN25: Sea 3D 42
William Morris Ct.
BN14: Broadw 6F 21
Williams Rd. BN43: Shor S 2D 24
William St. BN2: Brig 4D 44 (5E 29)
William St. BN41: Ports 3B 26
William Sutton Ho.
BN1: Brig 4C 44 (5E 29)
(off Tichborne St.)
Willingdon Rd. BN2: Brig 1A 30
Willowbrook Pk. BN15: S Lan 5E 23
Willowbrook Rd. BN14: Broadw 6G 21
Willow Cl. BN15: S Lan 5G 23
Willow Cl. BN2: W'dean 2G 31
Willow Cl. BN44: Stey 2C 4
Willow Ct. BN11: Worth 1A 34
Willow Ct. BN3: Hove 3B 28
Willow Cres. BN13: Durr 5E 19
Willow Dr. BN25: Sea 4H 43
Willow Est., The BN9: Newh 3G 41
Willow Ho. BN12: Gor S 6C 18
(off Goring Chase)
Willows, The BN14: Fin 2C 6
Willows, The BN15: Lan 5C 22
(off Grinstead La.)
Willows, The BN2: Brig 2F 29
(off Prince's Cres.)
Willows, The BN25: Sea 4D 42
Willows Dr. BN15: Lan 3C 22
Willow Wlk. BN9: Newh 3E 41
Wilmington Cl. BN1: Brig 3E 13
Wilmington Ct. BN11: Worth 3A 34
Wilmington Pde. BN1: Brig 3D 12
(off Wilmington Way)
Wilmington Rd. BN25: Sea 3C 42
Wilmington Rd. BN9: Newh 5D 40
Wilmington Way BN1: Brig 3D 12
Wilmot Ct. BN43: Shor S 2E 25
(off Wilmot Rd.)
Wilmot Rd. BN43: Shor S 2D 24
Wilson Av. BN2: Brig 4B 36
Wiltshire Ho. BN2: Brig 5F 29
(off Lavender St.)
Wimborne Ct. BN11: Worth 2H 33
Winchelsea Cl. BN25: Sea 2G 43
Winchelsea Ct. BN11: Worth 3A 34
Winchelsea Gdns. BN11: Worth 3H 33
Winchester Ct. BN11: Worth 2B 34
Winchester Ho. BN12: Gor S 1C 32
(off Goring St.)
Winchester Rd. BN11: Worth 2B 34
Winchester St. BN1: Brig 2E 29
Wincombe Rd. BN1: Brig 1B 28
Windermere Ct. BN12: Gor S 2D 32
Windermere Ct. BN2: Brig 4G 29
Windermere Cres. BN12: Gor S 5F 19
Windlesham Av. BN1: Brig 4C 28
Windlesham Cl. BN41: Ports 1A 26
Windlesham Ct.
BN1: Brig 1A 44 (3C 28)
(off Windlesham Gdns.)
Windlesham Gdns. BN1: Brig 4C 28
Windlesham Gdns. BN43: Shor S 2B 24
Windlesham Ho. BN1: Brig 4C 28
(off Windlesham Rd.)
Windlesham Mans. BN3: Hove 3C 28
(off Davigdor Rd.)
Windlesham Rd. BN1: Brig 4C 28
Windlesham Rd. BN43: Shor S 2B 24
Windmill Cl. BN3: Hove 6F 11
Windmill Cl. BN44: Up B 4G 5
Windmill Dr. BN1: Brig 2A 12

A-Z Brighton & Worthing 67

Y

Z

Published by Geographers' A-Z Map Company Limited
An imprint of HarperCollins Publishers
Westerhill Road
Bishopbriggs
Glasgow
G64 2QT

www.az.co.uk
a-z.maps@harpercollins.co.uk

7th edition 2021